FAVORITE BRAND NAME
COOKIE
COLLECTION

CRESCENT BOOKS

ISBN: 0-517-05674-7

Library of Congress Catalog Card Number: 91-62651

Pictured on the front cover: *Top row, left :* Cranberry Ricotta Cheese Brownies (*page 187*); *Center:* Lemon Cookies (*page 111*); *Right:* Peanut Butter Bears (*page 158*). *Bottom row, left:* Preserve Thumbprints (*page 192*), Choco-Orange Slices (*page 192*), Snowmen (*page 192*), Chocolate Mint Cutouts (*page 192*); *Center:* Peanut Butter Secrets (*page 144*); *Left:* Buttery Caramel Crisps (*page 75*).

Pictured on the back cover: *Top row, left:* Double Peanut Butter Supremes (*page 106*), Nutty Toppers (*page 105*), Oatmeal Lemon-Cheese Cookies (*page 105*); *Center:* Magic Rainbow Cookie Bars (*page 51*); *Right:* Pineapple Raisin Jumbles (*page 94*). *Bottom row, left:* Fruit and Chocolate Dream Bars (*page 48*), Chocolate Cheese Ripple Bars (*page 49*), Chocolate Pecan Pie Bars (*page 48*); *Center:* Lemon Cut-Out Cookies (*page 165*); *Right:* Chocolate Almond Buttons (*page 98*).

This edition published by
Crescent Books
Distributed by Outlet Book Company, Inc.
A Random House Company
225 Park Avenue South
New York, New York 10003

8 7 6 5 4 3 2 1

Manufactured in U.S.A.

Microwave ovens vary in wattage and power output; cooking times given with microwave directions in this book may need to be adjusted. Consult manufacturer's instructions for suitable microwave-safe cooking dishes.

Contents

Tips and Techniques   4
Helpful hints for successful cookie baking

Chock-Full O' Chips   10
Cookies bursting with chips and chunks of all kinds

Luscious Brownies   30
Satisfy your chocolate cravings with these sinfully rich creations

Delectable Bars   46
Quick-to-fix sweets sure to become all-time family favorites

Extra-Easy Cookies   82
Simple dropped and shaped cookies for fast treats on busy days

Tea-Time Treasures   116
Fancy cookies suitable for serving at any elegant occasion

Just for Kids   148
Yummy after-school treats to satisfy hungry cookie monsters

Festive Holiday Cookies   176
Celebrate the season with these delightful Christmas classics

Acknowledgments   214

Index   215

TIPS AND TECHNIQUES

The word cookie comes from the Dutch word, "koekje," meaning "little cake." The Dutch brought these little cakes to their first settlements in America, and they have been popular ever since. With so many flavors, shapes and sizes to choose from, cookies have definitely earned their place as America's favorite snack food.

Whether you're a newcomer to the cookie-baking scene or a real pro, these tips and techniques will help make the most of your time in the kitchen. Everything from simple drop cookies to pretty pinwheels will be a breeze to make if you follow the general guidelines below. Then read on for additional information on preparing, baking and storing all kinds of cookies. Whether you prefer cookies that are crispy or chewy, iced or spiced, it's easy to achieve baking success every time.

GENERAL GUIDELINES
Take the guesswork out of cookie baking by practicing the following techniques.

• Read the entire recipe before beginning to make sure you have all the necessary ingredients and baking utensils.

• Remove butter, margarine and cream cheese from the refrigerator to soften, if necessary.

• Toast and chop nuts, pare and slice fruit, and melt chocolate before preparing the cookie dough.

• Measure all the ingredients accurately and assemble them in the order they are called for in the recipe.

• When making bar cookies or brownies, use the pan size specified in the recipe. Prepare the pans according to the recipe directions. Adjust oven racks and preheat the oven. Check oven temperature for accuracy with an oven thermometer.

• Follow recipe directions and baking times exactly. Check for doneness using the test given in the recipe.

Measuring Ingredients
Dry Ingredients: Always use standardized measuring spoons and cups. Fill the correct measuring spoon or cup to overflowing and level it off with a metal spatula or knife. When measuring flour, lightly spoon it into a measuring cup and then level it off. Do not tap or bang the measuring cup as this will pack the flour. If a recipe calls for "sifted flour," sift the flour before it is measured. If a recipe calls for "flour, sifted," measure the flour first and then sift it.

Liquid Ingredients: Use a standardized glass or plastic measuring cup with a pouring spout. Place the cup on a flat surface, fill to the desired mark and check the measurement at eye level. When measuring sticky liquids such as honey and molasses, grease the measuring cup or spray it with vegetable cooking spray before adding the liquid to make their removal easier.

Melting Chocolate
Make sure the utensils you use for melting chocolate are completely dry. Moisture makes the chocolate become stiff and grainy. If this happens, add ½ teaspoon shortening (not butter) for each ounce of

chocolate and stir until smooth. Chocolate scorches easily, and once scorched cannot be used. Follow one of these three methods for successful melting.

Double Boiler: This is the safest method because it prevents scorching. Place the chocolate in the top of a double boiler or in a bowl over hot, not boiling, water; stir until smooth. (Make sure that the water remains just below a simmer and is one inch below the top pan.) Be careful that no steam or water gets into the chocolate.

Direct Heat: Place the chocolate in a heavy saucepan and melt over very low heat, stirring constantly. Remove the chocolate from the heat as soon as it is melted. Be sure to watch the chocolate carefully since it is easily scorched with this method.

Microwave Oven: Place an unwrapped 1-ounce square or 1 cup of chips in a small microwavable bowl. Microwave on High (100%) 1 to 1½ minutes, stirring after 1 minute. Stir the chocolate at 30-second intervals until smooth. Be sure to stir microwaved chocolate since it retains its original shape even when melted.

Toasting Nuts

Toasting nuts brings out their flavor and makes them crisp. Spread the nuts in a single layer on a rimmed baking sheet. Bake in a 325°F oven for 8 to 10 minutes or until golden. Shake the pan or stir the nuts occasionally during baking to ensure even toasting. The nuts will darken and become crisper as they cool. To toast a small amount of nuts, place them in a dry skillet over low heat. Stir constantly for 2 to 4 minutes, until the nuts darken slightly.

Toasting Coconut

Spread the flaked coconut in a thin layer on a rimmed baking sheet. Bake in a 325°F oven for 7 to 10 minutes. Shake the pan occasionally during baking to promote even browning and prevent burning.

Tinting Coconut

Dilute a few drops of food coloring with ½ teaspoon milk or water in a small bowl. Add 1 to 1⅓ cups flaked coconut and toss with a fork until evenly tinted.

PREPARATION

The seemingly endless variety of cookies can actually be divided into five basic types: bar, drop, refrigerator, rolled and shaped. These types are determined by the consistency of the dough and how it is formed into cookies.

Bar Cookies: Bar cookies and brownies are some of the easiest cookies to make—simply mix the batter, spread in the pan and bake. These cookies are also quick to prepare since they bake all at once rather than in batches on a cookie sheet.

Always use the pan size called for in the recipe. Substituting a different pan will affect the cookies' texture. A smaller pan will give the bars a more cakelike texture and a larger pan will produce a flatter bar with a drier texture.

Most bar cookies should cool in the pan on a wire rack until barely warm before cutting into squares. Try cutting bar cookies into triangles or diamonds for a festive new shape. To make serving easy, remove a corner piece first; then remove the rest.

Sprinkle bar cookies with powdered sugar for a simple garnish. Dress up frosted bar cookies by topping with nuts, chocolate chips or curls, or dried or candied fruit.

Drop Cookies: These cookies are named for the way they are formed on the cookie sheet. The soft dough mounds when dropped from a spoon and then flattens slightly during baking. Space the mounds of dough about 2 inches apart on cookie sheets to allow for spreading unless the recipe directs otherwise.

Cookies that are uniform in size and shape will finish baking at the same time. To easily shape drop cookies into a uniform size, use an ice cream scoop with a release bar. The bar usually has a number on it indicating the number of scoops that can be made from one quart of ice cream. The handiest size for cookies is a #80 or #90 scoop. This will yield about one rounded teaspoonful of dough for each cookie.

Refrigerator Cookies: Refrigerator doughs are perfect for preparing in advance. Tightly wrapped rolls of dough can be stored in the refrigerator for up to one week or frozen for up to six weeks. These rich doughs are ready to be sliced and baked at a moment's notice.

Always shape the dough into rolls before chilling. Shaping is easier if you first place the dough on a piece of waxed paper or plastic wrap. If desired, you can gently press chopped nuts, flaked coconut or colored sugar into the roll. Before chilling, wrap the rolls securely in plastic wrap or air may penetrate the dough and cause it to dry out.

Use gentle pressure and a back-and-forth sawing motion when slicing the rolls so the cookies will keep their nice round shape. Rotating the roll while slicing also prevents one side from flattening.

Rolled Cookies: Rolled or cutout cookies are made from stiff doughs that are rolled out and cut into fancy shapes with floured cookie cutters, a knife or a pastry wheel.

Chill the cookie dough before rolling for easier handling. Remove only enough dough from the refrigerator to work with at one time. Save any trimmings and reroll them all at once to prevent the dough from becoming tough.

To make your own custom-designed cookie cutters, cut a simple shape out of clean, heavy cardboard or poster board. Place the cardboard pattern on the rolled out dough and cut around it using a sharp knife.

Shaped Cookies: These cookies can be simply hand-shaped into balls or crescents, forced through a cookie press into more complex shapes or baked in cookie molds.

Be sure to use the specific cookie press or mold called for in the recipe. The consistency of the dough may not lend itself to using a different tool.

By using different plates in a cookie press, spritz cookies can be formed into many shapes. If your first efforts are not successful, just transfer the dough back to the cookie press and try again. The dough itself can be flavored or tinted with food coloring and the pressed shapes can be decorated before baking with colored sugar or candied fruit.

Madeleines are cookies baked in a special madeleine pan that has scallop-shell indentations. Originally from France, they have a light, sponge-cake-like texture.

BAKING
The best cookie sheets to use are those with little or no sides. They allow the heat to circulate easily during baking and promote even browning. Another way to promote even baking and browning is to place only one cookie sheet at a time in the center of the oven. If the cookies brown unevenly, rotate the cookie sheet from front to back halfway through the baking time. If you do use more than one sheet at a time, rotate the cookie sheets from top to bottom halfway through the baking time.

When a recipe calls for greasing the cookie sheets, use shortening or a vegetable cooking spray for best results. Lining the cookie sheets with parchment paper is an alternative to greasing. It eliminates cleanup, bakes the cookies more evenly and allows them to cool right on the paper instead of on wire racks. Allow cookie sheets to cool between batches; the dough will spread if placed on a hot cookie sheet.

Most cookies bake quickly and should be watched carefully to avoid overbaking.

Check them at the minimum baking time, then watch carefully to make sure they don't burn. It is generally better to slightly underbake, rather than to overbake, cookies. Here are some guidelines that describe when different types of cookies are finished baking:

Fudgelike Bar Cookies: the surface appears dull and a slight imprint remains after touching the surface with a fingertip. **Cakelike Bar Cookies:** a wooden toothpick inserted into the center comes out clean and dry. **Drop Cookies:** lightly browned and a slight imprint remains after touching the surface with a fingertip. **Refrigerator Cookies:** the edges are firm and the bottoms are lightly browned. **Rolled Cookies:** the edges are firm and the bottoms are lightly browned. **Shaped Cookies:** the edges are lightly browned.

Most cookies should be removed from cookie sheets immediately after baking and placed in a single layer on wire racks to cool. Fragile cookies may need to cool slightly on the cookie sheet before being moved. Always cool cookies completely before stacking and storing. Bar cookies and brownies may be cooled and stored in the baking pan.

STORING

Unbaked cookie dough can be refrigerated for up to one week or frozen for up to six weeks. Rolls of dough should be sealed tightly in plastic wrap; other doughs should be stored in airtight containers. Label dough with baking information for convenience.

Store soft and crisp cookies separately at room temperature to prevent changes in texture and flavor. Keep soft cookies in airtight containers. If they begin to dry out, add a piece of apple or bread to the container to help them retain moisture. Store crisp cookies in containers with loose-fitting lids to prevent moisture buildup. If they become soggy, heat undecorated cookies in a 300°F oven for 3 to 5 minutes to restore crispness. Store cookies with sticky glazes, fragile decorations and icings in single layers between sheets of waxed paper. Bar cookies and brownies may be stored in their own baking pan, covered with aluminum foil or plastic wrap when cool.

As a rule, crisp cookies freeze better than soft, moist cookies. Rich, buttery bar cookies and brownies are an exception to this rule since they freeze extremely well. Freeze baked cookies in airtight containers or freezer bags for up to six months. Thaw cookies and brownies unwrapped at room temperature. Meringue-based cookies do *not* freeze well and chocolate-dipped cookies will discolor if frozen.

TIPS FOR SENDING COOKIES

Prepare soft, moist cookies that can handle jostling rather than fragile, brittle cookies that might crumble. Brownies and bar cookies are generally sturdy although avoid shipping those with moist fillings and frostings since they become sticky at room temperature. For the same reason, shipping anything with chocolate during the summer or to warm climates is also risky.

Wrap each type of cookie separately to retain flavors and textures. Cookies can also be wrapped back-to-back in pairs with either plastic wrap or foil. Bar cookies should be packed in layers the size of the container, or they can be sent in a covered foil pan as long as the pan is well-cushioned inside the shipping box. Place wrapped cookies as tightly as possible in snug rows inside a sturdy shipping box or container.

Fill the bottom of the shipping container with an even layer of packing material. Do *not* use popped popcorn or puffed cereal as it may attract insects. Place crumpled waxed paper, newspaper or paper toweling between layers of wrapped cookies. Fill any crevices with packing material, and add a final layer at the top of the box.

WEIGHTS AND MEASURES

Dash = less than ⅛ teaspoon

½ tablespoon = 1½ teaspoons

1 tablespoon = 3 teaspoons

2 tablespoons = ⅛ cup

¼ cup = 4 tablespoons

⅓ cup = 5 tablespoons plus 1 teaspoon

½ cup = 8 tablespoons

¾ cup = 12 tablespoons

1 cup = 16 tablespoons

½ pint = 1 cup or 8 fluid ounces

1 pint = 2 cups or 16 fluid ounces

1 quart = 4 cups or 2 pints or 32 fluid ounces

1 gallon = 16 cups or 4 quarts

1 pound = 16 ounces

SUBSTITUTION LIST

If you don't have:	Use:
1 teaspoon baking powder	¼ teaspoon baking soda + ½ teaspoon cream of tartar
½ cup firmly packed brown sugar	½ cup granulated sugar mixed with 2 tablespoons molasses
1 cup buttermilk	1 tablespoon lemon juice or vinegar plus milk to equal 1 cup (Stir; let mixture stand 5 minutes.)
1 ounce (1 square) unsweetened baking chocolate	3 tablespoons unsweetened cocoa + 1 tablespoon shortening
3 ounces (3 squares) semi-sweet baking chocolate	3 ounces (½ cup) semi-sweet chocolate morsels
½ cup corn syrup	½ cup granulated sugar + 2 tablespoons liquid
1 whole egg	2 egg yolks + 1 tablespoon water
1 cup honey	1¼ cups granulated sugar + ¼ cup water
1 teaspoon freshly grated orange or lemon peel	½ teaspoon dried peel
1 teaspoon pumpkin pie spice	Combine: ½ teaspoon cinnamon, ¼ teaspoon nutmeg and ⅛ teaspoon *each* allspice and cardamom

EQUIVALENTS

Almonds, blanched, slivered	4 oz. = 1 cup
Apples	1 medium = 1 cup sliced
Bananas	1 medium, mashed = ⅓ cup
Butter or margarine	2 cups = 1 lb. or 4 sticks 1 cup = ½ lb. or 2 sticks ½ cup = 1 stick or 8 tablespoons ¼ cup = ½ stick or 4 tablespoons
Chocolate	1 (6-ounce) package chocolate chips = 1 cup chips or 6 (1-ounce) squares semisweet chocolate
Cocoa, unsweetened	1 (8-ounce) can = 2 cups
Coconut, flaked	3½ oz. = 1⅓ cups
Cream cheese	3-oz. package = 6 tablespoons 8-oz. package = 1 cup

Flour
    White or all-purpose
    Whole-wheat
	
	1 lb. = 3½ to 4 cups
	1 lb. = 3¾ to 4 cups

Honey, liquid	16 oz. = 1⅓ cups
Lemons	1 medium = 1 to 3 tablespoons juice and 2 to 3 teaspoons grated peel
Marshmallows	1 cup cut-up = 16 large or 160 miniature

Milk
    Evaporated
 	
    Sweetened, condensed
	
	5-oz. can = ⅔ cup
	12-oz. can = 1⅔ cups
	14-oz. can = 1¼ cups

Oranges	1 medium = 6 to 8 tablespoons juice and 2 to 3 teaspoons grated peel
Pecans, shelled	1 lb. = 4 cups halved, 3½ to 4 cups chopped
Raisins, seedless, whole	1 lb. = 2¾ to 3 cups
Shortening	1 lb. = 2½ cups

Sugar
    Granulated
    Brown, packed
    Confectioners' or
        powdered
	
	1 lb. = 2½ cups
	1 lb. = 2¼ cups
	1 lb. = 3¾ to 4 cups, unsifted

Walnuts, chopped	4½ oz. = 1 cup

CHOCK-FULL O' CHIPS

Original Toll House® Chocolate Chip Cookies

2¼ cups all-purpose flour
1 teaspoon baking soda
1 teaspoon salt
1 cup (2 sticks) butter, softened
¾ cup granulated sugar
¾ cup firmly packed brown sugar
1 teaspoon vanilla extract
2 eggs
One 12-oz. pkg. (2 cups) NESTLÉ®
    Toll House® Semi-Sweet
    Chocolate Morsels
1 cup nuts, chopped

Preheat oven to 375°F. In small bowl, combine flour, baking soda and salt; set aside.

In large mixer bowl, beat butter, granulated sugar, brown sugar and vanilla extract until creamy. Beat in eggs. Gradually beat in flour mixture. Stir in NESTLÉ® Toll House® Semi-Sweet Chocolate Morsels and nuts. Drop by rounded measuring tablespoonfuls onto ungreased cookie sheets.

Bake 9 to 11 minutes until edges are golden brown. Let stand on cookie sheets 2 minutes. Remove from cookie sheets; cool completely on wire racks.
Makes about 5 dozen cookies

Pan Cookies: Preheat oven to 375°F. Spread dough in greased 15½×10½×1-inch baking pan. Bake 20 to 25 minutes. Cool completely on wire racks. Cut into 2-inch squares. *Makes about 35 squares*

Giant Toll House® Cookies: Preheat oven to 375°F. Prepare dough as directed. Drop dough by ¼ cupfuls onto ungreased cookie sheets. Press lightly into 3-inch circles. Bake 10 to 12 minutes until edges are golden brown. Let stand on cookie sheets 2 minutes. Remove from cookie sheets; cool completely on wire racks.
Makes about 20 (4-inch) cookies

Triple Chocolate Cookies

1 package DUNCAN HINES® Moist
    Deluxe Swiss Chocolate
    Cake Mix
½ cup butter or margarine, melted
1 egg
½ cup semi-sweet chocolate chips
½ cup milk chocolate chips
½ cup coarsely chopped white
    chocolate
½ cup chopped pecans

1. Preheat oven to 375°F.

2. Combine cake mix, melted butter and egg in large bowl. Stir in all 3 chocolates and pecans.

3. Drop rounded tablespoonfuls of dough onto ungreased cookie sheet. Bake 9 to 11 minutes. Cool 1 minute on cookie sheet. Remove to cooling rack.
Makes 3½ to 4 dozen cookies

Original Toll House® Chocolate Chip Cookies

Left to right: Peanut Butter Jumbos,
White Chocolate Biggies

Peanut Butter Jumbos

½ cup butter or margarine, softened
1 cup packed brown sugar
1 cup granulated sugar
1½ cups peanut butter
3 eggs
2 teaspoons baking soda
1 teaspoon vanilla
4½ cups uncooked rolled oats
1 cup (6 ounces) semisweet chocolate chips
1 cup candy-coated chocolate pieces

Preheat oven to 350°F. Lightly grease cookie sheets or line with parchment paper.

Cream butter, sugars, peanut butter and eggs in large bowl until light. Blend in baking soda, vanilla and oats until well mixed. Stir in chocolate chips and candy pieces.

Scoop out about ⅓ cupful of dough for each cookie. Place on prepared cookie sheets, spacing about 4 inches apart. Press each cookie to flatten slightly. Bake 15 to 20 minutes or until firm in center. Remove to wire racks to cool.

Makes about 1½ dozen cookies

White Chocolate Biggies

1½ cups butter or margarine, softened
1 cup granulated sugar
¾ cup packed light brown sugar
2 teaspoons vanilla
2 eggs
2½ cups all-purpose flour
⅔ cup unsweetened cocoa
1 teaspoon baking soda
½ teaspoon salt
1 package (10 ounces) large white chocolate chips
¾ cup pecan halves, coarsely chopped
½ cup golden raisins

Preheat oven to 350°F. Lightly grease cookie sheets or line with parchment paper. Cream butter, sugars, vanilla and eggs in large bowl until light. Combine flour, cocoa, baking soda and salt in medium bowl; blend into creamed mixture until smooth. Stir in white chocolate chips, pecans and raisins.

Scoop out about ⅓ cupful of dough for each cookie. Place on prepared cookie sheets, spacing about 4 inches apart. Press each cookie to flatten slightly.

Bake 12 to 14 minutes or until firm in center. Cool 5 minutes on cookie sheet, then remove to wire racks to cool completely.

Makes about 2 dozen cookies

Oatmeal Chocolate Chip Cookies

1 can (20 oz.) DOLE® Crushed
    Pineapple in Syrup*
1½ cups brown sugar, packed
1 cup margarine, softened
1 egg
¼ teaspoon almond extract
4 cups rolled oats, uncooked
2 cups flour
1 teaspoon baking powder
1 teaspoon salt
1 teaspoon ground cinnamon
½ teaspoon ground nutmeg
1 pkg. (12 oz.) semisweet chocolate
    chips
¾ cup DOLE® Slivered Almonds,
    toasted
2 cups flaked coconut

Preheat oven to 350°F. Grease cookie sheets. Drain pineapple well, reserving ½ cup syrup.

In large bowl, cream brown sugar and margarine until light and fluffy. Beat in egg. Beat in pineapple, reserved syrup and almond extract. In small bowl, combine oats, flour, baking powder, salt, cinnamon and nutmeg. Add to creamed mixture; beat until blended. Stir in chocolate chips, almonds and coconut. Drop by heaping tablespoonfuls onto cookie sheets. Flatten cookies slightly with back of spoon. Bake 20 to 25 minutes or until golden. Cool on wire racks.

Makes about 5 dozen cookies

*May use pineapple packed in juice, if desired.

Hershey's® Vanilla Chip Chocolate Cookies

1¼ cups butter or margarine, softened
2 cups sugar
2 eggs
2 teaspoons vanilla extract
2 cups all-purpose flour
¾ cup HERSHEY'S® Cocoa
1 teaspoon baking soda
½ teaspoon salt
1⅔ cups (10-ounce package)
    HERSHEY'S® Vanilla Milk Chips

Preheat oven to 350°F. In large mixer bowl, beat butter and sugar until creamy. Add eggs and vanilla extract; beat until light and fluffy. Stir together flour, cocoa, baking soda and salt; gradually blend into butter mixture. Stir in vanilla milk chips. Drop by rounded teaspoonfuls onto ungreased cookie sheet.

Bake 8 to 9 minutes. (Do not overbake; cookies will be soft. They will puff while baking; flatten upon cooling.) Cool slightly; remove from cookie sheet to wire rack. Cool completely.

Makes about 4½ dozen cookies

Hershey's® Vanilla Chip Chocolate Cookies

Tracy's Pizza-Pan Cookies

1 cup butter or margarine, softened
¾ cup granulated sugar
¾ cup packed brown sugar
1 package (8 ounces) cream cheese,
    softened
1 teaspoon vanilla
2 eggs
2¼ cups all-purpose flour
1 teaspoon baking soda
¼ teaspoon salt
1 package (12 ounces) semisweet
    chocolate chips
1 cup chopped walnuts or pecans

Preheat oven to 375°F. Lightly grease two
12-inch pizza pans.

Cream butter, sugars, cream cheese and
vanilla in large bowl. Add eggs; beat until
light. Combine flour, baking soda and salt
in small bowl. Add to creamed mixture;
blend well. Stir in chocolate chips and
nuts. Divide dough in half; press each half
evenly into a prepared pan.

Bake 20 to 25 minutes or until lightly
browned around edges. Cool completely
in pans on wire racks. To serve, cut into
slim wedges or break into pieces.

Makes two 12-inch cookies

Pistachio Chip Cookies

½ cup butter or margarine
⅓ cup light corn syrup
2 tablespoons frozen orange juice
    concentrate, thawed
1 tablespoon grated orange zest
⅔ cup packed dark brown sugar
1 cup all-purpose flour
½ cup chopped pistachio nuts
1 cup (6 ounces) semisweet chocolate
    chips

Preheat oven to 375°F. Line cookie sheets
with foil; lightly grease foil.

Combine butter, corn syrup, orange juice
concentrate, orange zest and sugar in
medium saucepan. Bring mixture to a boil
over medium heat, stirring constantly.
Remove from heat; gradually stir in flour
and nuts. Cool completely. Stir in
chocolate chips. Drop batter by
teaspoonfuls 3 inches apart onto prepared
cookie sheets.

Bake 8 to 10 minutes or until golden and
lacy. (Cookies are soft when hot, but
become crispy as they cool.) Cool
completely on foil, then peel foil from
cookies. *Makes about 4 dozen cookies*

Simply Delicious Minty Cookies

1 cup BUTTER FLAVOR CRISCO®
1 package (8 ounces) cream cheese,
    softened
¾ cup granulated sugar
½ cup firmly packed brown sugar
1 teaspoon vanilla
2 cups all-purpose flour
1¾ cups mint chocolate chips

1. Preheat oven to 350°F. Combine
BUTTER FLAVOR CRISCO®, cream
cheese, granulated sugar, brown sugar and
vanilla in large bowl. Beat at medium
speed of electric mixer until well blended.

2. Mix flour into creamed mixture at low
speed until just blended. Stir in mint
chocolate chips. Drop dough by rounded
teaspoonfuls 2 inches apart onto
ungreased cookie sheet.

3. Bake 8 minutes or until lightly browned.
Cool 2 minutes on cookie sheet. Remove
to cooling rack.

Makes about 5 dozen cookies

Oatmeal Scotch Chippers

1¼ cups BUTTER FLAVOR CRISCO®
1½ cups firmly packed brown sugar
  1 cup granulated sugar
  3 eggs
1¼ cups JIF® Extra Crunchy Peanut
    Butter
4½ cups old fashioned oats (not instant
    or quick), uncooked
  2 teaspoons baking soda
  1 cup semi-sweet chocolate chips
  1 cup butterscotch-flavored chips
  1 cup chopped walnuts

1. Preheat oven to 350°F. Combine
BUTTER FLAVOR CRISCO®, brown sugar
and granulated sugar in large bowl. Beat at
medium speed of electric mixer until well
blended. Beat in eggs. Add JIF® Extra
Crunchy Peanut Butter. Beat until blended.

2. Combine oats and baking soda. Stir into
creamed mixture with spoon. Stir in
chocolate chips, butterscotch chips and
nuts until blended.

3. Drop rounded teaspoonfuls of dough 2
inches apart onto ungreased cookie sheet.

4. Bake 10 to 11 minutes or until lightly
browned. Cool 2 minutes on cookie sheet.
Remove to cooling rack.
Makes about 6 dozen cookies

Oatmeal Scotch Chippers

Hershey's® More Chips Chocolate Chip Cookies

1½ cups butter, softened
  1 cup granulated sugar
  1 cup packed light brown sugar
  3 eggs
  2 teaspoons vanilla extract
3⅓ cups all-purpose flour
1½ teaspoons baking soda
 ¾ teaspoon salt
  4 cups (24-ounce package)
    HERSHEY'S® Semi-Sweet
    Chocolate Chips

Preheat oven to 375°F. In large mixer
bowl, beat butter, granulated sugar and
brown sugar until creamy. Add eggs and
vanilla; beat until light and fluffy. Stir
together flour, baking soda and salt;
gradually beat into butter mixture. Stir in
chocolate chips. Drop by rounded
teaspoonfuls onto ungreased cookie sheet.

Bake 8 to 10 minutes or until lightly
browned. Cool slightly; remove from
cookie sheet to wire rack. Cool completely.
Makes about 7½ dozen cookies

Chewy Cherry Chocolate Chip Cookies

½ cup BUTTER FLAVOR CRISCO®
½ cup firmly packed brown sugar
½ cup granulated sugar
½ cup dairy sour cream
  1 egg
  1 tablespoon maraschino cherry juice
¾ teaspoon vanilla
1¼ cups all-purpose flour
½ teaspoon baking soda
¼ teaspoon salt
  1 cup semi-sweet chocolate chips
½ cup chopped pecans
¼ cup well-drained chopped
    maraschino cherries

1. Preheat oven to 375°F. Combine BUTTER FLAVOR CRISCO®, brown sugar and granulated sugar in large bowl. Beat at medium speed of electric mixer until well blended. Beat in sour cream, egg, cherry juice and vanilla.

2. Combine flour, baking soda and salt. Mix into creamed mixture at low speed until well blended. Stir in chocolate chips, nuts and cherries.

3. Drop rounded tablespoonfuls of dough 2 inches apart onto ungreased cookie sheet.

4. Bake 10 to 12 minutes or until set. Cool 2 minutes on cookie sheet. Remove to cooling rack.

Makes about 3 dozen cookies

San Francisco Cookies

Party Cookies

2¼ cups flour
1 teaspoon salt
1 teaspoon baking soda
1 cup butter or margarine, softened
1 cup firmly packed light brown sugar
½ cup granulated sugar
2 eggs
2 teaspoons vanilla
1½ cups "M&M's"® Plain Chocolate Candies, divided

Preheat oven to 375°F. In small bowl, combine flour, salt and baking soda. Set aside.

In large mixer bowl, beat butter, brown sugar and granulated sugar until light and fluffy. Blend in eggs and vanilla. Gradually beat in flour mixture; mix well. Stir in ½ cup candies. Drop dough by rounded teaspoonfuls onto ungreased cookie sheet. Press 2 or 3 additional candies into each cookie.

Bake for 10 to 12 minutes or until golden brown. Cool completely on wire racks.

Makes about 6 dozen cookies

San Francisco Cookies

2 extra-ripe, medium DOLE® Bananas, peeled and cut into chunks
2 cups granola
1½ cups flour
1 cup packed brown sugar
1 teaspoon baking powder
1 teaspoon ground cinnamon
2 eggs
½ cup margarine, melted
¼ cup vegetable oil
1 cup chocolate chips

Preheat oven to 350°F. In food processor or blender, process bananas until puréed (1 cup). Combine granola, flour, sugar, baking powder and cinnamon in large mixing bowl. Beat in puréed bananas, eggs, margarine and oil. Fold in chocolate chips.

Drop dough by ¼ cupfuls onto greased cookie sheets. Spread dough into 2½-to 3-inch circles Bake 16 minutes. Remove to wire racks to cool.

Makes about 16 cookies

Chocolate Chip 'n Oatmeal Cookies

1 package (18.25 or 18.5 ounces) yellow cake mix
1 cup quick-cooking rolled oats, uncooked
¾ cup butter or margarine, softened
2 eggs
1 cup HERSHEY'S® Semi-Sweet Chocolate Chips

Preheat oven to 350°F. In large mixer bowl, combine cake mix, oats, butter and eggs; mix well. Stir in chocolate chips. Drop by rounded teaspoonfuls onto ungreased cookie sheet.

Bake 10 to 12 minutes or until very lightly browned. Cool slightly; remove from cookie sheet to wire rack. Cool completely.
Makes about 4 dozen cookies

Caramel-Chocolate Delights

¾ cup BUTTER FLAVOR CRISCO®
¾ cup firmly packed brown sugar
¾ cup granulated sugar
1 teaspoon vanilla
2 eggs
2 cups all-purpose flour
½ cup unsweetened cocoa powder
1 teaspoon baking soda
1 teaspoon salt
¾ cup milk
1 cup semi-sweet chocolate chips
1 cup chopped pecans
26 caramels, unwrapped

1. Preheat oven to 375°F. Generously grease cookie sheet with BUTTER FLAVOR CRISCO®.

2. Combine BUTTER FLAVOR CRISCO®, brown sugar, granulated sugar and vanilla in large bowl. Beat at medium speed of electric mixer until well blended. Beat in eggs.

3. Combine flour, cocoa, baking soda and salt. Add alternately with milk to creamed mixture at low speed. Beat until well blended. Stir in chocolate chips and nuts.

4. Melt caramels in top of double boiler over hot, not boiling, water. Stir occasionally. Fold melted caramels into dough with spatula. (If caramel mixture is allowed to sit, it will harden.)

5. Drop level tablespoonfuls of dough 2 inches apart onto cookie sheet.

6. Bake 9 to 10 minutes or until set. Cool 4 to 5 minutes on cookie sheet. Remove to cooling rack.
Makes about 5 dozen cookies

Easy Peanutty Snickerdoodles

2 tablespoons sugar
2 teaspoons ground cinnamon
1 package (15 ounces) golden sugar cookie mix
1 egg
1 tablespoon water
1 cup REESE'S® Peanut Butter Chips

Preheat oven to 375°F. In small bowl combine sugar and cinnamon. In medium bowl combine cookie mix (and enclosed flavor packet), egg and water; mix with spoon or fork until thoroughly blended. Stir in peanut butter chips. Shape dough into 1-inch balls. (If dough is too soft, cover and chill about 1 hour.) Roll balls in cinnamon-sugar. Place on ungreased cookie sheet.

Bake 8 to 10 minutes or until very lightly browned. Cool slightly; remove from cookie sheet to wire rack. Cool completely.
Makes about 2 dozen cookies

Left to right:
Chocolate Kiss Cookies (page 89),
Chocolate Chip 'n Oatmeal Cookies,
Easy Peanutty Snickerdoodles

Double Nut Chocolate Chip Cookies

1 package DUNCAN HINES® Moist Deluxe Yellow Cake Mix
½ cup butter or margarine, melted
1 egg
1 cup semi-sweet chocolate chips
½ cup finely chopped pecans
1 cup sliced almonds, divided

1. Preheat oven to 375°F. Grease cookie sheet.

2. Combine cake mix, butter and egg in large bowl. Mix at low speed with electric mixer until just blended. Stir in chocolate chips, pecans and ¼ cup of the almonds. Shape rounded tablespoonfuls of dough into balls. Place remaining ¾ cup almonds in shallow bowl. Press tops of cookies in almonds. Place on cookie sheet, 1 inch apart.

3. Bake 9 to 11 minutes or until lightly browned. Cool 2 minutes on cookie sheet. Remove to cooling rack.

Makes 3 to 3½ dozen cookies

Double Nut Chocolate Chip Cookies

Pudding Chip Cookies

1 cup PARKAY® Margarine, softened
¾ cup firmly packed light brown sugar
¼ cup granulated sugar
1 package (4-serving size) JELL-O® Instant Pudding and Pie Filling, Butter Pecan, Butterscotch, Chocolate, Milk Chocolate, Chocolate Fudge, French Vanilla or Vanilla Flavor
1 teaspoon vanilla
2 eggs
2¼ cups all-purpose flour
1 teaspoon baking soda
1 package (12 ounces) BAKER'S® Semi-Sweet Real Chocolate Chips
1 cup chopped nuts (optional)

Preheat oven to 375°F. Beat margarine, sugars, pudding mix and vanilla in large bowl until smooth and creamy. Beat in eggs. Gradually add flour and baking soda. Stir in chips and nuts. (Dough will be stiff.) Drop by teaspoonfuls 2 inches apart onto ungreased cookie sheets.

Bake 8 to 10 minutes or until lightly browned. Remove from cookie sheets; cool on racks. *Makes about 7 dozen cookies*

Prep time: 30 minutes
Baking time: 30 minutes

Peanut Butter Sunshine Cookies

½ cup BUTTER FLAVOR CRISCO®
¾ cup JIF® Extra Crunchy Peanut Butter
1 cup sugar
½ cup orange marmalade
2 eggs
1 teaspoon vanilla
2 cups all-purpose flour
1 tablespoon baking powder
½ teaspoon salt
1 cup butterscotch-flavored chips

1. Preheat oven to 350°F. Grease cookie sheet with BUTTER FLAVOR CRISCO®.

2. Combine BUTTER FLAVOR CRISCO®, JIF® Extra Crunchy Peanut Butter and sugar in large bowl. Beat at medium speed of electric mixer until well blended. Beat in marmalade, eggs and vanilla.

3. Combine flour, baking powder and salt. Mix into creamed mixture at low speed until just blended. Stir in butterscotch chips.

4. Drop rounded teaspoonfuls of dough 2 inches apart onto cookie sheet.

5. Bake 10 to 12 minutes or until lightly browned. Cool 2 minutes on cookie sheet. Remove to cooling rack.

Makes about 4 dozen cookies

Black Forest Oatmeal Fancies

Black Forest Oatmeal Fancies

1 cup BUTTER FLAVOR CRISCO®
1 cup firmly packed brown sugar
1 cup granulated sugar
2 eggs
2 teaspoons vanilla
1⅔ cups all-purpose flour
1 teaspoon baking soda
1 teaspoon salt
½ teaspoon baking powder
3 cups quick oats (not instant or old fashioned), uncooked
1 baking bar (6 ounces) white chocolate, coarsely chopped
6 squares (1 ounce each) semi-sweet chocolate, coarsely chopped
½ cup coarsely chopped red candied cherries
½ cup sliced almonds

1. Preheat oven to 375°F. Combine BUTTER FLAVOR CRISCO®, brown sugar, granulated sugar, eggs and vanilla in large bowl. Beat at medium speed of electric mixer until well blended.

2. Combine flour, baking soda, salt and baking powder. Mix into creamed mixture at low speed until well blended. Stir in, one at a time, oats, white chocolate, semi-sweet chocolate, cherries and nuts with spoon.

3. Drop rounded tablespoonfuls of dough 2 inches apart onto ungreased cookie sheet.

4. Bake 9 to 11 minutes or until set. Cool 2 minutes on cookie sheet. Remove to cooling rack.

Makes about 3 dozen cookies

Double Chocolate Cookies

2 cups biscuit baking mix
1 (14-ounce) can EAGLE® Brand
    Sweetened Condensed Milk
    (NOT evaporated milk)
8 (1-ounce) squares semi-sweet
    chocolate *or* 1 (12-ounce) package
    semi-sweet chocolate chips,
    melted
3 tablespoons margarine or butter,
    melted
1 egg
1 teaspoon vanilla extract
6 (1¼-ounce) white candy bars with
    almonds, broken into small pieces
¾ cup chopped nuts

Preheat oven to 350°F. In large mixer bowl, combine all ingredients except candy pieces and nuts; beat until smooth. Stir in remaining ingredients. Drop by rounded teaspoonfuls, 2 inches apart, onto ungreased cookie sheets.

Bake 10 minutes or until tops are slightly crusted (*do not overbake*). Cool. Store tightly covered at room temperature.

Mint Chocolate: Omit white candy bars. Stir in ¾ cup mint-flavored chocolate chips. Proceed as above.

Chocolate Chip Whole Wheat Cookies

¾ cup shortening
1½ cups packed light brown sugar
 1 egg
¼ cup water
 1 teaspoon vanilla extract
 1 cup whole wheat flour
½ teaspoon baking soda
½ teaspoon salt
 2 cups quick-cooking oats, uncooked
 1 cup chopped dried apricots or
    raisins
 1 cup HERSHEY'S® MINI CHIPS®
    Semi-Sweet Chocolate

Preheat oven to 350°F. In large mixer bowl, beat shortening and brown sugar until light and fluffy. Add egg, water and vanilla; beat well. Stir together whole wheat flour, baking soda and salt; stir into brown sugar mixture. Stir in oats, apricots and MINI CHIPS® chocolate. Drop by rounded teaspoonfuls onto lightly greased cookie sheet; flatten slightly.

Bake 10 to 12 minutes or until golden brown. Remove to wire rack. Cool completely.   *Makes about 5 dozen cookies*

Chocolate-Orange Chip Cookies

(Pictured on page 113)

½ cup BUTTER FLAVOR CRISCO®
1¼ cups firmly packed brown sugar
 2 squares (1 ounce each) unsweetened
    chocolate, melted and cooled
 1 egg
 2 tablespoons orange juice
    concentrate
 2 tablespoons grated orange peel
 1 teaspoon vanilla
1½ cups all-purpose flour
¾ teaspoon baking soda
¼ teaspoon salt
 1 cup semi-sweet chocolate chips
½ cup blanched slivered almonds

1. Preheat oven to 375°F. Combine BUTTER FLAVOR CRISCO®, brown sugar and melted chocolate in large bowl. Beat at medium speed of electric mixer until well blended. Beat in egg, concentrate, peel and vanilla.

2. Combine flour, baking soda and salt. Mix into creamed mixture at low speed until well blended. Stir in chocolate chips and nuts.

3. Drop tablespoonfuls of dough 2 inches apart onto ungreased cookie sheet.

4. Bake 7 to 9 minutes or until set. Cool 2 minutes on cookie sheet. Remove to cooling rack.

Makes about 3½ dozen cookies

Cowboy Cookies

½ cup butter or margarine, softened
½ cup packed light brown sugar
¼ cup granulated sugar
1 egg
1 teaspoon vanilla
1 cup all-purpose flour
2 tablespoons unsweetened cocoa
½ teaspoon baking powder
¼ teaspoon baking soda
1 cup uncooked rolled oats
1 cup (6 ounces) semisweet chocolate chips
½ cup raisins
½ cup chopped nuts

Preheat oven to 375°F. Lightly grease cookie sheets or line with parchment paper.

Cream butter with sugars in large bowl until blended. Add egg and vanilla; beat until fluffy. Combine flour, cocoa, baking powder and baking soda in small bowl; stir into creamed mixture with oats, chocolate chips, raisins and nuts. Drop dough by teaspoonfuls 2 inches apart onto prepared cookie sheets.

Bake 10 to 12 minutes or until lightly browned around edges. Remove to wire racks to cool.

Makes about 4 dozen cookies

Cowboy Cookies

Island Treasure Cookies

1⅔ cups all-purpose flour
¾ teaspoon baking powder
½ teaspoon baking soda
½ teaspoon salt
14 tablespoons (1¾ sticks) butter, softened
¾ cup firmly packed brown sugar
⅓ cup granulated sugar
1 teaspoon vanilla extract
1 egg
¾ cup shredded coconut, toasted if desired
¾ cup macadamia nuts or walnuts, chopped
One 10-oz. pkg. (1½ cups) NESTLÉ® Toll House® Treasures® Milk Chocolate Deluxe Baking Pieces

Preheat oven to 375°F. In small bowl, combine flour, baking powder, baking soda and salt; set aside.

In large mixer bowl, beat butter, brown sugar, granulated sugar and vanilla extract until creamy. Beat in egg. Gradually blend in flour mixture. Stir in coconut, nuts and NESTLÉ® Toll House® Treasures® Milk Chocolate Deluxe Baking Pieces. Drop dough by slightly rounded measuring tablespoonfuls onto ungreased cookie sheets.

Bake 10 to 12 minutes until edges are lightly browned. Let stand on cookie sheets 2 minutes. Remove from cookie sheets; cool completely on wire racks.

Makes about 2 dozen cookies

Ivory Chip Strawberry Fudge Drops

⅔ cup BUTTER FLAVOR CRISCO®
1 cup sugar
1 egg
½ teaspoon strawberry extract
½ cup buttermilk*
6 tablespoons puréed frozen
    sweetened strawberries
1¾ cups all-purpose flour
6 tablespoons unsweetened cocoa
    powder
¾ teaspoon baking soda
½ teaspoon salt
1½ cups white chocolate baking chips

1. Preheat oven to 350°F. Grease cookie sheet with BUTTER FLAVOR CRISCO®.

2. Combine BUTTER FLAVOR CRISCO®, sugar, egg and strawberry extract in large bowl. Beat at medium speed of electric mixer until well blended. Beat in buttermilk and strawberry purée.

3. Combine flour, cocoa, baking soda and salt. Mix into creamed mixture at low speed of electric mixer until blended. Stir in white chocolate chips.

4. Drop rounded tablespoonfuls of dough 2 inches apart onto cookie sheet.

5. Bake 11 to 12 minutes or until tops spring back when pressed lightly. Remove immediately to cooling rack.

Makes about 2½ dozen cookies

*You may substitute 1½ teaspoons lemon juice or vinegar plus enough milk to make ½ cup for the buttermilk. Stir. Wait 5 minutes before using.

Brownie Cookie Bites

One 10-oz. pkg. (1½ cups) NESTLÉ®
    Toll House® Treasures®
    Semi-Sweet Chocolate Deluxe
    Baking Pieces, divided
1 tablespoon butter
¼ cup all-purpose flour
¼ teaspoon baking powder
1 egg
⅓ cup sugar
½ teaspoon vanilla extract

Over hot (not boiling) water, melt ½ cup NESTLÉ® Toll House® Treasures® Semi-Sweet Chocolate Deluxe Baking Pieces and butter, stirring until smooth.* In small bowl, combine flour and baking powder; set aside.

Preheat oven to 350°F. In small mixer bowl, beat egg and sugar at high speed until mixture is thick, about 3 minutes. Stir in vanilla and melted chocolate mixture. Gradually blend in flour mixture; stir in remaining NESTLÉ® Toll House® Treasures® Semi-Sweet Chocolate Deluxe Baking Pieces. Drop by level measuring tablespoonfuls onto greased cookie sheets.

Bake 8 to 10 minutes until cookies are puffed and tops are cracked and moist. (Cookies will look slightly underbaked.) Let stand on cookie sheets 5 minutes; cool on wire racks.

Makes about 1½ dozen cookies

*Or, place ½ cup NESTLÉ® Toll House® Treasures® Semi-Sweet Chocolate Deluxe Baking Pieces and butter in microwave-safe bowl. Microwave on HIGH power 1 minute; stir. Microwave on HIGH power 30 seconds longer; stir until smooth.

Ivory Chip Strawberry Fudge Drops

Double Chocolate Black-Eyed Susans

Double Chocolate Black-Eyed Susans

**1 package (18.25 or 19.75 ounces)
  fudge marble cake mix
1 egg
⅓ cup vegetable oil
4 tablespoons water, divided
1 cup HERSHEY'S® MINI CHIPS®
  Semi-Sweet Chocolate**

Preheat oven to 350°F. In large bowl, combine cake mix, egg, oil and 3 tablespoons water; mix with spoon until thoroughly blended. Stir in MINI CHIPS® chocolate. In separate bowl, combine ⅔ cup batter, chocolate packet from cake mix and remaining 1 tablespoon water; mix well. Drop vanilla batter by rounded teaspoonfuls onto lightly greased cookie sheet; gently press down center with thumb or back of spoon. Drop chocolate batter by rounded half teaspoonfuls onto top of each cookie.

Bake 10 to 12 minutes or until very lightly browned. Cool slightly; remove from cookie sheet to wire rack. Cool completely.
Makes about 3 dozen cookies

Ricotta Cookies with Chocolate and Pecans

**2 cups sugar
1 cup butter or margarine, softened
3 eggs
1 container (2 pounds) POLLY-O®
  Ricotta Cheese
1 tablespoon vanilla extract
1 tablespoon almond extract
4½ cups all-purpose flour
2 tablespoons baking powder
3 tablespoons coffee-flavored liqueur
¾ cup coarsely chopped pecans
3 squares (1 ounce each) semi-sweet
  chocolate, coarsely chopped**

Preheat oven to 350°F. Grease cookie sheets.

In large bowl, cream sugar and butter until well blended. Add eggs, ricotta cheese, vanilla and almond extract; mix well. In small bowl, sift together flour and baking powder. Alternately fold flour mixture, one cup at a time, and liqueur into ricotta mixture. Add pecans and chocolate. Drop by tablespoonfuls onto prepared cookie sheets.

Bake 20 to 25 minutes until lightly browned. Remove to wire racks to cool.
Makes about 60 cookies

Chunky Fruit Chews

**4 cups QUAKER® Oats (quick or old
  fashioned, uncooked)
1¼ teaspoons ground cinnamon
¾ cup non-fat dry milk
½ cup KRETSCHMER® Wheat Germ,
  any flavor *or* QUAKER®
  Unprocessed Bran
¾ cup (1½ sticks) margarine or butter,
  softened
2 eggs
⅔ cup honey
1 cup mixed dried fruit, chopped
½ cup semi-sweet chocolate pieces**

Preheat oven to 325°F. In small bowl, combine oats, cinnamon, non-fat dry milk and wheat germ; set aside.

In large mixer bowl, beat margarine, eggs and honey until creamy. Gradually add flour mixture. Stir in fruit and chocolate pieces. Drop by rounded teaspoonfuls onto ungreased cookie sheets.

Bake 10 to 12 minutes or until edges are firm. Cool 2 minutes on cookie sheets; remove to wire racks. Cool completely. Store tightly covered.

Makes about 5½ dozen cookies

Whole Grain Chippers

  1 cup butter or margarine, softened
⅔ cup granulated sugar
  1 cup packed light brown sugar
  2 eggs
  1 teaspoon baking soda
  1 teaspoon vanilla
    Pinch salt
  1 cup whole wheat flour
  1 cup all-purpose flour
  2 cups uncooked rolled oats
  1 package (12 ounces) semisweet
    chocolate chips
  1 cup sunflower seeds

Preheat oven to 375°F. Lightly grease cookie sheets or line with parchment paper.

Cream butter with sugars and eggs in large bowl until light and fluffy. Beat in baking soda, vanilla and salt. Blend in flours and oats to make a stiff dough. Stir in chocolate chips. Shape rounded teaspoonfuls of dough into balls; roll in sunflower seeds. Place 2 inches apart on prepared cookie sheets.

Bake 8 to 10 minutes or until firm. Do not overbake. Cool a few minutes on cookie sheets, then remove to wire racks to cool completely.

Makes about 6 dozen cookies

Reese's® Chewy Chocolate Cookies

1¼ cups butter or margarine, softened
  2 cups sugar
  2 eggs
  2 teaspoons vanilla extract
  2 cups all-purpose flour
¾ cup HERSHEY'S® Cocoa
  1 teaspoon baking soda
½ teaspoon salt
1⅔ cups (10-ounce package) REESE'S®
    Peanut Butter Chips
½ cup finely chopped nuts (optional)

Preheat oven to 350°F. In large mixer bowl, beat butter and sugar until light and fluffy. Add eggs and vanilla; beat well. Combine flour, cocoa, baking soda and salt; gradually blend into creamed mixture. Stir in peanut butter chips and nuts, if desired. Drop by teaspoonfuls onto ungreased cookie sheet.

Bake 8 to 9 minutes. (Do not overbake; cookies will be soft. They will puff while baking and flatten while cooling). Cool slightly; remove from cookie sheet to wire rack. Cool completely.

Makes about 4½ dozen cookies

Whole Grain Chippers

Sour Cream Chocolate Chip Cookies

1. Preheat oven to 375°F. Grease cookie sheet with BUTTER FLAVOR CRISCO®.

2. Combine BUTTER FLAVOR CRISCO®, brown sugar and granulated sugar in large bowl. Beat at medium speed of electric mixer until well blended. Beat in egg, sour cream, honey and vanilla. Beat until just blended.

3. Combine flour, baking powder and salt. Mix into creamed mixture at low speed until just blended. Stir in chocolate chips and nuts.

4. Drop slightly rounded measuring tablespoonfuls of dough 2 inches apart onto cookie sheet.

5. Bake 10 to 12 minutes or until set. Cool 2 minutes on cookie sheet. Remove to cooling rack.

Makes about 5 dozen cookies

Sour Cream Chocolate Chip Cookies

1 cup BUTTER FLAVOR CRISCO®
1 cup firmly packed brown sugar
½ cup granulated sugar
1 egg
½ cup dairy sour cream
¼ cup warm honey
2 teaspoons vanilla
2½ cups all-purpose flour
1½ teaspoons baking powder
½ teaspoon salt
2 cups semi-sweet or milk chocolate chips
1 cup coarsely chopped walnuts

Quick Peanut Butter Chocolate Chip Cookies

1 package DUNCAN HINES® Moist Deluxe Yellow Cake Mix
½ cup JIF® Creamy Peanut Butter
½ cup butter or margarine, softened
2 eggs
1 cup milk chocolate chips

1. Preheat oven to 350°F. Grease cookie sheet.

2. Combine cake mix, peanut butter, butter and eggs in large bowl. Mix at low speed with electric mixer until blended. Stir in chocolate chips.

3. Drop rounded teaspoonfuls of dough onto cookie sheet. Bake 9 to 11 minutes or until lightly browned. Cool 2 minutes on cookie sheet. Remove to cooling rack.

Makes about 4 dozen cookies

Tip: You can use JIF® Extra Crunchy Peanut Butter in place of regular peanut butter.

Crunchy Chocolate Chipsters

½ cup BUTTER FLAVOR CRISCO®
½ cup firmly packed brown sugar
½ cup granulated sugar
2 tablespoons milk
1 egg
1 teaspoon vanilla
1¼ cups all-purpose flour
½ teaspoon baking soda
¼ teaspoon salt
2 cups crisp rice cereal
1 cup semi-sweet miniature chocolate chips

1. Preheat oven to 350°F. Grease cookie sheet with BUTTER FLAVOR CRISCO®.

2. Combine BUTTER FLAVOR CRISCO®, brown sugar, granulated sugar and milk in large bowl. Beat at medium speed of electric mixer until well blended. Beat in egg and vanilla.

3. Combine flour, baking soda and salt. Mix into creamed mixture at low speed until blended. Stir in cereal and chocolate chips. Drop level measuring tablespoonfuls of dough 2 inches apart onto cookie sheet.

4. Bake 9 minutes or until set. Remove immediately to cooling rack.

Makes about 4 dozen cookies

Almond Chocolate Chip Cookies

2½ cups all-purpose flour
1 teaspoon baking soda
¼ teaspoon salt
1 can SOLO® Almond Paste
1 cup butter or margarine, softened
½ cup granulated sugar
½ cup firmly packed brown sugar
2 eggs
½ teaspoon almond extract
1 package (12 ounces) semisweet chocolate morsels
1 cup toasted slivered almonds

Preheat oven to 350°F. Grease 2 large cookie sheets. In small bowl, combine flour, baking soda and salt; set aside.

In medium-size bowl, break almond paste into small pieces. Add butter; beat with electric mixer until mixture is creamy and smooth. Add sugars, eggs and almond extract; beat until thoroughly blended. Add flour mixture; stir until well combined. Stir in chocolate and almonds. Drop heaping teaspoonfuls of dough 1½ inches apart onto prepared cookie sheets.

Bake 12 to 15 minutes or until golden brown. Remove from cookie sheets; cool on wire racks.

Makes about 6½ dozen cookies

Scrumptious Chocolate Fruit and Nut Cookies

1¼ cups butter or margarine, softened
2 cups sugar
2 eggs
2 teaspoons vanilla extract
2 cups all-purpose flour
¾ cup HERSHEY'S® Cocoa
1 teaspoon baking soda
½ teaspoon salt
2 cups (12-ounce package) HERSHEY'S® Semi-Sweet Chocolate Chips
1 cup chopped dried apricots
1 cup coarsely chopped macadamia nuts

Preheat oven to 350°F. In large mixer bowl, beat butter and sugar until light and fluffy. Add eggs and vanilla; beat well. Stir together flour, cocoa, baking soda and salt; blend into butter mixture. Stir in chocolate chips, apricots and nuts. Using ice cream scoop or ¼ cup measuring cup, drop dough 3 to 4 inches apart onto ungreased cookie sheet.

Bake 12 to 14 minutes or until set. Cool slightly; remove from cookie sheet to wire rack. Cool completely.

Makes about 24 (3½-inch) cookies

LUSCIOUS BROWNIES

One Bowl Brownies

4 squares BAKER'S® Unsweetened
    Chocolate
¾ cup (1½ sticks) margarine or butter
2 cups sugar
3 eggs
1 teaspoon vanilla
1 cup all-purpose flour
1 cup chopped nuts (optional)

Preheat oven to 350°F.

Microwave chocolate and margarine in
large microwavable bowl on HIGH 2
minutes or until margarine is melted. **Stir
until chocolate is completely melted.**

Stir sugar into melted chocolate mixture.
Mix in eggs and vanilla until well blended.
Stir in flour and nuts. Spread in greased
13×9-inch pan.

Bake for 30 to 35 minutes or until
toothpick inserted into center comes out
with fudgy crumbs. **Do not overbake.**
Cool in pan; cut into squares.

Makes about 24 brownies

Prep time: 10 minutes
Baking time: 30 to 35 minutes

Peanut Butter Swirl Brownies: Prepare
One Bowl Brownie batter as directed,
reserving 1 tablespoon of the margarine
and 2 tablespoons of the sugar. Add
reserved ingredients to ⅔ cup peanut
butter; mix well.

Place spoonfuls of peanut butter mixture
over brownie batter. Swirl with knife to
marbleize. Bake for 30 to 35 minutes or
until toothpick inserted into center comes
out with fudgy crumbs. Cool in pan; cut
into squares. *Makes about 24 brownies*

Prep time: 15 minutes
Baking time: 30 to 35 minutes

Rocky Road Brownies: Prepare One Bowl
Brownies as directed. Bake for 30 minutes.

Sprinkle 2 cups KRAFT® Miniature
Marshmallows, 1 cup BAKER'S® Semi-
Sweet Real Chocolate Chips and 1 cup
chopped nuts over brownies immediately.
Continue baking 3 to 5 minutes or until
topping begins to melt together. Cool in
pan; cut into squares.

Makes about 24 brownies

Prep time: 15 minutes
Baking time: 35 minutes

Top to bottom:
Peanut Butter Swirl Brownies,
Rocky Road Brownies

Left to right: Brownie Fudge,
White Chocolate & Almond Brownies

White Chocolate & Almond Brownies

12 ounces white chocolate, broken into
**   pieces**
1 cup unsalted butter
3 eggs
¾ cup all-purpose flour
1 teaspoon vanilla
½ cup slivered almonds

Preheat oven to 325°F. Grease and flour
9-inch square pan. Melt chocolate and
butter in large saucepan over low heat,
stirring constantly. (Do not be concerned if
the white chocolate separates.) Remove
from heat when chocolate is just melted.
With electric mixer, beat in eggs until
mixture is smooth. Beat in flour and
vanilla. Spread batter evenly in prepared
pan. Sprinkle almonds evenly over top.

Bake 30 to 35 minutes or just until set in
center. Cool completely in pan on wire
rack. Cut into 2-inch squares.
Makes about 16 brownies

Brownie Fudge

4 squares (1 ounce each) unsweetened
**   chocolate**
1 cup butter or margarine
2 cups sugar
4 eggs
1 cup all-purpose flour
1 cup chopped walnuts
2 teaspoons vanilla
**   Fudge Topping (recipe follows)**

Preheat oven to 350°F. Butter 13×9-inch
pan. Melt chocolate and butter in small
heavy saucepan over low heat, stirring
until completely melted; cool. Beat sugar
and eggs in large bowl until light and
fluffy. Gradually whisk chocolate mixture
into egg mixture. Stir in flour, walnuts and
vanilla. Spread evenly in prepared pan.

Bake 25 to 35 minutes or just until set. Do
not overbake. Meanwhile, prepare Fudge
Topping. Remove brownies from oven.
Immediately pour topping evenly over hot
brownies. Cool in pan on wire rack. Place
in freezer until firm. Cut into 1-inch
squares.   *Makes about 9 dozen brownies*

Fudge Topping

4½ cups sugar
⅓ cup butter or margarine
1 can (12 ounces) evaporated milk
1 jar (7 ounces) marshmallow creme
1 package (12 ounces) semisweet
**   chocolate chips**
1 package (12 ounces) milk chocolate
**   chips**
2 teaspoons vanilla
2 cups walnuts, coarsely chopped

Combine sugar, butter and milk in large
saucepan. Bring to a boil over medium
heat; boil 5 minutes, stirring constantly.
Remove from heat; add remaining
ingredients *except* walnuts. Beat until
smooth. Stir in walnuts.

Sour Cream Brownies

Brownies
- 1 cup water
- 1 cup butter
- 3 tablespoons unsweetened cocoa
- 2 cups all-purpose flour
- 2 cups granulated sugar
- 1 teaspoon baking soda
- ½ teaspoon salt
- 1 (8-ounce) container sour cream
- 2 eggs

Frosting
- 4 cups sifted powdered sugar
- 3 tablespoons unsweetened cocoa
- ½ cup butter, softened
- 6 tablespoons milk
- 1 cup chopped nuts

For Brownies, preheat oven to 350°F. In medium saucepan, combine water, butter and cocoa. Cook, stirring constantly, until mixture boils. Remove from heat; set aside. In medium bowl, combine flour, granulated sugar, baking soda and salt; set aside.

In large mixing bowl, beat sour cream with eggs. Gradually add hot cocoa mixture, beating well. Blend in flour mixture; beat until smooth. Pour batter into greased 15×10×1-inch baking pan. Bake 25 to 30 minutes. Cool completely in pan on wire rack.

For Frosting, combine powdered sugar and cocoa; set aside. Beat butter in medium mixing bowl until creamy. Add powdered sugar mixture alternately with milk, beating well after each addition. Spread over cooled bars. Sprinkle nuts over frosting. Cut into bars.

Makes about 40 brownies

Favorite recipe from **Wisconsin Milk Marketing Board**
© 1992

Cappucino Bon Bons

- 1 package DUNCAN HINES® Fudge Brownie Mix, Family Size
- 2 eggs
- ⅓ cup water
- ⅓ cup CRISCO® Oil or PURITAN® Oil
- 1½ tablespoons FOLGERS® Instant Coffee
- 1 teaspoon ground cinnamon
  Whipped topping
  Cinnamon

1. Preheat oven to 350°F. Place 2-inch foil cupcake liners on cookie sheet.

2. Combine brownie mix, eggs, water, oil, instant coffee and cinnamon. Stir with spoon until well blended, about 50 strokes. Fill each cupcake liner with 1 measuring tablespoon batter. Bake 12 to 15 minutes or until wooden toothpick inserted in center comes out clean. Cool completely. Garnish with whipped topping and a dash of cinnamon. Refrigerate until ready to serve.

Makes about 40 bon bons

Tip: To make larger Bon Bons, use twelve 2½-inch foil cupcake liners and fill with ¼ cup batter. Bake 28 to 30 minutes.

Cappucino Bon Bons

Toffee Brownie Bars

Crust
- ¾ cup butter or margarine, softened
- ¾ cup firmly packed brown sugar
- 1 egg yolk
- ¾ teaspoon vanilla extract
- 1½ cups all-purpose flour

Filling
- 1 package DUNCAN HINES® Fudge Brownie Mix, Family Size
- 1 egg
- ⅓ cup water
- ⅓ cup CRISCO® Oil or PURITAN® Oil

Topping
- 1 package (12 ounces) milk chocolate chips, melted
- ¾ cup finely chopped pecans

1. Preheat oven to 350°F. Grease 15½×10½×1-inch pan.

2. For Crust, combine butter, brown sugar, egg yolk and vanilla extract in large bowl. Stir in flour. Spread in pan. Bake 15 minutes or until golden.

3. For Filling, prepare brownie mix following package directions. Spread over hot crust. Bake 15 minutes or until surface appears set. Cool 30 minutes.

4. For Topping, spread melted chocolate on top of brownie layer; garnish with pecans. Cool completely in pan on wire rack. *Makes about 48 brownies*

Chewy Chocolate Brownies

- 1 cup (2 sticks) butter
- 3 foil-wrapped bars (6 oz.) NESTLÉ® Unsweetened Chocolate Baking Bars
- 2½ cups sugar
- 5 eggs
- 2 teaspoons vanilla extract
- ½ teaspoon salt
- 1½ cups all-purpose flour
- 2 cups chopped walnuts

Preheat oven to 375°F. In small saucepan, combine butter and Nestlé® Unsweetened Chocolate Baking Bars. Cook over low heat, stirring constantly, until chocolate is melted and mixture is smooth. Remove from heat; cool 10 minutes.

In large mixer bowl, beat sugar, eggs, vanilla extract and salt until foamy. Stir in chocolate mixture. Gradually add flour. Stir in nuts. Pour into greased 13×9-inch baking pan.

Bake 35 to 40 minutes. Cool completely. Cut into 2-inch squares.

Makes 24 brownies

Bittersweet Brownies

- MAZOLA® No Stick cooking spray
- 4 squares (1 ounce each) unsweetened chocolate, melted
- 1 cup sugar
- ½ cup HELLMANN'S® or BEST FOODS® Real, Light or Cholesterol Free Reduced Calorie Mayonnaise
- 2 eggs
- 1 teaspoon vanilla
- ¾ cup flour
- ½ teaspoon baking powder
- ¼ teaspoon salt
- ½ cup chopped walnuts

Preheat oven to 350°F. Spray 8×8×2-inch baking pan with cooking spray. In large bowl, stir chocolate, sugar, mayonnaise, eggs and vanilla until smooth. Stir in flour, baking powder and salt until well blended. Stir in walnuts. Spread evenly in prepared pan.

Bake 25 to 30 minutes or until wooden toothpick inserted into center comes out clean. Cool in pan on wire rack. Cut into 2-inch squares. *Makes 16 brownies*

Toffee Brownie Bars

Deep Dish Brownies

¾ cup butter or margarine, melted
1½ cups sugar
1½ teaspoons vanilla extract
 3 eggs
¾ cup all-purpose flour
½ cup HERSHEY'S® Cocoa
½ teaspoon baking powder
½ teaspoon salt

Preheat oven to 350°F. Grease 8-inch square baking pan.

In medium bowl blend butter, sugar and vanilla. Add eggs; using spoon, beat well. Combine flour, cocoa, baking powder and salt; gradually add to egg mixture, beating until well blended. Spread batter into prepared pan.

Bake 40 to 45 minutes or until brownies begin to pull away from sides of pan. Cool completely in pan on wire rack. Cut into squares.   *Makes about 16 brownies*

Variation: Stir 1 cup REESE'S® Peanut Butter Chips or HERSHEY'S® Semi-Sweet Chocolate Chips into batter.

Chocolate-Mint Brownies

½ cup butter or margarine
 2 squares (1 ounce each) unsweetened chocolate
 2 eggs
 1 cup packed light brown sugar
½ cup all-purpose flour
 1 teaspoon vanilla
   Creamy Mint Frosting (recipe follows)
   Chocolate Glaze (recipe follows)

Preheat oven to 350°F. Grease and flour 8-inch square pan. Melt butter and chocolate in small heavy saucepan over low heat; stir until blended. Remove from heat; cool. Beat eggs in medium bowl until light. Add brown sugar, beating well. Blend in chocolate mixture. Stir in flour and vanilla. Spread batter evenly in prepared pan.

Bake 30 minutes or until firm in center. Cool in pan on wire rack. Prepare Creamy Mint Frosting. Spread over top; refrigerate until firm. Prepare Chocolate Glaze. Drizzle over frosting; refrigerate until firm. Cut into 2-inch squares.
Makes 16 brownies

Creamy Mint Frosting

1½ cups powdered sugar
 2 to 3 tablespoons light cream or milk
 1 tablespoon butter or margarine, softened
½ teaspoon peppermint extract
 1 to 2 drops green food coloring

Blend powdered sugar, 2 tablespoons of the cream and the butter in small bowl until smooth. Add more cream, if necessary, to make frosting of spreading consistency. Blend in peppermint extract and enough green food coloring to make a pale mint-green color.

Chocolate Glaze

½ cup semisweet chocolate chips
 2 tablespoons butter or margarine

Place chocolate chips and butter in small bowl over hot water. Stir until melted and smooth.

Deep Dish Brownies

Madison Avenue Mocha Brownies

1 (20 or 23 oz.) pkg. brownie mix
1 (8 oz.) pkg. PHILADELPHIA
  BRAND® Cream Cheese,
  softened
⅓ cup sugar
1 egg
1½ teaspoons MAXWELL HOUSE®
  Instant Coffee
1 teaspoon vanilla

- Preheat oven to 350°F.
- Prepare brownie mix according to package directions. Pour into greased 13×9-inch baking pan.
- Beat cream cheese, sugar and egg in small mixing bowl at medium speed with electric mixer until well blended.
- Dissolve coffee in vanilla; add to cream cheese mixture, mixing until well blended.
- Spoon cream cheese mixture over brownie batter; cut through batter with knife several times for marble effect.
- Bake 35 to 40 minutes or until cream cheese mixture is set. Cool; cut into bars.

Makes about 4 dozen brownies

Prep time: 20 minutes
Cooking time: 40 minutes

Raspberry Fudge Brownies

½ cup butter or margarine
3 squares (1 ounce each) bittersweet
  chocolate*
2 eggs
1 cup sugar
1 teaspoon vanilla
¾ cup all-purpose flour
¼ teaspoon baking powder
  Dash salt
½ cup sliced or slivered almonds
½ cup raspberry preserves
1 cup (6 ounces) milk chocolate chips

Preheat oven to 350°F. Butter and flour 8-inch square pan.

Raspberry Fudge Brownies

Melt butter and bittersweet chocolate in small heavy saucepan over low heat. Remove from heat; cool. Beat eggs, sugar and vanilla in large bowl until light. Beat in chocolate mixture. Stir in flour, baking powder and salt until just blended. Spread ¾ of batter in prepared pan; sprinkle almonds over top.

Bake 10 minutes. Remove from oven; spread preserves over almonds. Carefully spoon remaining batter over preserves, smoothing top. Bake 25 to 30 minutes or just until top feels firm.

Remove from oven; sprinkle chocolate chips over top. Let stand a few minutes until chips melt, then spread evenly over brownies. Cool completely in pan on wire rack. When chocolate is set, cut into 2-inch squares.   *Makes 16 brownies*

*Bittersweet chocolate is available in specialty food stores. One square unsweetened chocolate plus two squares semisweet chocolate may be substituted.

Peanut-Layered Brownies

Brownie Layer:
- 4 squares BAKER'S® Unsweetened Chocolate
- ¾ cup (1½ sticks) margarine or butter
- 2 cups granulated sugar
- 3 eggs
- 1 teaspoon vanilla
- 1 cup all-purpose flour
- 1 cup chopped peanuts

Peanut Butter Layer:
- 1 cup peanut butter
- ½ cup powdered sugar
- 1 teaspoon vanilla

Glaze:
- 4 squares BAKER'S® Semi-Sweet Chocolate
- ¼ cup (½ stick) margarine or butter

Preheat oven to 350°F.

Microwave unsweetened chocolate and ¾ cup margarine in large microwavable bowl on HIGH 2 minutes or until margarine is melted. **Stir until chocolate is completely melted.**

Stir granulated sugar into melted chocolate mixture. Mix in eggs and 1 teaspoon vanilla until well blended. Stir in flour and peanuts. Spread batter in greased 13×9-inch pan.

Bake for 30 to 35 minutes or until toothpick inserted into center comes out with fudgy crumbs. **Do not overbake.** Cool in pan.

Mix peanut butter, powdered sugar and 1 teaspoon vanilla in separate bowl until well blended and smooth. Spread over brownies.

Microwave semi-sweet chocolate and ¼ cup margarine in small microwavable bowl on HIGH 2 minutes or until margarine is melted. **Stir until chocolate is completely melted.** Spread over peanut butter layer. Cool until set. Cut into squares. *Makes about 24 brownies*

Prep time: 20 minutes
Baking time: 30 to 35 minutes

Walnut Crunch Brownies

Brownie Layer:
- 4 squares BAKER'S® Unsweetened Chocolate
- ¾ cup (1½ sticks) margarine or butter
- 2 cups granulated sugar
- 4 eggs
- 1 teaspoon vanilla
- 1 cup all-purpose flour

Walnut Topping:
- ¼ cup (½ stick) margarine or butter
- ¾ cup firmly packed brown sugar
- 2 eggs
- 2 tablespoons all-purpose flour
- 1 teaspoon vanilla
- 4 cups chopped walnuts

Preheat oven to 350°F.

Microwave unsweetened chocolate and ¾ cup margarine in large microwavable bowl on HIGH 2 minutes or until margarine is melted. **Stir until chocolate is completely melted.**

Stir granulated sugar into melted chocolate mixture. Mix in 4 eggs and 1 teaspoon vanilla until well blended. Stir in 1 cup flour. Spread in greased 13×9-inch pan.

Microwave ¼ cup margarine and brown sugar in same bowl on HIGH 1 minute or until margarine is melted. Stir in 2 eggs, 2 tablespoons flour and 1 teaspoon vanilla until completely mixed. Stir in walnuts. Spread mixture evenly over brownie batter.

Bake for 45 minutes or until toothpick inserted into center comes out with fudgy crumbs. **Do not overbake.** Cool in pan; cut into squares.

Makes about 24 brownies

Prep time: 20 minutes
Baking time: 45 minutes

Clockwise from top left:
Peanut-Layered Brownies,
Walnut Crunch Brownies,
Almond Macaroon Brownies (page 40)

Almond Macaroon Brownies

Brownie Layer:
    6 squares BAKER'S® Semi-Sweet
        Chocolate
  ½ cup (1 stick) margarine or butter
  ⅔ cup sugar
  2 eggs
  1 teaspoon vanilla
  1 cup all-purpose flour
  ⅔ cup toasted chopped almonds
Cream Cheese Topping:
    4 ounces PHILADELPHIA BRAND®
        Cream Cheese, softened
  ⅓ cup sugar
  1 egg
  1 tablespoon all-purpose flour
  1 cup BAKER'S® ANGEL FLAKE®
        Coconut
    Whole almonds (optional)
  1 square BAKER'S® Semi-Sweet
        Chocolate, melted* (optional)

Preheat oven to 350°F.

Microwave 6 squares chocolate and margarine in large microwavable bowl on HIGH 2 minutes or until margarine is melted. **Stir until chocolate is completely melted.**

Stir ⅔ cup sugar into melted chocolate mixture. Mix in 2 eggs and vanilla until well blended. Stir in 1 cup flour and ⅓ cup of the chopped almonds. Spread in greased 8-inch square pan.

Mix cream cheese, ⅓ cup sugar, 1 egg and 1 tablespoon flour in same bowl until smooth. Stir in the remaining ⅓ cup

*Place chocolate in zipper-style plastic sandwich bag. Close bag tightly. Microwave on HIGH about 1 minute or until chocolate is melted. Fold down top of bag tightly and snip a tiny piece off 1 corner (about ⅛ inch). Holding top of bag tightly, drizzle chocolate through opening over brownies.

chopped almonds and the coconut. Spread over brownie batter. Garnish with whole almonds, if desired.

Bake for 35 minutes or until toothpick inserted into center comes out with fudgy crumbs. **Do not overbake.** Cool in pan. Drizzle with 1 square melted chocolate, if desired.   *Makes about 16 brownies*

Prep time: 20 minutes
Baking time: 35 minutes

Double Fudge Saucepan Brownies

  ½ cup sugar
  2 tablespoons butter or margarine
  2 tablespoons water
  2 cups (12-ounce package)
      HERSHEY'S® Semi-Sweet
      Chocolate Chips, divided
  2 eggs, slightly beaten
  1 teaspoon vanilla extract
  ⅔ cup all-purpose flour
  ¼ teaspoon baking soda
  ¼ teaspoon salt
  ½ cup chopped nuts (optional)

Preheat oven to 325°F. Grease 9-inch square baking pan.

In medium saucepan over low heat, cook sugar, butter and water, stirring constantly, until mixture comes to boil. Remove from heat; immediately add 1 cup of the chocolate chips, stirring until melted. Stir in eggs and vanilla until blended. Stir together flour, baking soda and salt; stir into chocolate mixture. Stir in remaining 1 cup chips and nuts, if desired. Pour batter into prepared pan.

Bake 25 to 30 minutes or until brownies begin to pull away from sides of pan. Cool completely in pan on wire rack; cut into squares.   *Makes about 18 brownies*

Fudgy Brownie Bars

Fudgy Brownie Bars

1¼ cups unsifted flour
¼ cup sugar
½ cup cold margarine or butter
1 (14-ounce) can EAGLE® Brand
    Sweetened Condensed Milk
    (NOT evaporated milk)
¼ cup unsweetened cocoa
1 egg
1 teaspoon vanilla extract
½ teaspoon baking powder
1 (8-ounce) bar milk chocolate candy,
    broken into small pieces
¾ cup chopped nuts
    Confectioners' sugar, optional

Preheat oven to 350°F. In medium bowl, combine *1 cup* flour and sugar; cut in margarine until crumbly. Press on bottom of 13×9-inch baking pan. Bake 15 minutes. In large mixer bowl, beat sweetened condensed milk, cocoa, egg, remaining *¼ cup* flour, vanilla and baking powder. Stir in chocolate pieces and nuts.

Spread over prepared crust. Bake 20 minutes or until center is set. Cool. Sprinkle with confectioners' sugar if desired. Cut into bars. Store loosely covered at room temperature.

Makes 24 to 36 brownies

Blonde Brickle Brownies

1⅓ cups flour
½ teaspoon baking powder
¼ teaspoon salt
2 eggs
½ cup granulated sugar
½ cup packed brown sugar
⅓ cup butter or margarine, melted
1 teaspoon vanilla extract
¼ teaspoon almond extract
1 package (6 ounces) BITS 'O
    BRICKLE®, divided
½ cup chopped pecans (optional)

Preheat oven to 350°F. Grease 8-inch square pan. Mix flour with baking powder and salt; set aside. In large bowl, beat eggs well. Gradually beat in granulated sugar and brown sugar until thick and creamy. Add melted butter, vanilla and almond extract; mix well. Gently stir in flour mixture until moistened. Fold in ⅔ cup BITS 'O BRICKLE® and nuts. Pour into prepared pan.

Bake 30 minutes. Remove from oven; immediately sprinkle remaining BITS 'O BRICKLE® over top. Cool completely in pan on wire rack. Cut into squares.

Makes about 16 brownies

Cheesecake Topped Brownies

1 (21.5- or 23.6-ounce) package fudge
  brownie mix
1 (8-ounce) package cream cheese,
  softened
2 tablespoons margarine or butter,
  softened
1 tablespoon cornstarch
1 (14-ounce) can EAGLE® Brand
  Sweetened Condensed Milk
  (NOT evaporated milk)
1 egg
1 teaspoon vanilla extract
  Ready-to-spread chocolate frosting,
  optional

Preheat oven to 350°F. Prepare brownie mix as package directs. Spread into well-greased 13×9-inch baking pan. In small mixer bowl, beat cheese, margarine and cornstarch until fluffy. Gradually beat in sweetened condensed milk, then egg and vanilla until smooth. Pour evenly over brownie batter. Bake 45 minutes or until top is lightly browned. Cool. Spread with frosting if desired. Cut into bars. Store covered in refrigerator.

Makes 36 to 40 brownies

Cheesecake Topped Brownies

Chocolate Almond Brownies

1¼ cups unsifted flour
2 tablespoons sugar
½ cup cold margarine or butter
1 cup chopped almonds, toasted
1 (14-ounce) can EAGLE® Brand
    Sweetened Condensed Milk
    (NOT evaporated milk)
¼ cup unsweetened cocoa
1 egg
2 tablespoons amaretto liqueur *or*
    1 teaspoon almond extract
½ teaspoon baking powder
6 (1¼-ounce) white candy bars with
    almonds, broken into small pieces

Preheat oven to 350°F. In medium bowl, combine *1 cup* flour and sugar; cut in margarine until crumbly. Add *¼ cup* nuts. Press on bottom of ungreased 9-inch round or square baking pan. Bake 15 minutes. In large mixer bowl, beat sweetened condensed milk, remaining *¼ cup* flour, cocoa, egg, amaretto and baking powder until smooth. Stir in candy pieces and *½ cup* nuts. Spread over prepared crust. Top with remaining *¼ cup* nuts. Bake 30 minutes or until center is set. Cool. Cut into wedges. Store tightly covered at room temperature.

Makes about 16 brownies

Prep time: 20 minutes
Baking time: 45 minutes

Our Best Bran Brownies

1 cup NABISCO® 100% Bran
4 eggs
1 cup unsweetened cocoa
⅔ cup all-purpose flour
1 teaspoon DAVIS® Baking Powder
¾ cup BLUE BONNET® Margarine,
    softened
1½ cups sugar
2 teaspoons vanilla extract
½ cup chopped walnuts

Preheat oven to 350°F. In small bowl, mix bran and eggs; let stand for 5 minutes. In separate bowl, combine cocoa, flour and baking powder; set aside.

In large bowl, with electric mixer at medium speed, beat margarine and sugar until creamy. Beat in vanilla and bran mixture; blend in flour mixture. Spread batter into greased 13×9×2-inch baking pan. Sprinkle with walnuts.

Bake 25 to 30 minutes or until knife inserted in center comes out clean. Cool completely in pan on wire rack. Cut into 2×1½-inch bars. Store in airtight container.

Makes 32 brownies

Semi-Sweet Chocolate Brownies

6 squares BAKER'S® Semi-Sweet
    Chocolate
½ cup (1 stick) margarine or butter
⅔ cup sugar
2 eggs
1 teaspoon vanilla
1 cup all-purpose flour
⅓ cup chopped nuts (optional)

Preheat oven to 350°F.

Microwave chocolate and margarine in large microwavable bowl on HIGH 2 minutes or until margarine is melted. **Stir until chocolate is completely melted.**

Stir sugar into melted chocolate mixture. Mix in eggs and vanilla until well blended. Stir in flour and nuts. Spread in greased 8-inch square pan.

Bake for 30 minutes or until toothpick inserted into center comes out with fudgy crumbs. **Do not overbake.** Cool in pan; cut into squares.

Makes about 16 brownies

Prep time: 10 minutes
Baking time: 30 minutes

Caramel-Layered Brownies

4 squares BAKER'S® Unsweetened Chocolate
¾ cup (1½ sticks) margarine or butter
2 cups sugar
3 eggs
1 teaspoon vanilla
1 cup all-purpose flour
1 cup BAKER'S® Semi-Sweet Real Chocolate Chips
1½ cups chopped nuts
1 package (14 ounces) KRAFT® Caramels
⅓ cup evaporated milk

Preheat oven to 350°F.

Microwave unsweetened chocolate and margarine in large microwavable bowl on HIGH 2 minutes or until margarine is melted. **Stir until chocolate is completely melted.**

Stir sugar into melted chocolate mixture. Mix in eggs and vanilla until well blended. Stir in flour. Remove 1 cup of batter; set aside. Spread remaining batter in greased 13×9-inch pan. Sprinkle with chips and 1 cup of the nuts.

Microwave caramels and milk in same bowl on HIGH 4 minutes, stirring after 2 minutes. Stir until caramels are completely melted and smooth. Spoon over chips and nuts, spreading to edges of pan. Gently spread reserved batter over caramel mixture. Sprinkle with the remaining ½ cup nuts.

Bake for 40 minutes or until toothpick inserted into center comes out with fudgy crumbs. **Do not overbake.** Cool in pan; cut into squares.

Makes about 24 brownies

Prep time: 20 minutes
Baking time: 40 minutes

Rocky Road Fudge Brownies

Bars
½ cup LAND O LAKES® Butter
2 squares (1 ounce each) unsweetened chocolate
2 eggs
1 cup sugar
⅔ cup all-purpose flour
¼ teaspoon salt
1 teaspoon vanilla

Topping
½ cup chopped salted peanuts
½ cup butterscotch chips
1 cup miniature marshmallows
¼ cup chocolate ice cream topping

Preheat oven to 350°F. Grease 9-inch square baking pan. For Bars, in heavy, small saucepan, combine butter and chocolate. Cook, stirring constantly, over medium heat, until melted, 3 to 5 minutes; set aside.

In small mixer bowl, beat eggs at medium speed until light and fluffy, 2 to 3 minutes. Gradually beat in cooled chocolate mixture, sugar, flour, salt and vanilla, scraping bowl often, until well mixed, 1 to 2 minutes. Spread into prepared pan. Bake 20 to 25 minutes, or until brownies begin to pull away from sides of pan.

For Topping, sprinkle nuts, butterscotch chips and marshmallows over hot brownies. Drizzle with ice cream topping. Continue baking for 12 to 18 minutes, or until lightly browned. Cool completely in pan on wire rack. Cut into bars.

Makes about 2 dozen brownies

Caramel-Layered Brownies

Ultimate Chocolate Brownies

¾ cup HERSHEY'S® Cocoa
½ teaspoon baking soda
⅔ cup butter or margarine, melted and divided
½ cup boiling water
2 cups sugar
2 eggs
1⅓ cups all-purpose flour
1 teaspoon vanilla extract
¼ teaspoon salt
1 cup HERSHEY'S® Semi-Sweet Chocolate Chips
One-Bowl Buttercream Frosting (recipe follows)

Preheat oven to 350°F. Grease 13×9×2-inch baking pan or two 8-inch square baking pans.

In large bowl, stir together cocoa and baking soda; blend in ⅓ cup butter. Add boiling water; stir until mixture thickens. Stir in sugar, eggs and remaining ⅓ cup butter; mix until smooth. Add flour, vanilla and salt; mix until well blended. Stir in chocolate chips. Pour batter into prepared pan.

Bake 35 to 40 minutes for rectangular pan and 30 to 35 minutes for square pans or until brownies begin to pull away from sides of pan. Cool completely in pan on wire rack. Frost with One-Bowl Buttercream Frosting. Cut into squares.

Makes about 36 brownies

Ultimate Chocolate Brownies

One-Bowl Buttercream Frosting

6 tablespoons butter or margarine, softened
½ cup HERSHEY'S® Cocoa
2⅔ cups powdered sugar
⅓ cup milk
1 teaspoon vanilla extract

In small mixer bowl, beat butter. Blend in cocoa and powdered sugar alternately with milk; beat to spreading consistency (additional milk may be needed). Blend in vanilla. *Makes about 2 cups frosting*

DELECTABLE BARS

Toffee-Bran Bars

¾ cup all-purpose flour
¾ cup NABISCO® 100% Bran, divided
1¼ cups firmly packed light brown
    sugar, divided
½ cup BLUE BONNET® Margarine,
    melted
2 eggs, slightly beaten
1 teaspoon DAVIS® Baking Powder
1 teaspoon vanilla extract
1 cup semisweet chocolate chips
½ cup flaked coconut, toasted
⅓ cup chopped walnuts

Preheat oven to 350°F. In small bowl, combine flour, ½ cup of the bran, ½ cup brown sugar and the margarine. Press on bottom of 13×9×2-inch baking pan. Bake 10 minutes; set aside.

In medium bowl, with electric mixer at high speed, beat remaining ¼ cup bran, ¾ cup brown sugar, eggs, baking powder and vanilla until thick and foamy. Spread over prepared crust. Bake for 25 minutes more or until set. Remove pan from oven. Sprinkle with chocolate chips; let stand for 5 minutes. Spread softened chocolate evenly over baked layer. Immediately sprinkle coconut and chopped walnuts in alternating diagonal strips over chocolate. Cool completely in pan on wire rack. Cut into 3×1½-inch bars. Store in airtight container. *Makes 2 dozen bars*

Chewy Bar Cookies

½ cup BLUE BONNET® Margarine,
    softened
1 cup firmly packed light brown
    sugar
2 eggs
3 (1¼-ounce) packages Mix 'n Eat
    CREAM OF WHEAT® Cereal
    Apple 'n Cinnamon Flavor
⅔ cup all-purpose flour
2 teaspoons baking powder
1 cup finely chopped walnuts

Preheat oven to 350°F. In large bowl, with electric mixer at medium speed, beat margarine and brown sugar until creamy. Beat in eggs until light and fluffy. Stir in cereal, flour and baking powder. Mix in walnuts. Spread batter in greased 15½×10½×1-inch baking pan. Bake 20 to 25 minutes or until golden brown. Cool completely in pan on wire rack. Cut into bars. *Makes about 4 dozen bars*

Clockwise from bottom: Fruit and Chocolate Dream Bars, Chocolate Pecan Pie Bars, Chocolate Cheese Ripple Bars

Fruit and Chocolate Dream Bars

Base:
   1¼ cups all-purpose flour
   ½ cup granulated sugar
   ½ cup (1 stick) butter, softened
   ½ cup strawberry or raspberry jam
One 10-oz. pkg. (1½ cups) NESTLÉ®
      Toll House® Treasures® Milk
      Chocolate Deluxe Baking Pieces

Crumb Topping:
   ⅔ cup all-purpose flour
   ½ cup pecans, chopped
   ⅓ cup firmly packed brown sugar
   6 tablespoons (¾ stick) butter, softened

Base: Preheat oven to 375°F. In small bowl, combine flour and granulated sugar. With pastry blender or 2 knives, cut in butter until mixture resembles fine

crumbs. Press into greased 9-inch square pan.

Bake 20 to 25 minutes until set but not brown. Remove from oven. Spread with jam. Top with NESTLÉ® Toll House® Treasures® Milk Chocolate Deluxe Baking Pieces and Crumb Topping.

Bake 15 to 20 minutes longer until top is lightly browned. Cool completely in pan on wire rack. Cut into 2¼-inch squares.

Crumb Topping: In small bowl, combine flour, pecans and brown sugar. With pastry blender or 2 knives, cut in butter until mixture resembles coarse crumbs.

Makes 16 squares

Chocolate Pecan Pie Bars

Crust:
   1½ cups all-purpose flour
   ½ cup (1 stick) butter, softened
   ¼ cup firmly packed brown sugar
Filling:
   3 eggs
   ¾ cup dark or light corn syrup
   ¾ cup granulated sugar
   2 tablespoons (¼ stick) butter, melted
   1 teaspoon vanilla extract
   1½ cups pecans, coarsely chopped
One 10-oz. pkg. (1½ cups) NESTLÉ®
      Toll House® Treasures®
      Semi-Sweet Chocolate Deluxe
      Baking Pieces

Crust: Preheat oven to 350°F. In small mixer bowl, beat flour, butter and brown sugar until crumbly. Press into greased 13×9-inch baking pan. Bake 12 to 15 minutes until lightly browned.

Filling: In medium bowl with wire whisk, beat eggs, corn syrup, granulated sugar, melted butter and vanilla extract. Stir in pecans and NESTLÉ® Toll House® Treasures® Semi-Sweet Chocolate Deluxe Baking Pieces. Pour evenly over baked Crust.

Bake 25 to 30 minutes until set. Cool completely in pan on wire rack; cut into 2×1½-inch bars.   *Makes 3 dozen bars*

Chocolate Cheese Ripple Bars

Cheese Batter:
Two 3-oz. pkgs. cream cheese, softened
   2 eggs
   ¼ cup sugar
   2 tablespoons all-purpose flour
   2 tablespoons (¼ stick) butter, softened

Chocolate Batter:
   1 cup all-purpose flour
   1 cup sugar
   ¾ teaspoon baking soda
   ¾ teaspoon salt
   ½ cup milk
   1¼ teaspoons vinegar
   ⅓ cup (5⅓ tablespoons) butter, softened
   3 envelopes (3 oz.) NESTLÉ® Choco Bake® Unsweetened Baking Chocolate Flavor
   2 eggs
   1¼ teaspoons vanilla extract

Cheese Batter: Preheat oven to 350°F. In small mixer bowl, beat cream cheese, eggs, sugar, flour and butter until creamy; set aside.

Chocolate Batter: In large mixer bowl, combine flour, sugar, baking soda and salt. Beat in milk, vinegar, butter and NESTLÉ® Choco Bake® Unsweetened Baking Chocolate Flavor. Blend in eggs and vanilla extract until smooth. Pour into greased 13×9×2-inch baking pan. Spoon Cheese Batter over top. Swirl knife through batters to ripple slightly.

Bake 25 to 30 minutes. Cool completely in pan on wire rack; cut into 2-inch squares.

Makes 2 dozen squares

Quick and Easy Nutty Cheese Bars

Base
   1 package DUNCAN HINES® Butter Recipe Golden Cake Mix
   ¾ cup chopped pecans or walnuts
   ¾ cup butter or margarine, melted

Topping
   2 packages (8 ounces each) cream cheese, softened
   1 cup firmly packed brown sugar
   ¾ cup chopped pecans or walnuts

1. Preheat oven to 350°F. Grease and flour 13×9×2-inch pan.

2. For Base, combine cake mix, ¾ cup pecans and melted butter in large bowl. Stir until well blended. Press mixture into bottom of pan.

3. For Topping, combine cream cheese and brown sugar in medium bowl. Stir with spoon until well mixed. Spread evenly over base. Sprinkle with ¾ cup pecans.

4. Bake 25 to 30 minutes or until edges are browned and cheese topping is set. Cool completely in pan on wire rack. Cut into 2¼×2-inch bars. Refrigerate leftovers.

Makes 24 bars

Quick and Easy Nutty Cheese Bars

Butterscotch Peanut Bars

1 (8 oz.) pkg. PHILADELPHIA
    BRAND® Cream Cheese,
    softened
½ cup packed brown sugar
½ cup granulated sugar
¼ cup PARKAY® Margarine
½ cup milk
1 egg
2 teaspoons vanilla
2¼ cups flour
1 teaspoon CALUMET® Baking
    Powder
¼ teaspoon salt
1 cup chopped salted peanuts
1 cup butterscotch chips
    Butterscotch Frosting
½ cup chopped salted peanuts

• Preheat oven to 350°F.

• Beat cream cheese, sugars and ¼ cup margarine in large mixing bowl at medium speed with electric mixer until well blended. Blend in ½ cup milk, egg and vanilla.

• Add combined dry ingredients; mix well. Stir in 1 cup peanuts and 1 cup butterscotch chips. Spread in greased 15×10×1-inch jelly roll pan.

• Bake 20 to 25 minutes or until wooden toothpick inserted in center comes out clean. Spread with Butterscotch Frosting. Sprinkle with ½ cup peanuts. Cut into bars. *Makes about 3 dozen bars*

Butterscotch Frosting

1 cup butterscotch chips
½ cup creamy peanut butter
2 tablespoons PARKAY® Margarine
1 tablespoon milk

• Stir together all ingredients in small saucepan over low heat until smooth.

Prep time: 20 minutes
Cooking time: 25 minutes

Double Chocolate Raspberry Bars

Bars
1¾ cups all-purpose flour
1 cup granulated sugar
¼ cup unsweetened cocoa powder
1 cup butter or margarine
1 egg, lightly beaten
1 teaspoon vanilla
1 can SOLO® or 1 jar BAKER®
    Raspberry Filling
1 cup chopped almonds *or* pecans
6 squares (6 ounces) semisweet
    chocolate, finely chopped, *or*
    1 package (6 ounces) semisweet
    chocolate morsels

Glaze
1 cup confectioners' sugar
1 to 2 tablespoons milk

Preheat oven to 350°F. Grease 13×9-inch baking pan; set aside.

For Bars, stir flour, granulated sugar and cocoa in medium-size bowl until blended. Cut in butter until mixture resembles coarse crumbs. Add egg and vanilla; stir until dry ingredients are thoroughly moistened. Measure 1 cup mixture and set aside. Press remaining mixture evenly into bottom of prepared pan. Cover with raspberry filling, spreading evenly. Combine reserved 1 cup crumb mixture, chopped almonds and chopped chocolate. Sprinkle over raspberry filling. Bake 40 minutes. Cool completely in pan on wire rack.

For Glaze, combine confectioners' sugar and milk in small bowl; stir until smooth. Drizzle glaze in zig-zag pattern over cooled bars. Let stand until glaze is set. Cut into 2×1½-inch bars.
Makes about 48 bars

Magic Rainbow Cookie Bars

½ cup margarine or butter
1½ cups graham cracker crumbs
1 (14-ounce) can EAGLE® Brand Sweetened Condensed Milk (NOT evaporated milk)
1 (3½-ounce) can flaked coconut (1⅓ cups)
1 cup chopped nuts
1 cup plain multi-colored candy-coated chocolate pieces

Preheat oven to 350°F (325°F for glass dish). In 13×9-inch baking pan, melt margarine in oven. Sprinkle crumbs over margarine; pour sweetened condensed milk evenly over crumbs. Top with remaining ingredients; press down firmly. Bake 25 to 30 minutes or until lightly browned. Cool. Chill if desired. Cut into bars. Store loosely covered at room temperature. *Makes 24 to 36 bars*

Pear Blondies

1 cup packed brown sugar
¼ cup butter or margarine, melted
1 egg
½ teaspoon vanilla
¾ cup all-purpose flour
½ teaspoon baking powder
½ teaspoon salt
1 cup chopped firm-ripe fresh U.S.A. Anjou, Bosc, Bartlett, Nelis or Seckel pears
⅓ cup semisweet chocolate chips

Preheat oven to 350°F. In medium bowl, mix brown sugar, butter, egg and vanilla; blend well. In small bowl, combine flour, baking powder and salt; stir into brown sugar mixture. Stir in pears and chips. Spread in greased 8-inch square pan. Bake 30 to 35 minutes or until golden brown. Cool completely in pan on wire rack. Cut into 2-inch squares. *Makes 16 bars*

Favorite recipe from **Oregon Washington California Pear Bureau**

Magic Rainbow Cookie Bars

Apple Pie Bars

Crust
>   Milk
>   **1 egg yolk, reserve egg white**
>   **2½ cups all-purpose flour**
>   **1 teaspoon salt**
>   **1 cup LAND O LAKES® Butter**

Filling
>   **1 cup crushed corn flake cereal**
>   **8 cups peeled, cored, ¼-inch sliced, tart cooking apples (about 8 to 10 medium)**
>   **1 cup granulated sugar**
>   **1½ teaspoons ground cinnamon**
>   **½ teaspoon ground nutmeg**
>   **1 reserved egg white**
>   **2 tablespoons granulated sugar**
>   **½ teaspoon ground cinnamon**

Glaze
>   **1 cup powdered sugar**
>   **1 to 2 tablespoons milk**
>   **½ teaspoon vanilla**

Preheat oven to 350°F. For Crust, add enough milk to egg yolk to measure ⅔ cup; set aside. In medium bowl, combine flour and salt. Cut in butter until crumbly. With fork, stir in milk mixture until dough forms a ball; divide into halves. Roll out half of the dough, on lightly floured surface, into a 15×10-inch rectangle. Place on bottom of ungreased 15×10×1-inch jelly-roll pan.

For Filling, sprinkle cereal over top of crust; layer apples over cereal. In small bowl, combine 1 cup granulated sugar, 1½ teaspoons cinnamon and nutmeg. Sprinkle over apples. Roll remaining half of dough into a 15½×10½-inch rectangle; place over apples. In small bowl, with fork beat egg white until foamy; brush over top crust. In another small bowl, stir together 2 tablespoons granulated sugar and ½ teaspoon cinnamon; sprinkle over crust. Bake for 45 to 60 minutes, or until lightly browned.

For Glaze, in small bowl, stir together all glaze ingredients. Drizzle over warm bars. Cut into bars.   *Makes about 3 dozen bars*

Fudgy Cookie Wedges

1 (20-ounce) package refrigerated cookie dough, any flavor
1 (12-ounce) package semi-sweet chocolate chips
2 tablespoons margarine or butter
1 (14-ounce) can EAGLE® Brand Sweetened Condensed Milk (NOT evaporated milk)
1 teaspoon vanilla extract
Chopped nuts

Preheat oven to 350°F. Divide cookie dough into thirds. With floured hands, press on bottom of three aluminum foil-lined 9-inch round cake pans *or* press into 9-inch circles on ungreased baking sheets. Bake 10 to 12 minutes or until golden. Cool.

In heavy saucepan, over medium heat, melt chips and margarine with sweetened condensed milk and vanilla. Cook and stir until thickened, about 5 minutes. Spread over cookie circles; top with nuts. Chill. Cut into wedges. Store loosely covered at room temperature.   *Makes 36 wedges*

Microwave: Bake cookie dough as above. In 1-quart glass measure, combine remaining ingredients except nuts. Cook on 100% power (high) 4 minutes, stirring after each minute. Proceed as above.

Apple Pie Bars

Double Chocolate Crispy Bars

6 cups crispy rice cereal
½ cup peanut butter
⅓ cup butter or margarine
2 squares (1 ounce each) unsweetened
    chocolate
1 package (8 ounces) marshmallows
1 cup (6 ounces) semisweet chocolate
    chips *or* 6 ounces bittersweet
    chocolate, chopped
6 ounces white chocolate, chopped
2 teaspoons shortening, divided

Preheat oven to 350°F. Line 13×9-inch
pan with waxed paper. Spread cereal on
cookie sheet; toast in oven 10 minutes or
until crispy. Place in large bowl.

Meanwhile, combine peanut butter, butter
and unsweetened chocolate in large heavy
saucepan. Stir over low heat until chocolate
is melted. Add marshmallows; stir until
melted and smooth. Pour chocolate
mixture over cereal; mix until evenly
coated. Press firmly into prepared pan.

Place semisweet and white chocolates into
separate bowls. Add 1 teaspoon shortening
to each bowl. Place bowls over very warm
water; stir until chocolates are melted.
Spread top of bars with melted semisweet
chocolate; cool until chocolate is set. Turn
bars out of pan onto sheet of waxed paper,
chocolate side down. Remove waxed
paper from bottom of bars; spread white
chocolate over surface. Cool until
chocolate is set. Cut into 2×1½-inch bars
using sharp, thin knife.

Makes 3 dozen bars

Clockwise from top left: Double Chocolate Crispy Bars,
Chocolate Macadamia Bars, Naomi's Revel Bars

Chocolate Macadamia Bars

12 squares (1 ounce each) bittersweet
    chocolate *or* 1 package (12 ounces)
    semisweet chocolate chips
1 package (8 ounces) cream cheese,
    softened
⅔ cup whipping cream *or* undiluted
    evaporated milk
1 cup chopped macadamia nuts or
    almonds
1 teaspoon vanilla, divided
1 cup butter or margarine, softened
1½ cups sugar
1 egg
3 cups all-purpose flour
1 teaspoon baking powder
¼ teaspoon salt

Preheat oven to 375°F. Lightly grease
13×9-inch pan.

Combine chocolate, cream cheese and cream in large heavy saucepan. Stir over low heat until chocolate is melted and mixture is smooth. Remove from heat; stir in nuts and ½ teaspoon of the vanilla. Cream butter and sugar in large bowl. Beat in egg and remaining ½ teaspoon vanilla. Add flour, baking powder and salt, blending well. Press half of butter mixture on bottom of prepared pan. Spread chocolate mixture evenly over top. Sprinkle remaining butter mixture over chocolate.

Bake 35 to 40 minutes or until golden brown. Cool in pan on wire rack. Cut into 2×1½-inch bars.   *Makes 3 dozen bars*

Naomi's Revel Bars

1 cup plus 2 tablespoons butter or margarine, softened
2 cups packed brown sugar
2 eggs
2 teaspoons vanilla
2½ cups all-purpose flour
1 teaspoon baking soda
3 cups uncooked rolled oats
1 package (12 ounces) semisweet chocolate chips
1 can (14 ounces) sweetened condensed milk

Preheat oven to 325°F. Lightly grease 13×9-inch pan.

Cream the 1 cup butter and the brown sugar in large bowl. Add eggs; beat until light. Blend in vanilla. Combine flour and baking soda; stir into creamed mixture. Blend in oats. Spread ¾ of the oat mixture evenly in prepared pan. Combine chocolate chips, milk and the remaining 2 tablespoons butter in small heavy saucepan. Stir over low heat until chocolate is melted. Pour chocolate mixture evenly over oat mixture in pan. Dot with remaining oat mixture.

Bake 20 to 25 minutes or until edges are browned and center feels firm. Cool in pan on wire rack. Cut into 2×1½-inch bars.   *Makes 3 dozen bars*

Mocha Almond Bars

Bars
2¼ cups all-purpose flour
1 cup granulated sugar
1 cup LAND O LAKES® Butter, softened
1 egg
1 teaspoon instant coffee granules
1 cup sliced almonds

Glaze
¾ cup powdered sugar
1 to 2 tablespoons milk
¼ teaspoon almond extract

Preheat oven to 350°F. For Bars, in small mixer bowl, combine flour, granulated sugar, butter, egg and instant coffee. Beat at low speed, scraping bowl often, until well mixed, 2 to 3 minutes. Stir in nuts. Press on bottom of greased 13×9×2-inch baking pan. Bake for 25 to 30 minutes, or until edges are lightly browned.

For Glaze, in small bowl, stir together all glaze ingredients. Drizzle glaze over warm bars. Cool completely in pan on wire rack. Cut into bars.   *Makes about 3 dozen bars*

Mocha Almond Bars

Caramel Chocolate Pecan Bars

Crust
  2 cups all-purpose flour
  1 cup firmly packed brown sugar
  ½ cup LAND O LAKES® Butter,
    softened
  1 cup pecan halves

Filling
  ½ cup firmly packed brown sugar
  ⅔ cup LAND O LAKES® Butter
  ½ cup semi-sweet chocolate chips
  ½ cup butterscotch chips

Preheat oven to 350°F. For Crust, in large mixer bowl, combine flour, brown sugar and butter. Beat at medium speed, scraping bowl often, until particles are fine, 2 to 3 minutes. Press on bottom of ungreased 13×9×2-inch baking pan. Sprinkle nuts over crust.

For Filling, in small saucepan, combine brown sugar and butter. Cook, stirring constantly, over medium heat until mixture comes to a full boil, 4 to 5 minutes. Boil, stirring constantly, until candy thermometer reaches 242°F, or small amount of mixture dropped into ice water forms a firm ball, about 1 minute. Pour over pecans and crust.

Bake for 18 to 20 minutes, or until entire caramel layer is bubbly. Immediately sprinkle with chocolate and butterscotch chips. Let stand 3 to 5 minutes to melt chips. Swirl chips with tip of knife, leaving some whole for marbled effect. Cool completely in pan on wire rack. Cut into bars.   *Makes about 3 dozen bars*

Caramel Chocolate Pecan Bars

Caramel Granola Bars

  7 oz. caramel candies
  ¼ cup (½ stick) butter
  ¼ cup water
  1 lb. granola cereal
One 11½-oz. pkg. (2 cups) NESTLÉ®
    Toll House® Milk Chocolate
    Morsels

In large saucepan, combine caramels, butter and water. Stir over low heat until caramels are melted and mixture is smooth. Remove from heat. Stir in cereal and NESTLÉ® Toll House® Milk Chocolate Morsels until well mixed. Press into foil-lined 9-inch square pan. Chill until firm, about 1 hour. Cut into 1-inch squares.   *Makes 81 bars*

Lemon Iced Ambrosia Bars

1½ cups unsifted flour
⅓ cup confectioners' sugar
¾ cup cold margarine or butter
2 cups firmly packed light brown sugar
4 eggs, beaten
1 cup flaked coconut
1 cup finely chopped pecans
3 tablespoons flour
½ teaspoon baking powder
Lemon Icing

Preheat oven to 350°F. In medium bowl, combine flour and confectioners' sugar; cut in margarine until crumbly. Press onto bottom of lightly greased 13×9-inch baking pan; bake 15 minutes. Meanwhile, in large bowl, combine remaining ingredients except icing; mix well. Spread evenly over baked crust; bake 20 to 25 minutes. Cool. Spread with Lemon Icing; chill. Cut into bars. Store covered in refrigerator.   *Makes 24 to 36 bars*

Lemon Icing: Mix 2 cups confectioners' sugar, 3 tablespoons REALEMON® Lemon Juice from Concentrate and 2 tablespoons softened margarine until smooth.   *Makes about ⅔ cup icing*

Choco-Coconut Layer Bars

⅓ cup margarine or butter, melted
¾ cup unsifted flour
½ cup sugar
2 tablespoons unsweetened cocoa
1 egg
1 (14-ounce) can EAGLE® Brand Sweetened Condensed Milk (NOT evaporated milk)
1 (3½-ounce) can flaked coconut (1⅓ cups)
Flavor Variations*
1 (6-ounce) package semi-sweet chocolate chips (1 cup)

Preheat oven to 350°F (325°F for glass dish). In medium bowl, combine margarine, flour, sugar, cocoa and egg; mix well. Spread evenly into lightly greased 9-inch square baking pan. In small bowl, combine ¾ *cup* sweetened condensed milk, coconut and desired flavor variation; spread over chocolate layer.

Bake 20 minutes or until lightly browned around edges. In heavy saucepan, over low heat, melt chips with remaining sweetened condensed milk. Remove from heat; spread evenly over coconut layer. Cool. Chill. Cut into bars. Store loosely covered at room temperature.
          Makes about 24 bars

*Flavor Variations:

Almond: Add 1 cup chopped slivered almonds and ½ teaspoon almond extract.

Mint: Add ½ teaspoon peppermint extract and 4 drops green food coloring if desired.

Cherry: Add 2 (6-ounce) jars maraschino cherries, chopped and well drained on paper towels.

Crispy Chocolate Logs

1 cup (6 ounces) semisweet chocolate chips
½ cup butter or margarine
1 package (10 ounces) marshmallows
6 cups crispy rice cereal

Lightly oil 13×9-inch baking pan. Melt chocolate chips and butter in large bowl over hot water, stirring constantly. Add marshmallows; stir until melted. Add cereal; stir until evenly coated with chocolate mixture. Press into prepared pan; cool until mixture is firm. Cut into 2×1½-inch logs using sharp, thin knife.
          Makes 36 logs

Layered Chocolate Cheese Bars

¼ cup (½ stick) margarine or butter
1½ cups graham cracker crumbs
¾ cup sugar
1 package (4 ounces) BAKER'S®
 GERMAN'S® Sweet Chocolate
1 package (8 ounces) PHILADELPHIA
 BRAND® Cream Cheese,
 softened
1 egg
1 cup BAKER'S® ANGEL FLAKE®
 Coconut
1 cup chopped nuts

Preheat oven to 350°F.

Melt margarine in oven in 13×9-inch pan. Add graham cracker crumbs and ¼ cup of the sugar; mix well. Press into pan. Bake for 10 minutes.

Melt chocolate.* Stir in the remaining ½ cup sugar, the cream cheese and egg. Spread over crust. Sprinkle with coconut and nuts; press lightly.

Bake for 30 minutes. Cool; cut into bars.
Makes about 24 bars

Prep time: 20 minutes
Baking time: 40 minutes

*Place unwrapped chocolate in microwave-safe dish. Microwave on HIGH 1½ to 2½ minutes or until almost melted, stirring after each minute. Remove from microwave. Stir until completely melted. *Or,* place chocolate, unwrapped, in heavy saucepan over very low heat, stirring constantly, until chocolate is just melted.

Chocolate Peanut Butter Bars

2 cups peanut butter
1 cup sugar
2 eggs
1 package (8 ounces) BAKER'S®
 Semi-Sweet Chocolate Squares
1 cup chopped peanuts

Preheat oven to 350°F.

Beat peanut butter, sugar and eggs in large bowl until light and fluffy. Reserve 1 cup peanut butter mixture; set aside.

Melt 4 squares of the chocolate.* Add to peanut butter mixture in bowl; mix well. Press into ungreased 13×9-inch pan. Top with reserved peanut butter mixture.

Bake for 30 minutes or until edges are lightly browned. Melt the remaining 4 squares chocolate; spread evenly over entire surface. Sprinkle with peanuts. Cool in pan until chocolate is set. Cut into bars.
Makes about 24 bars

Prep time: 15 minutes
Baking time: 30 minutes

*Place unwrapped chocolate in microwave-safe dish. Microwave on HIGH 1½ to 2½ minutes or until almost melted, stirring after each minute. Remove from microwave. Stir until completely melted. *Or,* place chocolate, unwrapped, in heavy saucepan over very low heat, stirring constantly, until chocolate is just melted.

*Top plate (clockwise from top):
Layered Chocolate Cheese Bars,
Banana Split Bars (page 60),
Chocolate Peanut Butter Bars*

Banana Split Bars

⅓ cup margarine or butter, softened
1 cup sugar
1 egg
1 banana, mashed
½ teaspoon vanilla
1¼ cups all-purpose flour
1 teaspoon CALUMET® Baking
    Powder
¼ teaspoon salt
⅓ cup chopped nuts
2 cups KRAFT® Miniature
    Marshmallows
1 cup BAKER'S® Semi-Sweet Real
    Chocolate Chips
⅓ cup maraschino cherries, drained
    and quartered

Preheat oven to 350°F.

Beat margarine and sugar until light and fluffy. Add egg, banana and vanilla; mix well. Mix in flour, baking powder and salt. Stir in nuts. Pour batter into greased 13×9-inch pan.

Bake for 20 minutes. Remove from oven. Sprinkle with marshmallows, chips and cherries. Bake 10 to 15 minutes longer or until wooden toothpick inserted in center comes out clean. Cool in pan; cut into bars. *Makes about 24 bars*

Prep time: 20 minutes
Baking time: 30 to 35 minutes

Double Peanut-Choco Bars

1 (18¼- or 18½-ounce) package white
    cake mix
½ cup plus ⅓ cup peanut butter
1 egg
1 (14-ounce) can EAGLE® Brand
    Sweetened Condensed Milk
    (NOT evaporated milk)
1 (6-ounce) package semi-sweet
    chocolate chips (1 cup)
¾ cup Spanish peanuts

Top to bottom: Double Peanut-Choco Bars, Chocolate Mint Bars, Layered Lemon Crumb Bars

Preheat oven to 350°F (325°F for glass dish). In large mixer bowl, combine cake mix, ½ *cup* peanut butter and egg; beat on low speed until crumbly. Press firmly on bottom of greased 13×9-inch baking pan. In medium bowl, combine sweetened condensed milk and remaining ⅓ *cup* peanut butter; mix well. Spread evenly over prepared crust. Top with chips and peanuts.

Bake 30 to 35 minutes or until lightly browned. Cool. Cut into bars. Store loosely covered at room temperature.

Makes 24 to 36 bars

Layered Lemon Crumb Bars

    1 (14-ounce) can EAGLE® Brand Sweetened Condensed Milk (NOT evaporated milk)
  ½ cup REALEMON® Lemon Juice from Concentrate
    1 teaspoon grated lemon rind
  ⅔ cup margarine or butter, softened
    1 cup firmly packed light brown sugar
 1½ cups unsifted flour
    1 cup quick-cooking oats, uncooked
    1 teaspoon baking powder
  ½ teaspoon salt
  ½ teaspoon ground cinnamon
  ½ teaspoon ground nutmeg

Preheat oven to 350°F (325°F for glass dish). In small bowl, combine sweetened condensed milk, REALEMON® brand and rind; set aside. In large mixer bowl, beat margarine and brown sugar until fluffy; add flour, oats, baking powder and salt. Mix until crumbly. Press half the oat mixture on bottom of lightly greased 13×9-inch baking pan. Top with lemon mixture. Stir spices into remaining crumb mixture; sprinkle evenly over lemon layer.

Bake 20 to 25 minutes or until lightly browned. Cool. Chill. Cut into bars. Store covered in refrigerator.

Makes 24 to 36 bars

Chocolate Mint Bars

    1 (6-ounce) package semi-sweet chocolate chips (1 cup)
    1 (14-ounce) can EAGLE® Brand Sweetened Condensed Milk (NOT evaporated milk)
  ¾ cup plus 2 tablespoons margarine or butter
  ½ teaspoon peppermint extract
 1¼ cups firmly packed light brown sugar
    1 egg
 1½ cups unsifted flour
 1½ cups quick-cooking oats, uncooked
  ¾ cup chopped nuts
  ⅓ cup crushed hard peppermint candy, optional

Preheat oven to 350°F. In heavy saucepan, over low heat, melt chips with sweetened condensed milk and *2 tablespoons* margarine; remove from heat. Add extract; set aside. In large mixer bowl, beat remaining ¾ *cup* margarine and brown sugar until fluffy; beat in egg. Add flour and oats; mix well. With floured hands, press two-thirds oat mixture on bottom of greased 15×10-inch baking pan; spread evenly with chocolate mixture. Add nuts to remaining oat mixture; crumble evenly over chocolate. Sprinkle with peppermint candy if desired.

Bake 15 to 18 minutes or until edges are lightly browned. Cool. Cut into bars. Store loosely covered at room temperature.

Makes 36 to 48 bars

Creative Pan Cookies

2¼ cups all-purpose flour
1 teaspoon baking soda
½ teaspoon salt
1 cup (2 sticks) butter, softened
¾ cup granulated sugar
¾ cup firmly packed brown sugar
1 teaspoon vanilla extract
2 eggs
One 12-oz. pkg. (2 cups) NESTLÉ®
    Toll House® Semi-Sweet
    Chocolate Morsels
    Flavor Options, if desired
    (see below)

Preheat oven to 375°F. In small bowl, combine flour, baking soda and salt; set aside. In large mixer bowl, beat butter, granulated sugar, brown sugar and vanilla extract until creamy. Beat in eggs. Gradually beat in flour mixture. Stir in NESTLÉ® Toll House® Semi-Sweet Chocolate Morsels and ingredients for 1 of the Flavor Options. Spread in ungreased 15½×10½×1-inch baking pan.

Bake 18 to 20 minutes. Cool completely in pan on wire rack. Cut into 2-inch squares.
Makes 35 squares

Flavor Options:

Granola-Nut: Stir in 2 cups granola cereal, 1 cup raisins and 1 cup chopped walnuts.

Apricot-Cashew: Stir in 2 cups granola cereal, 1 cup chopped dried apricots and 1 cup chopped dry-roasted cashews.

Apple-Oatmeal: Decrease all-purpose flour to 2 cups. Stir in 2¼ cups quick oats, uncooked, 1 cup diced peeled apples and ¾ teaspoon cinnamon.

Carrot-Pineapple: Increase all-purpose flour to 2¾ cups. Add ½ teaspoon cinnamon and ¼ teaspoon *each* allspice and nutmeg. Stir in 1 cup grated carrots, one 8-oz. can juice-packed crushed pineapple, *well drained*, and ¾ cup wheat germ.

Creative Pan Cookies

Almond Chinese Chews

1 cup granulated sugar
3 eggs
1 can SOLO® or 1 jar BAKER®
    Almond Filling
¾ cup all-purpose flour
1 teaspoon baking powder
¼ teaspoon salt
    Confectioners' sugar

Preheat oven to 300°F. Grease 13×9-inch baking pan; set aside.

Beat granulated sugar and eggs in medium-size bowl with electric mixer until thoroughly blended. Add almond filling; beat until blended. Stir flour, baking powder and salt until mixed; fold into almond mixture. Spread batter evenly in prepared pan.

Bake 40 to 45 minutes or until wooden toothpick inserted in center comes out clean. Cool completely in pan on wire rack. Cut into 2×1½-inch bars; dust with confectioners' sugar. *Makes 36 bars*

Orange Butter Cream Squares

Crust
- 1¼ cups finely crushed chocolate wafer cookies
- ⅓ cup LAND O LAKES® Butter, softened

Filling
- 1½ cups powdered sugar
- ⅓ cup LAND O LAKES® Butter, softened
- 1 tablespoon milk
- 2 teaspoons grated orange peel
- ½ teaspoon vanilla

Glaze
- 1 tablespoon unsweetened cocoa
- 1 tablespoon LAND O LAKES® Butter, melted

For Crust, in medium bowl, stir together cookie crumbs and butter. Press on bottom of ungreased 9-inch square baking pan. Refrigerate until firm, about 1 hour.

For Filling, in small mixer bowl, combine all filling ingredients. Beat at medium speed, scraping bowl often until light and fluffy, 3 to 4 minutes. Spread over crust.

For Glaze, in small bowl, stir together cocoa and butter. Drizzle over filling. Refrigerate until firm, about 2 hours. Cut into bars. Store in refrigerator.

Makes about 2 dozen bars

Prune Bars

- 2 cups all-purpose flour
- 1 cup sugar
- 1 teaspoon salt
- ½ teaspoon baking soda
- ¾ cup butter or margarine, softened
- 1½ cups shredded or flaked coconut
- 1 cup chopped nuts (walnuts, pecans or almonds)
- 1 can SOLO® or 1 jar BAKER® Prune or Date Filling

Preheat oven to 400°F. Grease 13×9-inch baking pan; set aside. Combine flour, sugar, salt and baking soda in medium-size bowl; stir until blended. Cut in butter until mixture resembles coarse crumbs. Add coconut and chopped nuts; stir until well mixed. Measure 2 cups flour-coconut mixture; set aside. Press remaining mixture into bottom of prepared pan.

Bake 10 minutes. Remove from oven and spread prune filling over baked crust. Sprinkle reserved flour-coconut mixture over filling. Bake 15 minutes or until top is golden brown. Cool completely in pan on wire rack. Cut into 2×1½-inch bars.

Makes 36 bars

Orange Butter Cream Squares

Toffee Bars

½ cup margarine or butter, melted
 1 cup quick-cooking oats, uncooked
½ cup firmly packed brown sugar
½ cup unsifted flour
½ cup finely chopped walnuts
¼ teaspoon baking soda
 1 (14-ounce) can EAGLE® Brand
    Sweetened Condensed Milk
    (NOT evaporated milk)
 2 teaspoons vanilla extract
 1 (6-ounce) package semi-sweet
    chocolate chips (1 cup)

Preheat oven to 350°F. In medium bowl, combine *6 tablespoons* margarine, oats, brown sugar, flour, nuts and baking soda. Press firmly on bottom of greased 13×9-inch baking pan; bake 10 to 15 minutes or until lightly browned.

Meanwhile, in medium saucepan, combine remaining *2 tablespoons* margarine and sweetened condensed milk. Over medium heat, cook and stir until mixture thickens slightly, about 15 minutes. Remove from heat; stir in vanilla. Pour over crust. Return to oven; bake 10 to 15 minutes longer or until golden brown. Remove from oven; *immediately* sprinkle chips on top. Let stand 1 minute; spread while still warm. Cool. Cut into bars. Store tightly covered at room temperature.

Makes 24 to 36 bars

Raspberry Meringue Bars

Bars
 1 package DUNCAN HINES® Moist
    Deluxe Yellow Cake Mix
½ cup butter or margarine, melted
 2 egg yolks
Meringue
 2 egg whites
½ cup sugar
 1 cup chopped walnuts
 1 cup raspberry preserves
½ cup flaked coconut

1. Preheat oven to 350°F. For Bars, combine cake mix, melted butter and egg yolks in large bowl. Beat at low speed with electric mixer for 1 minute. Spread in ungreased 13×9×2-inch pan. Bake 15 minutes or until lightly browned.

2. For Meringue, beat egg whites in medium bowl at high speed with electric mixer until foamy and double in volume. Beat in sugar. Continue beating until meringue forms firm peaks. Fold in walnuts. Spread raspberry preserves over crust. Sprinkle with coconut. Spread meringue over top. Bake 25 minutes. Cool completely in pan on wire rack. Cut into 1½×1-inch bars.   *Makes 48 bars*

Macaroon Almond Crumb Bars

 1 (18¼- or 18½-ounce) package
    chocolate cake mix
¼ cup vegetable oil
 2 eggs
 1 (14-ounce) can EAGLE® Brand
    Sweetened Condensed Milk
    (NOT evaporated milk)
½ to 1 teaspoon almond extract
 1½ cups coconut macaroon crumbs
    (about 8 macaroons)
 1 cup chopped slivered almonds

Preheat oven to 350°F (325°F for glass dish). In large mixer bowl, combine cake mix, oil and *1 egg*; beat on medium speed until crumbly. Press firmly on bottom of greased 13×9-inch baking pan. In medium bowl, combine sweetened condensed milk, remaining egg and extract; mix well. Add *1 cup* macaroon crumbs and almonds. Spread evenly over crust. Sprinkle with remaining *½ cup* crumbs.

Bake 30 to 35 minutes or until lightly browned. Cool. Cut into bars. Store loosely covered at room temperature.

Makes 24 to 36 bars

Top to bottom: Double Chocolate Fantasy Bars, Macaroon Almond Crumb Bars, Toffee Bars

Double Chocolate
Fantasy Bars

1 (18¼- or 18½-ounce) package
    chocolate cake mix
¼ cup vegetable oil
1 egg
1 cup chopped nuts
1 (14-ounce) can EAGLE® Brand
    Sweetened Condensed Milk
    (NOT evaporated milk)
1 (6-ounce) package semi-sweet
    chocolate chips (1 cup)
1 teaspoon vanilla extract
    Dash salt

Preheat oven to 350°F. In large mixer bowl, combine cake mix, oil and egg; beat on medium speed until crumbly. Stir in nuts. Reserving 1½ cups crumb mixture, press remainder firmly on bottom of greased 13×9-inch baking pan. In small saucepan, combine remaining ingredients. Over medium heat, cook and stir until chips melt. Pour over prepared crust. Top with reserved crumb mixture.

Bake 25 to 30 minutes or until bubbly. Cool. Cut into bars. Store loosely covered at room temperature.

Makes 24 to 36 bars

Almond Shortbread Bars

Mississippi Mud Bars

½ cup butter or margarine, softened
¾ cup packed brown sugar
1 teaspoon vanilla
1 egg
½ teaspoon baking soda
¼ teaspoon salt
1 cup plus 2 tablespoons all-purpose flour
1 cup (6 ounces) semisweet chocolate chips, divided
1 cup (6 ounces) white chocolate chips, divided
½ cup chopped walnuts or pecans

Preheat oven to 375°F. Line 9-inch square pan with foil; grease foil.

Cream butter and brown sugar in large bowl until blended and smooth. Beat in vanilla and egg until light. Blend in baking soda and salt. Add flour, mixing until well blended. Add ¾ cup *each* of the semisweet and white chocolate chips and the nuts; stir well. Spread dough in prepared pan.

Bake 23 to 25 minutes or until center feels firm. Do not overbake. Remove from oven; sprinkle remaining ¼ cup *each* semisweet and white chocolate chips over the top. Let stand a few minutes until chips melt, then spread evenly over bars. Cool in pan on wire rack until chocolate is set. Cut into 2×1-inch bars. *Makes 3 dozen bars*

Almond Shortbread Bars

2 cups all-purpose flour
1 cup sugar
1 cup LAND O LAKES® Butter, softened
1 egg, separated
¼ teaspoon almond extract
1 tablespoon water
½ cup chopped almonds

Preheat oven to 350°F. In large mixer bowl, combine flour, sugar, butter, egg yolk and almond extract. Beat at low speed, scraping bowl often, until particles are fine, 2 to 3 minutes. Press on bottom of greased 15×10×1-inch jelly-roll pan. In small bowl, beat egg white and water until frothy; brush on dough. Sprinkle nuts over top. Bake for 15 to 20 minutes, or until very lightly browned. Cool completely in pan on wire rack. Cut into bars.

Makes about 2½ dozen bars

Crunchy Peanut Brickle Bars

2 cups quick-cooking oats, uncooked
1½ cups unsifted flour
1 cup chopped dry-roasted peanuts
1 cup firmly packed brown sugar
1 teaspoon baking soda
½ teaspoon salt
1 cup margarine or butter, melted
1 (14-ounce) can EAGLE® Brand Sweetened Condensed Milk (NOT evaporated milk)
½ cup peanut butter
1 (6-ounce) package almond brickle chips, or 6 (1⅜-ounce) milk chocolate-covered English toffee candy bars, cut into small pieces

Preheat oven to 375°F. In large bowl, combine oats, flour, peanuts, brown sugar, baking soda and salt; stir in margarine until crumbly. Reserving 1½ cups crumb mixture, press remainder on bottom of greased 15×10-inch baking pan. Bake 12 minutes. Meanwhile, in small mixer bowl, beat sweetened condensed milk with peanut butter until smooth; spread evenly over prepared crust to within ¼ inch of edge. In medium bowl, combine reserved crumb mixture and brickle chips. Sprinkle evenly over peanut butter mixture; press down firmly.

Bake 20 minutes or until golden brown. Cool. Cut into bars. Store loosely covered at room temperature.

Makes 36 to 48 bars

Prep time: 20 minutes
Baking time: 32 minutes

Pineapple Walnut Bars

1 can (8¼ oz.) DOLE® Crushed Pineapple in Syrup*
2 cups flour
2 cups packed brown sugar
½ cup margarine, softened
1 cup chopped walnuts
1 teaspoon ground cinnamon
1 teaspoon baking soda
¼ teaspoon salt
1 egg
¾ cup dairy sour cream
1 teaspoon vanilla extract
Powdered sugar, optional

Preheat oven to 350°F. Drain pineapple well, pressing out excess syrup with back of spoon. Grease 13×9-inch baking pan.

In large bowl, combine flour, brown sugar and margarine; mix until fine crumbs form. Stir in walnuts. Press 2 cups mixture onto bottom of prepared baking pan. To remaining flour mixture, add cinnamon, baking soda and salt; blend well. Beat in egg, sour cream and vanilla until blended. Stir in pineapple. Spoon evenly over crust in pan.

Bake 40 minutes until bars pull away from sides of pan and wooden toothpick inserted in center comes out clean. Cool completely in pan on wire rack. Dust with powdered sugar. Cut into bars.

Makes about 16 bars

*May use pineapple packed in juice, if desired.

Peanut Butter Bars

½ cup BUTTER FLAVOR CRISCO®
1½ cups firmly packed brown sugar
⅔ cup JIF® Creamy *or* Extra Crunchy
      Peanut Butter
2 eggs
1 teaspoon vanilla
1½ cups all-purpose flour
½ teaspoon salt
¼ cup milk

1. Preheat oven to 350°F. Grease 13×9×2-inch baking pan with BUTTER FLAVOR CRISCO®.

2. Combine BUTTER FLAVOR CRISCO®, brown sugar and JIF® Creamy Peanut Butter in large bowl. Beat at medium speed of electric mixer until well blended. Beat in eggs and vanilla.

3. Combine flour and salt. Add alternately with milk to creamed mixture at low speed. Beat until well blended. Spread in pan.

4. Bake 28 to 32 minutes or until golden brown and center is set. Cool in pan on wire rack. Top with frosting or glaze, if desired. Cut into 2¼×1½-inch bars.

Makes 32 bars

Frosting and Glaze Variations

Chocolate Dream Frosting: Combine 2 tablespoons BUTTER FLAVOR CRISCO®, 1 cup miniature marshmallows, 1 square (1 ounce) unsweetened chocolate and 3 tablespoons milk in medium microwave-safe bowl. Cover with waxed paper. Microwave at 50% (MEDIUM). Stir after 1 minute. Repeat until smooth (or melt on rangetop in medium saucepan on low heat). Stir in 1¾ cups powdered sugar. Beat until well blended. Spread over top. Sprinkle ¼ cup finely chopped peanuts over frosting. Set aside until frosting is firm. Cut into bars.

"Peanut Butter Special" Frosting: Combine 2 tablespoons BUTTER FLAVOR CRISCO® and ⅓ cup JIF® Creamy Peanut Butter in medium bowl. Stir mixture until smooth. Add 1¼ cups powdered sugar, 2 tablespoons milk and ½ teaspoon vanilla. Stir until well blended. Spread over top. Set aside until frosting is firm. Cut into bars.

Microwave Chocolate Chip Glaze: Combine 1 tablespoon BUTTER FLAVOR CRISCO®, ¼ cup semi-sweet chocolate chips and 3 tablespoons milk in medium microwave-safe bowl. Microwave at 50% (MEDIUM). Stir after 1 minute. Repeat until smooth (or melt on rangetop in small saucepan on very low heat). Add ½ cup powdered sugar and ¼ teaspoon vanilla. Stir until smooth. (Add small amount of hot milk if thinner consistency is desired.) Drizzle over top. Set aside until glaze is firm. Cut into bars.

Peanut Butter Glaze: Combine 1 tablespoon BUTTER FLAVOR CRISCO® and 1 tablespoon JIF® Creamy Peanut Butter in small bowl. Stir mixture until smooth. Add ¾ cup powdered sugar and 2 to 2½ tablespoons hot milk (use enough milk to obtain drizzling consistency). Stir until well blended. Drizzle over top. Sprinkle 2 tablespoons finely chopped peanuts over glaze. Set aside until glaze is firm. Cut into bars.

Top to bottom: "Cordially Yours" Chocolate Chip Bars (page 70), Peanut Butter Bars

"Cordially Yours" Chocolate Chip Bars

¾ cup BUTTER FLAVOR CRISCO®
2 eggs
½ cup granulated sugar
¼ cup firmly packed brown sugar
1½ teaspoons vanilla
1 teaspoon almond extract
2 cups all-purpose flour
1 teaspoon baking soda
½ teaspoon cinnamon
1 can (21 ounces) cherry pie filling
1½ cups milk chocolate big chips
   Powdered sugar

1. Preheat oven to 350°F. Grease 15½×10½×1-inch pan with BUTTER FLAVOR CRISCO®.

2. Combine BUTTER FLAVOR CRISCO®, eggs, granulated sugar, brown sugar, vanilla and almond extract in large bowl. Beat at medium speed of electric mixer until well blended.

3. Combine flour, baking soda and cinnamon. Mix into creamed mixture at low speed until just blended. Stir in pie filling and chocolate chips. Spread in pan.

4. Bake 25 minutes or until lightly browned and top springs back when lightly pressed. Cool completely in pan on wire rack. Sprinkle with powdered sugar. Cut into 2½×2-inch bars.

Makes 30 bars

Breakfast Bars to Go

1 cup NABISCO® 100% Bran
⅔ cup applesauce
¾ cup chunky peanut butter
½ cup BLUE BONNET® Margarine
½ cup sugar
1 teaspoon vanilla extract
2 eggs
1 cup all-purpose flour
½ teaspoon baking soda
24 apple slices

Preheat oven to 350°F. In small bowl, combine bran and applesauce; let mixture stand for 5 minutes.

In large bowl, with electric mixer at medium speed, blend peanut butter and margarine. Beat in sugar and vanilla. Add eggs, one at a time, beating 1 minute after each addition. Stir in bran mixture, flour and baking soda until well blended. Spread in greased and floured 13×9×2-inch baking pan. Arrange apple slices in 4 rows on top of batter.

Bake 25 to 30 minutes or until knife inserted in center comes out clean. Cool completely in pan on wire rack. Cut into bars. Store in airtight container.

Makes 24 bars

Breakfast Bars to Go

Heath® Bars

1 cup butter
1 cup brown sugar
1 egg yolk
1 teaspoon vanilla
2 cups flour
18 to 19 Original HEATH® English
   Toffee Snack Size Bars, crushed,
   divided
½ cup finely chopped pecans

Preheat oven to 350°F. In large bowl, with electric mixer, cream butter well; blend in brown sugar, egg yolk and vanilla. By hand, mix in flour, ⅔ cup of the HEATH® Bars and the nuts. Press into ungreased 15½×10½-inch jelly roll pan.

Bake 18 to 20 minutes, or until browned. Remove from oven and immediately sprinkle remaining HEATH® Bars over top. Cool slightly; cut into bars while warm. *Makes about 48 bars*

Heath® Bars

Cocoa Shortbread

2 cups all-purpose flour
½ cup NESTLÉ® Cocoa
1 cup (2 sticks) butter, softened
1 cup sifted confectioners' sugar
1½ teaspoons vanilla extract

Preheat oven to 300°F. In small bowl, combine flour and NESTLÉ® Cocoa; set aside. In large mixer bowl, beat butter, confectioners' sugar and vanilla extract until creamy. Gradually blend in flour mixture. On lightly floured board, roll dough ½ inch thick; cut into 2×1-inch strips. With fork, pierce surface. Place on ungreased cookie sheets.

Bake 20 minutes or just until firm. Remove from cookie sheets; cool completely on wire rack. *Makes about 2 dozen cookies*

Pecan Pie Bars

Crust
  2 cups all-purpose flour
  ½ cup powdered sugar
  1 cup LAND O LAKES® Butter
Filling
  1 can (14 ounces) sweetened
     condensed milk
  1 egg
  1 teaspoon vanilla
  1 package (6 ounces) almond brickle
     bits
  1 cup chopped pecans

Preheat oven to 350°F. For Crust, in large bowl, combine flour and powdered sugar. Cut in butter until crumbly. Press firmly on bottom of ungreased 13×9×2-inch baking pan. Bake for 15 minutes.

For Filling, in large bowl, stir together sweetened condensed milk, egg and vanilla. Stir in almond brickle bits and nuts. Spread evenly over hot crust. Continue baking for 25 to 28 minutes, or until golden brown. Cool completely in pan on wire rack. Refrigerate until firm, 2 to 3 hours. Cut into bars. Store, covered, in refrigerator. *Makes about 3 dozen bars*

Kahlúa® Chocolate Nut Squares

1¼ cups sifted all-purpose flour
¾ teaspoon baking powder
½ teaspoon salt
½ cup butter, softened
¾ cup packed brown sugar
1 large egg
¼ cup *plus* 1 tablespoon KAHLÚA®
1 cup semi-sweet chocolate pieces
⅓ cup chopped walnuts or pecans
    Brown Butter Icing (recipe follows)
    Nut halves (optional)

Preheat oven to 350°F. Grease 11×7-inch baking pan.

Resift flour with baking powder and salt; set aside. Cream butter and brown sugar; beat in egg. Stir in ¼ cup KAHLÚA®, then flour mixture; blend well. Fold in chocolate pieces and chopped nuts. Spread batter evenly in prepared pan.

Bake 30 minutes or until top springs back when touched lightly in center. Do not overbake. Remove from oven; cool in pan 15 minutes. Brush top with remaining 1 tablespoon KAHLÚA®. Cool completely; frost with Brown Butter Icing. When icing is set, cut into bars. Garnish, if desired, with nut halves.

Makes about 2 dozen bars

Brown Butter Icing: In saucepan, heat 2 tablespoons butter until lightly browned. Remove from heat. Add 1 tablespoon KAHLÚA®, 2 teaspoons milk *or* cream and 1⅓ cups sifted powdered sugar; beat until smooth.

Chocolate-Frosted Almond Shortbread

¾ cup butter, softened
¼ cup packed light brown sugar
¼ cup powdered sugar
1 egg yolk
1 teaspoon almond extract
1½ cups all-purpose flour
⅛ teaspoon baking soda
7 ounces (about 1 cup) almond paste
½ cup granulated sugar
1 egg
½ cup milk chocolate chips

Preheat oven to 350°F. Cover bottom of 9-inch pie pan with parchment or waxed paper.

Cream butter, brown sugar, powdered sugar, egg yolk and almond extract in large bowl. Blend in flour and baking soda until smooth. Press half of dough into prepared pie pan. Beat almond paste, granulated sugar and whole egg in small bowl until smooth. Spread over dough in pan. Roll out remaining half of dough on lightly floured surface into a circle to fit on top of almond layer. Place over almond layer; press down to make smooth top.

Bake 30 to 40 minutes or until top appears very lightly browned and feels firm. Remove from oven; sprinkle chocolate chips over top. Let stand a few minutes until chips melt, then spread evenly over shortbread. Refrigerate until chocolate is set. Cut into slim wedges to serve.

Makes 16 to 20 cookies

Chocolate Meringue Peanut Squares

Chocolate Meringue Peanut Squares

Crust
  1½ cups all-purpose flour
  ½ cup sugar
  ¾ cup LAND O LAKES® Butter, softened
  2 egg yolks, reserve egg whites
  2 teaspoons vanilla

Filling
  2 reserved egg whites
  ⅓ cup sugar
  1 cup chopped salted peanuts
  ½ cup milk chocolate chips

Preheat oven to 325°F. For Crust, in large mixer bowl, combine all crust ingredients. Beat at low speed, scraping bowl often, until mixture is crumbly, 1 to 2 minutes. Press onto bottom of greased 13×9×2-inch baking pan.

For Filling, in small bowl, beat egg whites at high speed, scraping bowl often, until soft mounds form, 1 to 2 minutes. Gradually add sugar; beat until stiff peaks form, 1 to 2 minutes. Fold in peanuts and chocolate chips. Spread over crust. Bake for 30 to 35 minutes, or until lightly browned. Cool completely in pan on wire rack. Cut into squares.

Makes about 3 dozen squares

Oatmeal Caramel Bars

  1 cup quick-cooking oats, uncooked
  1 cup unsifted flour
  ¾ cup firmly packed light brown sugar
  1 teaspoon ground cinnamon
  1 egg, beaten
  ½ cup cold margarine or butter
  1 cup chopped nuts
  1 (14-ounce) package EAGLE™ Brand Caramels, unwrapped
  1 (14-ounce) can EAGLE® Brand Sweetened Condensed Milk (NOT evaporated milk)

Preheat oven to 350°F. In large bowl, combine oats, flour, brown sugar, cinnamon and egg; mix well. Cut in margarine until crumbly. Stir in nuts. Reserving 2 cups crumb mixture, press remainder firmly on bottom of 13×9-inch baking pan. Bake 15 minutes. Meanwhile, in heavy saucepan, over low heat, melt caramels with sweetened condensed milk, stirring constantly. Pour evenly over prepared crust. Top with reserved crumb mixture.

Bake 20 minutes or until golden. Cool. Chill if desired. Cut into bars. Store loosely covered in refrigerator.

Makes 24 to 36 bars

Buttery Caramel Crisps

12 double graham crackers
2 cups miniature marshmallows
¾ cup firmly packed brown sugar
¾ cup LAND O LAKES® Butter
1 teaspoon ground cinnamon
1 teaspoon vanilla
1 cup sliced almonds
1 cup flaked coconut

Preheat oven to 350°F. Line ungreased 15×10×1-inch jelly-roll pan with graham crackers. Sprinkle marshmallows evenly over crackers. In medium saucepan, combine brown sugar, butter, cinnamon and vanilla. Cook, stirring constantly, over medium heat until sugar is dissolved and butter is melted, 4 to 5 minutes. Pour evenly over crackers and marshmallows; sprinkle nuts and coconut over top. Bake for 8 to 12 minutes, or until lightly browned. Cool completely in pan on wire rack. Cut into bars.

Makes about 4 dozen bars

Lemon Chocolate Bars

1⅓ cups plus 3 tablespoons unsifted
    flour
½ cup confectioners' sugar
2 tablespoons unsweetened cocoa
¾ cup cold margarine or butter
1½ cups granulated sugar
1 teaspoon baking powder
½ cup REALEMON® Lemon Juice
    from Concentrate
4 eggs, beaten
    Quick Chocolate Drizzle

Preheat oven to 350°F. In large bowl, combine *1⅓ cups* flour, confectioners' sugar and cocoa; cut in margarine until crumbly. Press onto bottom of 13×9-inch baking pan; bake 20 minutes. Meanwhile, in medium bowl, combine granulated sugar, baking powder and remaining *3 tablespoons* flour. Add REALEMON® brand and eggs; mix well. Pour over baked crust; bake 20 minutes longer or until golden brown. Cool. Drizzle with Quick Chocolate Drizzle. Chill. Cut into bars. Store covered in refrigerator; serve at room temperature. *Makes 24 to 36 bars*

Quick Chocolate Drizzle: In small saucepan, over low heat, melt 1 (1-ounce) square semi-sweet chocolate with 1 tablespoon margarine or butter. Immediately drizzle over bars.

Spice 'n' Easy Apple Raisin Bars

Crumb Mixture
2 cups all-purpose flour
2 cups quick-cooking oats, uncooked
1½ cups sugar
1¼ cups LAND O LAKES® Butter,
    melted
1 teaspoon baking soda

Filling
½ cup raisins
½ cup chopped pecans
1 can (20 ounces) apple fruit filling
½ teaspoon ground cinnamon
½ teaspoon ground nutmeg

Preheat oven to 350°F. For Crumb Mixture, in large bowl, combine all crumb ingredients. Stir until well mixed, 1 to 2 minutes. Reserve 1½ cups of the crumb mixture. Press remaining crumb mixture on bottom of ungreased 13×9×2-inch baking pan. Bake for 15 to 20 minutes, or until edges are lightly browned.

For Filling, in medium bowl, combine all filling ingredients. Stir to blend. Spread over hot crust. Sprinkle 1½ cups reserved crumb mixture over top. Continue baking for 25 to 30 minutes, or until lightly browned. Cool completely in pan on wire rack. Cut into bars.

Makes about 3 dozen bars

Buttery Caramel Crisps

California Apricot Power Bars

2 cups California dried apricot
    halves, coarsely chopped
    (12 ounces)
1¼ cups pitted dates, coarsely chopped
    (8 ounces)
2½ cups pecans, coarsely chopped
    (10 ounces)
1¼ cups whole-wheat flour
  1 teaspoon baking powder
  3 large eggs
  1 cup firmly packed brown sugar
  ¼ cup apple juice *or* water
1½ teaspoons vanilla extract

Preheat oven to 350°F. Line 15½×10½×1-inch jelly roll pan with foil. In large bowl, stir together apricots, dates and pecans; divide in half. Combine flour and baking powder; add to half of fruit-nut mixture; toss to coat. In medium bowl, combine eggs and remaining ingredients; stir into flour mixture until thoroughly moistened. Spread batter evenly into prepared pan. Press remaining fruit-nut mixture lightly on top.

Bake 20 minutes or until golden and bars spring back when pressed lightly. Cool in pan 5 minutes. Turn out onto rack; cool 45 minutes. Peel off foil and cut into bars. Store in airtight container. Bars may be frozen. *Makes about 32 bars*

Favorite recipe from **California Apricot Advisory Board**

Chocolate Caramel Nut Bars

  1 (14 oz.) bag KRAFT® Caramels
  1 (5 fl. oz.) can evaporated milk,
    divided
  1 two-layer German chocolate cake
    mix with pudding
  ½ cup PARKAY® Margarine, melted
  1 cup BAKER'S® Semi-Sweet Real
    Chocolate Chips
1½ cups chopped walnuts, divided

• Preheat oven to 350°F.

• In medium saucepan, melt caramels with ⅓ cup milk over low heat, stirring until smooth. Set aside.

• In large bowl, mix together remaining milk, cake mix and margarine. Press *half* of cake mixture onto bottom of ungreased 13×9-inch baking pan. Bake 8 minutes.

• Sprinkle chocolate pieces and 1 cup walnuts over crust; top with caramel mixture, spreading to edges of pan. Top with teaspoonfuls of remaining cake mixture; press gently into caramel mixture. Sprinkle with remaining walnuts.

• Bake 16 to 18 minutes. Cool. Cut into bars. *Makes 2 dozen bars*

Prep time: 25 minutes
Cooking time: 18 minutes

Microwave Tip: Microwave caramels with milk in 2-quart bowl on HIGH 3 to 4 minutes or until sauce is smooth, stirring every 2 minutes.

California Apricot Power Bars

Sour Cream Cherry Bars

Crust
- 2 cups all-purpose flour
- ⅔ cup sugar
- ⅔ cup LAND O LAKES® Butter, softened

Filling
- 1 can (21 ounces) cherry fruit filling
- ¾ cup dairy sour cream
- 2 teaspoons almond extract
- ¾ cup sliced toasted almonds

Preheat oven to 350°F. For Crust, in large mixer bowl, combine all crust ingredients. Beat at low speed, scraping bowl often, until mixture is crumbly, 2 to 3 minutes. Press on bottom of ungreased 13×9×2-inch baking pan. Bake for 20 to 25 minutes, or until lightly browned around edges.

For Filling, in medium bowl, stir together fruit filling, sour cream and almond extract. Spread over hot crust. Sprinkle nuts over top. Continue baking for 15 to 20 minutes, or until edges are bubbly. Cool completely in pan on wire rack. Cut into bars. Store, covered, in refrigerator.

Makes about 3 dozen bars

Cherry Date Sparkle Bars

Cherry Date Sparkle Bars

Crust
- 1 cup all-purpose flour
- ¼ cup sugar
- ½ cup LAND O LAKES® Butter, softened

Filling
- ¾ cup sugar
- ½ cup all-purpose flour
- 2 eggs
- ½ teaspoon baking powder
- ¼ teaspoon salt
- 1½ teaspoons vanilla
- ¾ cup chopped dates
- ½ cup flaked coconut
- ½ cup chopped pecans
- ½ cup halved maraschino cherries, drained

Preheat oven to 350°F. For Crust, in small mixer bowl, combine all crust ingredients. Beat at low speed, scraping bowl often, until mixture is crumbly, 1 to 2 minutes. Press on bottom of ungreased 9-inch square baking pan. Bake for 15 to 20 minutes, or until edges are lightly browned.

For Filling, in same mixer bowl, combine sugar, flour, eggs, baking powder, salt and vanilla. Beat at medium speed, scraping bowl often, until well mixed, 1 to 2 minutes. Stir in remaining ingredients. Pour over hot crust. Continue baking for 25 to 30 minutes, or until lightly browned and filling is set. Cool completely in pan on wire rack. Cut into bars.

Makes about 3 dozen bars

Strawberry Wonders

Crust
- 1½ cups all-purpose flour
- ½ cup quick-cooking oats, uncooked
- ½ cup granulated sugar
- ¾ cup LAND O LAKES® Butter, softened
- ½ teaspoon baking soda

Topping
- ¾ cup flaked coconut
- ¾ cup chopped walnuts
- ¼ cup all-purpose flour
- ¼ cup firmly packed brown sugar
- 2 tablespoons LAND O LAKES® Butter, softened
- ½ teaspoon ground cinnamon
- 1 jar (10 ounces) strawberry preserves

Preheat oven to 350°F. For Crust, in large mixer bowl, combine all crust ingredients. Beat at low speed, scraping bowl often, until mixture is crumbly, 1 to 2 minutes. Press crust mixture on bottom of greased 13×9×2-inch baking pan. Bake for 18 to 22 minutes, or until edges are lightly browned.

For Topping, in same mixer bowl, combine coconut, nuts, flour, brown sugar, butter and cinnamon. Beat at low speed, scraping bowl often, until well mixed, 1 to 2 minutes. Spread preserves to ¼ inch of edges of hot crust. Sprinkle topping mixture over preserves. Continue baking for 18 to 22 minutes, or until edges are lightly browned. Cool completely in pan on wire rack. Cut into bars.

Makes about 3 dozen bars

Butterscotch Bars

- ¼ cup BUTTER FLAVOR CRISCO®
- 1 package (12 ounces) butterscotch chips*
- 1 cup JIF® Creamy Peanut Butter
- ⅓ cup milk
- 2 cups graham cracker crumbs
- 1 cup chopped salted peanuts
- 1 package (6 ounces) semi-sweet chocolate chips
- 3 tablespoons BUTTER FLAVOR CRISCO®
- Finely chopped peanuts

1. Combine ¼ cup BUTTER FLAVOR CRISCO®, butterscotch chips, JIF® Creamy Peanut Butter and milk in top of double boiler over hot water. Stir occasionally until mixture is melted and smooth.

2. Combine graham cracker crumbs and 1 cup chopped nuts in large bowl. Pour butterscotch mixture over crumbs. Stir until combined.

3. Spread mixture in ungreased 9×9×2-inch pan. Refrigerate until firm. Cut into 1¾×¾-inch bars.

4. Combine chocolate chips and 3 tablespoons BUTTER FLAVOR CRISCO® in top of double boiler over hot water. Stir occasionally until chocolate melts.

5. Place one bar at a time in melted chocolate. Turn with fork to coat evenly. Lift from chocolate on fork; allow excess to drip off. Place on waxed-paper-lined baking sheet. Sprinkle top with finely chopped nuts. Return to refrigerator to harden chocolate.

Makes 5½ to 6 dozen bars

*1 package (12 ounces) peanut butter chips may be substituted for butterscotch chips.

Crisp 'n' Crunchy Almond Coconut Bars, Strawberry Wonders

Crisp 'n' Crunchy Almond Coconut Bars

Crust
  1¼ cups all-purpose flour
  ¼ cup granulated sugar
  ½ cup LAND O LAKES® Butter,
    softened
  ½ teaspoon rum extract
  ¼ cup sliced almonds, toasted

Filling
  1 cup powdered sugar
  ¼ cup LAND O LAKES® Butter
  ¼ cup milk
  2 tablespoons all-purpose flour
  ½ teaspoon rum extract
  1 cup flaked coconut
  1 cup sliced almonds

Preheat oven to 375°F. For Crust, in small mixer bowl, combine flour, granulated sugar, butter and rum extract. Beat at low speed, scraping bowl often, until mixture is crumbly, 1 to 2 minutes. Stir in nuts. Press on bottom of ungreased 9-inch square baking pan. Bake for 12 to 18 minutes, or until edges are lightly browned.

For Filling, in small saucepan, combine powdered sugar, butter, milk, flour and rum extract. Cook, stirring constantly, over medium heat until mixture comes to a full boil, 5 to 7 minutes. Stir in coconut and nuts. Pour over crust. Continue baking for 11 to 16 minutes, or until lightly browned. Cool completely in pan on wire rack. Cut into bars.   *Makes about 2 dozen bars*

Frosted Honey Bars

Bars
- 1½ cups all-purpose flour
- 1 cup LAND O LAKES® Butter, melted
- 1 cup honey
- 3 eggs
- 1½ teaspoons baking soda
- 1 teaspoon ground cinnamon
- ¾ teaspoon salt
- 1½ cups shredded carrots (about 3 medium)
- ¾ cup chopped walnuts

Frosting
- 1 cup powdered sugar
- 1 package (8 ounces) cream cheese, softened
- 1 teaspoon milk
- 1 teaspoon vanilla

Frosted Honey Bars

Preheat oven to 350°F. For Bars, in large mixer bowl, combine flour, butter, honey, eggs, baking soda, cinnamon and salt. Beat at low speed, scraping bowl often, until well mixed, 1 to 2 minutes. Stir in carrots and nuts. Pour into greased 15×10×1-inch jelly-roll pan. Bake for 20 to 25 minutes, or until top springs back when touched lightly in center. Cool completely in pan on wire rack.

For Frosting, in small mixer bowl, combine all frosting ingredients. Beat at medium speed, scraping bowl often, until smooth, 1 to 2 minutes. Spread bars with frosting. Cut into bars. Store, covered, in refrigerator.

Makes about 3 dozen bars

Apricot Oatmeal Bars

- 1½ cups all-purpose flour
- ¾ cup firmly packed brown sugar
- 1 teaspoon baking powder
- 1 cup butter or margarine, softened
- 1½ cups quick-cooking rolled oats, uncooked
- ½ cup flaked coconut
- ½ cup coarsely chopped walnuts
- 1 can SOLO® or 1 jar BAKER® Apricot, Raspberry, or Strawberry Filling

Preheat oven to 350°F. Grease 13×9-inch pan. Combine flour, brown sugar and baking powder in large bowl. Cut in butter until mixture resembles coarse crumbs. Add oats, coconut and walnuts; mix until crumbly. Press half of mixture into pan. Top with apricot filling. Sprinkle remaining crumb mixture over apricot layer.

Bake 25 to 30 minutes or until lightly browned. (Center may seem soft but will set when cool.) Cool completely in pan on wire rack. Cut into 2×1½-inch bars.

Makes 36 bars

Zesty Fresh Lemon Bars

Crust:
- ½ cup butter or margarine, softened
- ½ cup granulated sugar
- Grated peel of ½ SUNKIST® Lemon
- 1¼ cups all-purpose flour

Filling:
- 1 cup packed brown sugar
- 1 cup chopped walnuts
- 2 eggs, slightly beaten
- ¼ cup all-purpose flour
- Grated peel of ½ SUNKIST® Lemon
- ¼ teaspoon baking powder

Glaze:
- 1 cup powdered sugar
- 1 tablespoon butter or margarine, softened
- 2 tablespoons fresh-squeezed SUNKIST® Lemon Juice

To prepare Crust: Preheat oven to 350°F. In medium bowl, cream butter, granulated sugar and lemon peel. Gradually stir in flour to form soft dough. Press evenly on bottom of 13×9×2-inch pan. Bake 15 minutes.

To prepare Filling: In medium bowl, mix all filling ingredients. Spread over baked crust. Bake 20 minutes. Meanwhile, prepare Glaze.

To prepare Glaze: In small bowl, gradually blend small amount of powdered sugar into butter. Add lemon juice and the remaining sugar; stir to blend well. Drizzle glaze over hot lemon bars. Cool in pan on wire rack; cut into bars.

Makes about 3 dozen bars

Glazed Rum Raisin Bars

Bars
- ½ cup water
- 1 cup raisins
- 2 cups all-purpose flour
- ¾ cup granulated sugar
- 1 cup LAND O LAKES® Butter, softened
- ½ cup milk
- 1 egg
- 1 teaspoon baking powder
- 1 teaspoon salt
- ½ teaspoon rum extract

Glaze
- ¼ cup LAND O LAKES® Butter
- ¾ cup powdered sugar
- 1 tablespoon water
- ¼ teaspoon rum extract

Preheat oven to 375°F. For Bars, in heavy, small saucepan, combine water and raisins. Cook over medium heat until water comes to a full boil, 3 to 4 minutes. Drain water; reserve raisins.

In large mixer bowl, combine flour, granulated sugar, butter, milk, egg, baking powder, salt and rum extract. Beat at low speed, scraping bowl often, until well mixed, 2 to 3 minutes. Stir in drained raisins. Spread into ungreased 13×9×2-inch baking pan. Bake for 20 to 25 minutes, or until wooden toothpick inserted in center comes out clean.

For Glaze, in same saucepan, melt butter over low heat, 3 to 4 minutes. Add powdered sugar, water and rum extract. Cook, stirring occasionally, until smooth, 1 to 2 minutes. Spread glaze over warm bars. Cool completely in pan on wire rack. Cut into bars.

Makes about 3 dozen bars

EXTRA-EASY COOKIES

Cocoa Snickerdoodles

1 cup butter or margarine, softened
¾ cup packed brown sugar
¾ cup plus 2 tablespoons granulated
    sugar
2 eggs
2 cups uncooked rolled oats
1½ cups all-purpose flour
¼ cup plus 2 tablespoons unsweetened
    cocoa
1 teaspoon baking soda
2 tablespoons ground cinnamon

Preheat oven to 375°F. Lightly grease cookie sheets or line with parchment paper.

Beat butter, brown sugar and the ¾ cup granulated sugar in large bowl until light and fluffy. Add eggs; mix well. Combine oats, flour, the ¼ cup cocoa and the baking soda in medium bowl. Stir into butter mixture until blended. Mix the 2 tablespoons granulated sugar, the cinnamon and the 2 tablespoons cocoa in small bowl. Drop dough by rounded teaspoonfuls into cinnamon mixture; toss to coat. Place 2 inches apart on prepared cookie sheets.

Bake 8 to 10 minutes or until firm in center. Do not overbake. Remove to wire racks to cool.

Makes about 4½ dozen cookies

Chocolate-Peanut Cookies

1 cup butter or margarine, softened
¾ cup granulated sugar
¾ cup packed light brown sugar
2 eggs
1 teaspoon vanilla
1 teaspoon baking soda
¼ teaspoon salt
2¼ cups all-purpose flour
2 cups chocolate-covered peanuts

Preheat oven to 375°F. Line cookie sheets with parchment paper or leave ungreased. Cream butter with sugars, eggs and vanilla in large bowl until light. Beat in baking soda and salt. Stir in flour to make stiff dough. Blend in chocolate-covered peanuts. Drop dough by rounded teaspoonfuls 2 inches apart onto cookie sheets.

Bake 9 to 11 minutes or until just barely golden. Do not overbake. Remove to wire racks to cool.

Makes about 5 dozen cookies

Cocoa Snickerdoodles,
Chocolate-Peanut Cookies

Lemon Meltaways

Cookies
- 1¼ cups all-purpose flour
- ½ cup cornstarch
- ⅓ cup powdered sugar
- ¾ cup LAND O LAKES® Butter, softened
- 1 tablespoon lemon juice
- 1 teaspoon lemon peel

Frosting
- ¾ cup powdered sugar
- ¼ cup LAND O LAKES® Butter, softened
- 1 teaspoon lemon juice
- 1 teaspoon grated lemon peel

For Cookies, in large mixer bowl, combine all cookie ingredients. Beat at low speed, scraping bowl often, until well mixed, 2 to 3 minutes. Shape dough into two 8×1-inch rolls. Wrap in waxed paper. Refrigerate until firm, 1 to 2 hours.

Preheat oven to 350°F. Cut rolls into ¼-inch slices. Place 2 inches apart on ungreased cookie sheets. Bake for 8 to 12 minutes, or until set; cookies will not brown. Remove immediately; cool completely on wire racks.

For Frosting, in small mixer bowl, combine all frosting ingredients. Beat at medium speed, scraping bowl often, until light and fluffy, 1 to 2 minutes. Spread on cooled cookies.   *Makes about 4 dozen cookies*

Top plate (clockwise from top left): Fruit Filled Thumbprints, Peanut Buttery Cookies, Lemon Meltaways

Fruit Filled Thumbprints

2 cups all-purpose flour
½ cup firmly packed brown sugar
1 cup LAND O LAKES® Butter, softened
2 eggs, separated
⅛ teaspoon salt
1 teaspoon vanilla
1½ cups finely chopped pecans
Fruit preserves

Preheat oven to 350°F. In large mixer bowl, combine flour, sugar, butter, egg yolks, salt and vanilla. Beat at low speed, scraping bowl often, until well mixed, 2 to 3 minutes. Shape rounded teaspoonfuls of dough into 1-inch balls. In small bowl, beat egg whites with fork until foamy. Dip each ball into whites; roll in nuts. Place 1 inch apart on greased cookie sheets. Make a depression in center of each cookie with back of teaspoon.

Bake for 8 minutes; remove from oven. Fill centers with preserves. Continue baking for 6 to 10 minutes, or until lightly browned. Cool on wire racks.

Makes about 3 dozen cookies

Peanut Buttery Cookies

1½ cups all-purpose flour
½ cup granulated sugar
½ cup firmly packed brown sugar
½ cup LAND O LAKES® Butter, softened
2 eggs
1 teaspoon salt
½ teaspoon baking soda
½ teaspoon vanilla
2 cups salted peanuts (about 12 ounces)

Preheat oven to 350°F. In large mixer bowl, combine flour, granulated sugar, brown sugar, butter, eggs, salt, baking soda and vanilla. Beat at low speed,

scraping bowl often, until well mixed, 2 to 3 minutes. Stir in nuts. Drop rounded teaspoonfuls of dough 2 inches apart onto greased cookie sheets. Bake for 8 to 12 minutes, or until lightly browned. Remove immediately; cool on wire racks.

Makes about 4 dozen cookies

German Chocolate Oatmeal Cookies

¾ cup BUTTER FLAVOR CRISCO®
1 cup firmly packed dark brown sugar
½ cup granulated sugar
2 eggs
2 packages (4 ounces each) German chocolate, melted and cooled
1 tablespoon water
1¼ cups all-purpose flour
½ teaspoon baking soda
½ teaspoon salt
3 cups quick oats (not instant or old fashioned), uncooked
1 cup coarsely chopped pecans
1 cup flake coconut

1. Preheat oven to 375°F. Grease cookie sheet with BUTTER FLAVOR CRISCO®.

2. Combine BUTTER FLAVOR CRISCO®, brown sugar, granulated sugar, eggs, chocolate and water in large bowl. Beat at medium speed of electric mixer until well blended.

3. Combine flour, baking soda and salt. Mix into creamed mixture at low speed until blended. Stir in oats, nuts and coconut with spoon.

4. Drop rounded tablespoonfuls of dough 2 inches apart onto cookie sheet.

5. Bake 10 minutes or until bottoms are browned, but tops are slightly soft. Cool 3 minutes on cookie sheet. Remove to cooling rack.

Makes about 4 dozen cookies

Swiss Chocolate Crispies

1 package DUNCAN HINES® Moist
    Deluxe Swiss Chocolate
    Cake Mix
½ cup BUTTER FLAVOR CRISCO®
½ cup butter or margarine, softened
2 eggs
2 tablespoons water
3 cups crisp rice cereal, divided

1. Combine cake mix, BUTTER FLAVOR CRISCO®, butter, eggs and water in large bowl. Beat at low speed with electric mixer for 2 minutes. Fold in 1 cup cereal. Refrigerate 1 hour.

2. Crush remaining 2 cups cereal into coarse crumbs.

3. Preheat oven to 350°F. Grease cookie sheets. Shape dough into 1-inch balls. Roll in crushed cereal. Place on cookie sheets about 1 inch apart.

4. Bake 11 to 13 minutes. Cool 1 minute on cookie sheets. Remove to cooling racks.

Makes about 4 dozen cookies

Whole Wheat Oatmeal Cookies

¾ cup BUTTER FLAVOR CRISCO®
¾ cup firmly packed brown sugar
¼ cup molasses
¼ cup honey
1 egg
⅓ cup apple juice
1 teaspoon vanilla
1 cup whole wheat flour
1 teaspoon cinnamon
½ teaspoon baking soda
¼ teaspoon salt
⅛ teaspoon nutmeg
3 cups quick oats (not instant or old
    fashioned), uncooked
¾ cup raisins
¾ cup chopped walnuts

1. Preheat oven to 350°F. Grease cookie sheet with BUTTER FLAVOR CRISCO®.

2. Combine BUTTER FLAVOR CRISCO®, brown sugar, molasses, honey, egg, juice and vanilla in large bowl. Beat at medium speed of electric mixer until blended.

3. Combine flour, cinnamon, baking soda, salt and nutmeg. Mix into creamed mixture at low speed until just blended. Stir in oats, raisins and nuts with spoon. Drop rounded tablespoonfuls of dough 2 inches apart onto cookie sheet.

4. Bake 13 to 14 minutes or until set. Cool 5 minutes on cookie sheet. Remove to cooling rack.

Makes about 3 dozen cookies

Peanutty Crisscrosses

3 cups QUAKER® Oats (quick or old
    fashioned, uncooked)
1½ cups all-purpose flour
½ teaspoon baking soda
1½ cups firmly packed brown sugar
1 cup peanut butter
¾ cup (1½ sticks) margarine or butter,
    softened
⅓ cup water
1 egg
1 teaspoon vanilla

Combine oats, flour and baking soda; set aside. In large bowl, beat brown sugar, peanut butter and margarine until creamy. Blend in water, egg and vanilla. Add dry ingredients; mix well. Chill dough about 1 hour.

Preheat oven to 350°F. Shape dough into 1-inch balls. Place on ungreased cookie sheet; flatten with tines of fork dipped in granulated sugar to form crisscross pattern.

Bake 9 to 10 minutes or until edges are golden brown. Cool 2 minutes on cookie sheet. Remove to wire rack to cool completely. Store tightly covered.

Makes about 7 dozen cookies

Maple Raisin Cookies

Cookies
- 2¼ cups all-purpose flour
- 1 cup granulated sugar
- ¾ cup LAND O LAKES® Butter, softened
- ¾ cup applesauce
- 1 egg
- 1 teaspoon pumpkin pie spice
- ½ teaspoon baking soda
- ½ teaspoon salt
- 1 cup raisins
- ½ cup chopped walnuts

Frosting
- 4 cups powdered sugar
- ½ cup LAND O LAKES® Butter, softened
- 3 to 4 tablespoons milk
- ½ teaspoon maple extract
- Raisins

Preheat oven to 375°F. For Cookies, in large mixer bowl, combine flour, granulated sugar, butter, applesauce, egg, pumpkin pie spice, baking soda and salt. Beat at low speed, scraping bowl often, until well mixed, 2 to 3 minutes. Stir in raisins and walnuts. Drop rounded teaspoonfuls of dough 2 inches apart onto greased cookie sheets. Bake for 10 to 12 minutes, or until lightly browned. Remove immediately; cool completely on wire racks.

For Frosting, in small mixer bowl, combine powdered sugar, butter, milk and maple extract. Beat at medium speed, scraping bowl often, until light and fluffy, 3 to 4 minutes. Spread over cooled cookies. Place 2 raisins in center of each cookie.

Makes about 3 dozen cookies

Maple Raisin Cookies

Peanut Butter Sensations

- ½ cup BUTTER FLAVOR CRISCO®
- 1 cup JIF® Creamy Peanut Butter
- ¾ cup granulated sugar
- ½ cup firmly packed brown sugar
- 1 tablespoon milk
- 1 teaspoon vanilla
- 1 egg
- 1¼ cups all-purpose flour
- ¾ teaspoon baking soda
- ½ teaspoon baking powder
- ¼ teaspoon salt

1. Preheat oven to 375°F. Combine BUTTER FLAVOR CRISCO®, JIF® Creamy Peanut Butter, granulated sugar, brown sugar, milk and vanilla in large bowl. Beat at medium speed of electric mixer until well blended. Beat in egg.

2. Combine flour, baking soda, baking powder and salt. Mix into creamed mixture at low speed until just blended. Drop rounded tablespoonfuls of dough 2 inches apart onto ungreased cookie sheet. Make crisscross pattern on dough with floured fork.

3. Bake 8 to 10 minutes. Cool 2 minutes on cookie sheet. Remove to cooling rack.

Makes about 2 dozen cookies

Mom's Best Oatmeal Cookies

1 cup BUTTER FLAVOR CRISCO®
1½ cups firmly packed brown sugar
2 eggs
2 teaspoons vanilla
1½ cups all-purpose flour
1 teaspoon salt
1 teaspoon baking powder
1 teaspoon cinnamon
¼ teaspoon baking soda
2 cups quick oats (not instant or old fashioned), uncooked
1 cup chopped pecans
⅔ cup sesame seeds
⅔ cup flake coconut

1. Preheat oven to 350°F. Combine BUTTER FLAVOR CRISCO® and brown sugar in large bowl. Beat at medium speed of electric mixer until well blended. Beat in eggs and vanilla.

2. Combine flour, salt, baking powder, cinnamon and baking soda. Mix into creamed mixture at low speed until blended. Stir in, one at a time, oats, nuts, sesame seeds and coconut with spoon. Drop rounded tablespoonfuls of dough 2 inches apart onto ungreased cookie sheet.

3. Bake 10 minutes or until lightly browned. Remove immediately to cooling rack. *Makes about 6 dozen cookies*

Chocolate Kiss Cookies

(Pictured on page 19)

1 package (15 ounces) golden sugar cookie mix
½ cup HERSHEY'S® Cocoa
1 egg
2 tablespoons water
¾ cup finely chopped nuts
1 bag (9 ounces) HERSHEY'S® KISSES® Chocolates, unwrapped (about 42)

Preheat oven to 350°F. In medium bowl combine cookie mix (and enclosed flavor packet), cocoa, egg and water; mix with spoon or fork until thoroughly blended. Shape dough into 1-inch balls. Roll balls in nuts; place on ungreased cookie sheet.

Bake 8 minutes. Immediately press KISS® into center of each warm cookie, allowing cookie to crack slightly. Cool slightly; remove from cookie sheet to wire rack. Cool completely.
Makes about 3½ dozen cookies

Ginger Snap Oats

¾ cup BUTTER FLAVOR CRISCO®
1 cup firmly packed brown sugar
½ cup granulated sugar
½ cup molasses
2 teaspoons vinegar
2 eggs
1¼ cups all-purpose flour
1 tablespoon ginger
1½ teaspoons baking soda
½ teaspoon cinnamon
¼ teaspoon ground cloves
2¾ cups quick oats (not instant or old fashioned), uncooked
1½ cups raisins

1. Preheat oven to 350°F. Grease cookie sheet with BUTTER FLAVOR CRISCO®.

2. Combine BUTTER FLAVOR CRISCO®, brown sugar, granulated sugar, molasses, vinegar and eggs in large bowl. Beat at medium speed of electric mixer until well blended.

3. Combine flour, ginger, baking soda, cinnamon and cloves. Mix into creamed mixture at low speed until blended. Stir in oats and raisins. Drop dough by rounded teaspoonfuls 2 inches apart onto cookie sheet.

4. Bake 11 to 14 minutes. Cool 2 minutes on cookie sheet. Remove to cooling rack.
Makes about 5 dozen cookies

Top to bottom: Ginger Snap Oats, Mom's Best Oatmeal Cookies

Granola Apple Cookies

1 cup firmly packed brown sugar
¾ cup margarine or butter, softened
1 egg
¾ cup MOTT'S® Natural Apple Sauce
1 teaspoon vanilla
3 cups granola with dates and raisins
1½ cups all-purpose flour
1 teaspoon baking powder
½ teaspoon baking soda
1 teaspoon cinnamon
½ teaspoon allspice
½ teaspoon salt
1 cup flaked coconut
1 cup unsalted sunflower nuts

In large bowl, combine brown sugar, margarine, egg, apple sauce and vanilla; beat well. Stir in remaining ingredients; mix well. Refrigerate 1 to 2 hours for ease in handling.

Preheat oven to 375°F. Grease cookie sheets. Drop dough by teaspoonfuls 2 inches apart onto prepared cookie sheets. Bake 11 to 13 minutes or until edges are light golden brown. Immediately remove from cookie sheets. Cool on wire racks. Store cookies in airtight container to retain their soft, chewy texture.

Makes about 5 dozen cookies

Variation: For larger cookies, press ¼ cup dough onto greased cookie sheet. Bake at 375°F for 13 to 15 minutes.

Granola Apple Cookies

Marvelous Macaroons

1 can (8 ounces) DOLE® Crushed Pineapple in Juice
1 can (14 ounces) sweetened condensed milk
1 package (7 ounces) flaked coconut
½ cup margarine, melted
¾ cup DOLE® Chopped Natural Almonds, toasted
Grated peel from 1 DOLE® Lemon
¼ teaspoon almond extract
1 cup flour
1 teaspoon baking powder

Preheat oven to 350°F. Drain pineapple well, pressing out excess juice with back of spoon. In large bowl, combine pineapple, condensed milk, coconut, margarine, nuts, lemon peel and extract. In small bowl, combine flour and baking powder. Beat into pineapple mixture until blended.

Drop heaping tablespoons of dough 1 inch apart onto greased cookie sheets. Bake 13 to 15 minutes or until lightly browned. Cool on wire rack. Store in covered container in refrigerator.

Makes about 3½ dozen cookies

Spicy Sour Cream Cookies

1 package DUNCAN HINES® Moist Deluxe Spice Cake Mix
1 cup dairy sour cream
1 cup chopped pecans or walnuts
¼ cup butter or margarine, softened
1 egg

1. Preheat oven to 350°F. Grease cookie sheets.

2. Combine cake mix, sour cream, pecans, butter and egg in large bowl. Mix at low speed with electric mixer until blended.

3. Drop by rounded teaspoonfuls onto cookie sheets. Bake 9 to 11 minutes or until lightly browned. Cool 2 minutes on cookie sheets. Remove to cooling racks.

Makes about 4½ dozen cookies

Double Mint Chocolate Cookies

Cookies
- 2 cups granulated sugar
- 1 cup unsweetened cocoa
- 1 cup LAND O LAKES® Butter, softened
- 1 cup buttermilk or sour milk
- 1 cup water
- 2 eggs
- 2 teaspoons baking soda
- 1 teaspoon baking powder
- ½ teaspoon salt
- 1 teaspoon vanilla
- 4 cups all-purpose flour

Frosting
- 4 cups powdered sugar
- 1 cup LAND O LAKES® Butter, softened
- 1 teaspoon salt
- 2 tablespoons milk
- 2 teaspoons vanilla
- ½ teaspoon mint extract
- ½ cup crushed starlight peppermint candy

Preheat oven to 400°F. For Cookies, in large mixer bowl, combine granulated sugar, cocoa, butter, buttermilk, water, eggs, baking soda, baking powder, salt and vanilla. Beat at low speed, scraping bowl often, until well mixed, 1 to 2 minutes. Stir in flour until well mixed, 3 to 4 minutes. Drop rounded teaspoonfuls of dough 2 inches apart onto greased cookie sheets. Bake for 7 to 9 minutes, or until top of cookie springs back when touched lightly in center. Remove immediately; cool completely on wire racks.

For Frosting, in small mixer bowl, combine powdered sugar, butter, salt, milk, vanilla and mint extract. Beat at medium speed, scraping bowl often, until light and fluffy, 2 to 3 minutes. Spread ½ tablespoonful of frosting on each cookie. Sprinkle with candy.   *Makes about 8 dozen cookies*

Double Mint Chocolate Cookies

Sour Cream Chocolate Cookies

- 2 eggs
- 1 cup granulated sugar
- 1 cup packed light brown sugar
- 1 teaspoon vanilla extract
- 1 cup dairy sour cream
- ½ cup butter or margarine, melted
- ½ cup shortening, melted
- 2½ cups all-purpose flour
- 1 cup HERSHEY'S® Cocoa
- 1 teaspoon baking powder
- ½ teaspoon baking soda
- 1 cup chopped walnuts

Preheat oven to 325°F. In large mixer bowl beat eggs, granulated sugar, brown sugar and vanilla. Blend in sour cream, butter and shortening. Combine flour, cocoa, baking powder and baking soda; add to sugar mixture. Stir in walnuts. Drop by tablespoonfuls onto greased cookie sheet. Bake 10 to 12 minutes or just until set. Cool slightly; remove from cookie sheet. Cool on wire rack.

Makes about 4 dozen cookies

Double Almond Butter Cookies

Dough
- 2 cups butter, softened
- 1 cup powdered sugar
- 4 cups flour
- 2 teaspoons vanilla

Filling
- ⅔ cup BLUE DIAMOND® Blanched Almond Paste
- ¼ cup firmly packed light brown sugar
- ½ cup BLUE DIAMOND® Chopped Natural Almonds, toasted
- ¼ teaspoon vanilla
- 1½ cups powdered sugar

For Dough, cream butter with 1 cup powdered sugar. Gradually beat in flour. Beat in 2 teaspoons vanilla. Chill dough ½ hour. For Filling, combine almond paste, brown sugar, almonds and ¼ teaspoon vanilla.

Top left to top right:
Almond Raspberry Thumbprint Cookies,
Double Almond Butter Cookies

Preheat oven to 350°F. Shape dough around ½ teaspoon filling mixture to form 1-inch balls. Place on ungreased cookie sheets. Bake 15 minutes. Cool on wire racks. Roll cookies in 1½ cups powdered sugar or sift over cookies.

Makes about 8 dozen cookies

Almond Raspberry Thumbprint Cookies

- 1 cup butter or margarine, softened
- 1 cup sugar
- 1 can SOLO® or 1 jar BAKER® Almond Filling
- 2 egg yolks
- 1 teaspoon almond extract
- 2½ cups all-purpose flour
- ½ teaspoon baking powder
- ½ teaspoon salt
- 1 can SOLO® or 1 jar BAKER® Raspberry or Strawberry Filling

Beat butter and sugar in medium-size bowl with electric mixer until light and fluffy. Add almond filling, egg yolks and almond extract; beat until blended. Stir in flour, baking powder and salt with wooden spoon to make soft dough. Cover and refrigerate at least 3 hours or overnight.

Preheat oven to 350°F. Shape dough into 1-inch balls. Place 1½ inches apart on ungreased cookie sheets. Press thumb into center of each ball to make deep depression. Spoon ½ teaspoon raspberry filling into depressions.

Bake 11 to 13 minutes or until edges of cookies are golden brown. Cool on cookie sheets 1 minute. Remove to wire racks; cool completely.

Makes about 60 cookies

Nutty Clusters

2 squares (1 ounce each) unsweetened
  chocolate
½ cup butter or margarine, softened
1 cup granulated sugar
1 egg
⅓ cup buttermilk
1 teaspoon vanilla
1¾ cups all-purpose flour
½ teaspoon baking soda
1 cup mixed salted nuts, coarsely
  chopped
Easy Chocolate Icing (recipe
  follows)

Preheat oven to 400°F. Line cookie sheets
with parchment paper or leave ungreased.
Melt chocolate in top of double boiler over
hot, not boiling, water. Remove from heat;
cool. Cream butter and granulated sugar
in large bowl until smooth. Beat in egg,
melted chocolate, buttermilk and vanilla
until light. Stir in flour, baking soda and
nuts. Drop dough by teaspoonfuls 2
inches apart onto cookie sheets.

Bake 8 to 10 minutes or until almost no
imprint remains when touched.
Immediately remove cookies from cookie
sheet to wire rack. While cookies bake,
prepare Easy Chocolate Icing. Frost
cookies while still warm.

Makes about 4 dozen cookies

Nutty Clusters

Easy Chocolate Icing

2 squares (1 ounce each) unsweetened
  chocolate
2 tablespoons butter or margarine
2 cups powdered sugar
2 to 3 tablespoons water

Melt chocolate and butter in small heavy
saucepan over low heat, stirring until
completely melted. Add powdered sugar
and water, mixing until smooth.

Drop Sugar Cookies

2½ cups sifted all-purpose flour
¾ teaspoon salt
½ teaspoon ARM & HAMMER® Pure
  Baking Soda
½ cup butter or margarine, softened
½ cup vegetable shortening
1 cup sugar
1 teaspoon vanilla
1 egg
2 tablespoons milk
Sugar

Preheat oven to 400°F. Sift together flour,
salt and baking soda. Set aside. Using an
electric mixer, cream together butter and
shortening in large bowl. Gradually add
sugar; continue beating until light and
fluffy. Beat in vanilla and egg. Add flour
mixture and beat until smooth; blend in
milk.

Drop dough by teaspoonfuls 3 inches
apart onto greased cookie sheets. Flatten
with bottom of glass that has been dipped
in sugar. Bake 12 minutes or until edges
are lightly browned. Cool on wire racks.

Makes about 5½ dozen cookies

Snickerdoodles

1 cup BUTTER FLAVOR CRISCO®
2 cups sugar, divided
2 eggs
2 tablespoons milk
1 teaspoon vanilla
2¾ cups all-purpose flour
2 teaspoons cream of tartar
1 teaspoon baking soda
¾ teaspoon salt
2 teaspoons cinnamon

1. Preheat oven to 400°F. Combine BUTTER FLAVOR CRISCO®, 1½ cups of the sugar, the eggs, milk and vanilla in large bowl. Beat at medium speed of electric mixer until well blended.

2. Combine flour, cream of tartar, baking soda and salt. Mix into creamed mixture. Shape dough into 1-inch balls.

3. Combine remaining ½ cup sugar and cinnamon in small bowl. Roll balls of dough in mixture. (Hint: Sugar mixture can be put in reclosable plastic bag. Put 2 to 3 dough balls at a time in bag. Shake to sugar coat dough.) Place 2 inches apart on ungreased cookie sheet.

5. Bake 7 to 8 minutes. Remove to cooling rack.   *Makes about 6 dozen cookies*

Colored Sugar Variation: Add 2 teaspoons cinnamon to flour mixture in Step #2. Combine 3 tablespoons colored sugar and 3 tablespoons granulated sugar for coating instead of cinnamon and sugar mixture.

Preparation Time: 30 minutes
Bake Time: 7 to 8 minutes

Pineapple Raisin Jumbles

2 cans (8 ounces each) DOLE®
   Crushed Pineapple
½ cup butter or margarine, softened
½ cup sugar
1 teaspoon vanilla extract
1 cup flour
4 teaspoons grated orange peel
1 cup DOLE® Blanched Slivered
   Almonds, toasted
1 cup DOLE® Raisins

Preheat oven to 350°F. Drain pineapple well, pressing out excess liquid with back of spoon. In large bowl, beat butter and sugar until light and fluffy. Stir in pineapple and vanilla. Beat in flour and orange peel. Stir in almonds and raisins. Drop heaping tablespoons of dough 2 inches apart onto greased cookie sheets. Bake 20 to 22 minutes or until firm. Cool on wire rack.

Makes 2 to 2½ dozen cookies

Pineapple Raisin Jumbles

Coconut Macaroons

2 (7-ounce) packages *flaked* coconut
    (5⅓ cups)
1 (14-ounce) can EAGLE® Brand
    Sweetened Condensed Milk
    (NOT evaporated milk)
2 teaspoons vanilla extract
1½ teaspoons almond extract

Preheat oven to 350°F. In large bowl,
combine coconut, sweetened condensed
milk and extracts; mix well. Drop by
rounded teaspoonfuls onto aluminum-
foil-lined and *generously greased* cookie
sheets.

Bake 8 to 10 minutes or until lightly
browned around edges. *Immediately*
remove from cookie sheets (macaroons
will stick if allowed to cool). Store loosely
covered at room temperature.

Makes about 4 dozen cookies

Variations:

Chocolate: Omit almond extract. Add 4
(1-ounce) squares unsweetened chocolate,
melted. Proceed as above.

Chocolate Chip: Omit almond extract.
Add 1 cup mini chocolate chips. Proceed
as above.

Cherry Nut: Omit almond extract. Add
1 cup chopped nuts and 2 tablespoons
maraschino cherry syrup. Before baking,
press maraschino cherry half into center of
each macaroon. Proceed as above.

Rum Raisin: Omit almond extract. Add
1 cup raisins and 1 teaspoon rum
flavoring. Proceed as above.

Almond Brickle: Add ½ cup almond
brickle chips. Proceed as above. Bake 10 to
12 minutes. Cool 3 minutes; remove from
cookie sheets.

Coconut Macaroons

Maple Walnut: Omit almond extract.
Add ½ cup finely chopped walnuts and
½ teaspoon maple flavoring. Proceed as
above.

Nutty Oat: Omit almond extract. Add
1 cup oats and 1 cup chopped nuts.
Proceed as above.

Chocolate Sugar Cookies

**3 squares BAKER'S® Unsweetened
   Chocolate
1 cup (2 sticks) margarine or butter
1 cup sugar
1 egg
1 teaspoon vanilla
2 cups all-purpose flour
1 teaspoon baking soda
¼ teaspoon salt
   Additional sugar**

Microwave chocolate and margarine in large microwavable bowl on HIGH 2 minutes or until margarine is melted. **Stir until chocolate is completely melted.**

Stir 1 cup sugar into melted chocolate mixture until well blended. Stir in egg and vanilla until completely mixed. Mix in flour, baking soda and salt. Refrigerate 30 minutes.

Preheat oven to 375°F. Shape dough into 1-inch balls; roll in additional sugar. Place on ungreased cookie sheets. (If a flatter, crisper cookie is desired, flatten ball with bottom of drinking glass.)

Bake for 8 to 10 minutes or until set. Remove from cookie sheets to cool on wire racks.   *Makes about 3½ dozen cookies*

Prep time: 15 minutes
Chill time: 30 minutes
Baking time: 8 to 10 minutes

Jam-Filled Chocolate Sugar Cookies:
Prepare Chocolate Sugar Cookie dough as directed; roll in finely chopped nuts in place of sugar. Make indentation in each ball; fill center with your favorite jam. Bake as directed.

Chocolate-Caramel Sugar Cookies:
Prepare Chocolate Sugar Cookie dough as directed. Roll in finely chopped nuts in place of sugar. Make indentation in each ball; bake as directed. Microwave 1 package (14 ounces) KRAFT® Caramels with 2 tablespoons milk in microwavable bowl on HIGH 3 minutes or until melted,

stirring after 2 minutes. Fill centers of cookies with caramel mixture. To drizzle with chocolate, place 1 square BAKER'S® Semi-Sweet Chocolate in zipper-style plastic sandwich bag. Close bag tightly. Microwave on High about 1 minute or until chocolate is melted. Fold down top of bag; snip a tiny piece off 1 bottom corner (about ⅛ inch). Holding top of bag tightly, drizzle chocolate through opening over cookies.

Lemon Tea Cookies

**3¼ cups all-purpose flour
1½ teaspoons baking powder
¼ teaspoon salt
¾ cup butter or margarine, softened
¾ cup granulated sugar
¾ cup confectioners sugar
½ cup CRISCO® Oil
2 eggs
2 teaspoons grated lemon peel
2 teaspoons lemon extract
   Granulated sugar**

1. Combine flour, baking powder and salt in small bowl. Combine butter, granulated sugar and confectioners sugar in large bowl. Beat at medium speed of electric mixer until well blended. Blend in CRISCO® Oil, eggs, lemon peel and lemon extract. Stir in flour mixture. Cover and refrigerate about 2 hours.

2. Preheat oven to 350°F. Shape dough into 1-inch balls. Place 2 to 3 inches apart on ungreased cookie sheet. Flatten to ⅛-inch thickness with bottom of greased drinking glass dipped in granulated sugar.

3. Bake 10 to 12 minutes or until edges are light golden brown. Remove to cooling rack.   *Makes 6 to 7 dozen cookies*

Lemon Crisps: Follow recipe above, except shape dough into ¾-inch balls and flatten to ¹⁄₁₆-inch thickness with sugar-dipped glass. Bake 7 to 9 minutes or until edges are light golden brown.

Chocolate Sugar Cookies, Jam-Filled Chocolate Sugar Cookies, Chocolate-Caramel Sugar Cookies

Easy Peanut Butter Cookies

Easy Peanut Butter Cookies

**1 (14-ounce) can EAGLE® Brand
  Sweetened Condensed Milk
  (NOT evaporated milk)**
¾ to 1 cup peanut butter
1 egg
1 teaspoon vanilla extract
**2 cups biscuit baking mix
  Granulated sugar**

In large mixer bowl, beat sweetened condensed milk, peanut butter, egg and vanilla until smooth. Add biscuit mix; mix well. Chill at least 1 hour.

Preheat oven to 350°F. Shape dough into 1-inch balls. Roll in sugar. Place 2 inches apart on ungreased cookie sheets. Flatten with fork. Bake 6 to 8 minutes or until *lightly* browned (*do not overbake*). Cool. Store tightly covered at room temperature.
Makes about 5 dozen cookies

Peanut Blossoms: Shape as above; *do not flatten.* Bake as above. Press solid milk chocolate candy drop in center of each ball immediately after baking.

Peanut Butter & Jelly Gems: Press thumb in center of each ball of dough; fill with jelly, jam or preserves. Bake as above.

Any-Way-You-Like 'em Cookies: Stir *1 cup* semi-sweet chocolate chips *or* chopped peanuts *or* raisins *or* flaked coconut into dough. Proceed as above.

Ice Cream Sandwiches

**2 squares (1 ounce each) unsweetened
  chocolate**
1 cup butter, softened
1 cup powdered sugar
4 egg yolks
1 teaspoon vanilla
**3 cups all-purpose flour
  Ice cream, softened
  Powdered sugar**

Melt chocolate in top of double boiler over hot, not boiling, water. Remove from heat; cool. Cream butter and 1 cup sugar in large bowl until blended. Add egg yolks, vanilla and melted chocolate; beat until light. Blend in flour to make stiff dough. Divide dough into 4 parts. Shape each part into a roll, about 1½ inches in diameter. Wrap in plastic wrap; refrigerate until firm, at least 30 minutes or up to 1 week. (For longer storage, freeze up to 6 weeks.)

Preheat oven to 350°F. Line cookie sheets with parchment paper or leave ungreased. Cut rolls into ⅛-inch-thick slices; place 2 inches apart on ungreased cookie sheets. Bake 8 to 10 minutes or just until set, but not browned. Remove to wire racks to cool completely.

Spread desired amount of softened ice cream on bottoms of half the cookies. Top with remaining cookies, bottom sides down, forming sandwiches. Dust tops with powdered sugar; serve immediately.
Makes about 4 dozen sandwich cookies

Note: Cookies can also be served on their own, without ice cream.

Date Fudge Cookies

1 cup (6 ounces) semisweet chocolate
   chips
½ cup butter or margarine, softened
1 cup granulated sugar
2 eggs
1½ cups all-purpose flour
   Dash salt
1 package (8 ounces) chopped pitted
   dates
½ cup coarsely chopped pecans or
   walnuts
   Brown-Sugar Icing (recipe follows)

Preheat oven to 375°F. Lightly grease cookie sheets or line with parchment paper. Melt chocolate chips in top of double boiler over hot, not boiling, water. Remove from heat; cool. Cream butter, granulated sugar and eggs in large bowl until smooth. Beat in melted chocolate. Gradually add flour and salt, mixing until smooth. Stir in dates and nuts. Drop dough by rounded teaspoonfuls 2 inches apart onto prepared cookie sheets.

Bake 10 to 12 minutes or until slightly firm. Cool 5 minutes on cookie sheets, then remove to wire racks. While cookies bake, prepare Brown-Sugar Icing. Spread over cookies while still warm. Cool until icing is set.   *Makes about 5 dozen cookies*

Brown-Sugar Icing

½ cup packed dark brown sugar
¼ cup water
2 squares (1 ounce each) unsweetened
   chocolate
2 cups powdered sugar
¼ cup butter or margarine
1 teaspoon vanilla

Combine brown sugar, water and chocolate in small heavy saucepan. Stir over medium heat until chocolate is melted and mixture boils. Boil 1 minute. Remove from heat; beat in powdered sugar, butter and vanilla. Continue beating until mixture has cooled slightly and thickens. Spread over cookies while icing is still warm.

Crispie Coconut Refrigerator Cookies

1 cup BUTTER FLAVOR CRISCO®
1 cup sugar
2 tablespoons milk
1 egg
2¼ cups all-purpose flour
½ teaspoon salt
½ teaspoon baking soda
3 cups flake coconut, divided
1 egg yolk
1 tablespoon milk
70 pecan halves (about 1¼ cups)

1. Cream BUTTER FLAVOR CRISCO®, sugar and 2 tablespoons of the milk in large bowl at medium speed of electric mixer until well blended. Beat in egg. Combine flour, salt and baking soda. Add to creamed mixture. Add 2 cups of the coconut. Mix until well blended.

2. Divide dough in half. Form each into a roll 1½ inches in diameter . Cut 2 pieces waxed paper 18 inches long. Sprinkle ½ cup coconut on each piece. Roll dough in coconut. Roll up in waxed paper. Refrigerate several hours or overnight.

3. Preheat oven to 325°F. Grease cookie sheet with BUTTER FLAVOR CRISCO®. Cut dough with sharp knife into ¼-inch slices. Place 2 inches apart on cookie sheet. Combine egg yolk and 1 tablespoon milk. Stir well. Brush on cookie slices. Top each slice with pecan half. Bake 12 minutes. Remove to cooling rack.
   Makes about 6 dozen cookies

Hint: Cookie rolls can be frozen for up to three months.

Preparation Time: 20 minutes
Chill Time: 2 hours or overnight
Bake Time: 12 minutes

Kentucky Oatmeal-Jam Cookies

½ cup BUTTER FLAVOR CRISCO®
¾ cup sugar
1 egg
¼ cup buttermilk*
½ cup strawberry jam
1 teaspoon vanilla
1 cup all-purpose flour
½ cup unsweetened cocoa powder
1 teaspoon cinnamon
½ teaspoon baking soda
¼ teaspoon nutmeg
¼ teaspoon ground cloves
1½ cups quick oats (not instant or old fashioned), uncooked
½ cup raisins
½ cup chopped pecans (optional)
  About 24 pecan halves (optional)

1. Preheat oven to 350°F. Grease cookie sheet with BUTTER FLAVOR CRISCO®.

2. Combine BUTTER FLAVOR CRISCO®, sugar, egg, buttermilk, jam and vanilla in large bowl. Beat at medium speed of electric mixer until well blended.

3. Combine flour, cocoa, cinnamon, baking soda, nutmeg and cloves. Mix into creamed mixture at low speed until blended. Stir in oats, raisins and chopped nuts with spoon.

4. Drop 2 tablespoonfuls of dough in a mound 3 inches apart onto cookie sheet. Repeat for each cookie. Top each with pecan half.

5. Bake 10 to 12 minutes or until set. Cool 2 minutes on cookie sheet. Remove to cooling rack.

Makes about 2 dozen cookies

*You may substitute ¾ teaspoon lemon juice or vinegar plus enough milk to make ¼ cup for buttermilk. Stir. Wait 5 minutes before using.

Macaroon Kiss Cookies

⅓ cup butter or margarine, softened
1 package (3 ounces) cream cheese, softened
¾ cup sugar
1 egg yolk
2 teaspoons almond extract
2 teaspoons orange juice
1¼ cups all-purpose flour
2 teaspoons baking powder
¼ teaspoon salt
5 cups (14-ounce package) flaked coconut, divided
54 HERSHEY'S® KISSES® Chocolates (9-ounce package), unwrapped

In large mixer bowl, beat together butter, cream cheese and sugar. Add egg yolk, almond extract and orange juice; beat well. Stir together flour, baking powder and salt; gradually add to butter mixture. Stir in 3 cups of the coconut. Cover tightly; refrigerate 1 hour or until firm enough to handle.

Preheat oven to 350°F. Shape dough into 1-inch balls; roll in remaining 2 cups coconut. Place on ungreased cookie sheet. Bake 10 to 12 minutes or until lightly browned. Remove from oven; immediately press KISS® on top of each cookie. Cool 1 minute. Carefully remove from cookie sheet; cool completely on wire rack.

Makes about 4½ dozen cookies

Macaroon Kiss Cookies

Gingersnaps

1 cup packed brown sugar
¾ cup unsalted butter, softened
¼ teaspoon salt
1 egg
¼ cup light molasses
1 tablespoon ground ginger
2 teaspoons baking soda
1 teaspoon ground cinnamon
½ teaspoon ground cloves
2¼ cups all-purpose flour
⅓ to ½ cup granulated sugar
½ cup powdered sugar, sifted
1 to 1½ teaspoons strong brewed
    coffee, cooled
¼ teaspoon lemon juice

In large bowl, beat brown sugar, butter and salt until light and fluffy. Beat in egg. Gradually add molasses; mix well. Add ginger, baking soda, cinnamon and cloves. Beat until blended. Using rubber spatula, gradually fold in flour. (Dough will be soft and sticky.) Divide dough into quarters. Wrap each portion; refrigerate until firm, about 1½ hours.

Preheat oven to 350°F. Shape slightly rounded tablespoonfuls of dough into balls. Roll balls in granulated sugar to coat generously. Place 4 inches apart on greased cookie sheets. Bake about 10 minutes or until centers of cookies feel slightly firm. Let cookies cool 5 minutes before removing them from cookie sheets to wire racks; cool completely.

In small bowl, mix powdered sugar, 1 teaspoon of the coffee and the lemon juice; stir until smooth. Stir in as much of the remaining coffee as needed to make stiff icing for piping. Fit pastry bag with small round tip. Pipe icing on cookies forming a spiral design. Let stand until icing is firm.

Makes about 4 dozen cookies

Chocolate Oat Chewies

Chocolate Oat Chewies

1 package DUNCAN HINES® Moist
    Deluxe Devil's Food Cake Mix
1⅓ cups old-fashioned oats, uncooked
1 cup flaked coconut, toasted and
    divided
¾ cup butter or margarine, melted
2 eggs, beaten
1 teaspoon vanilla extract
5 bars (1.55 ounces each) milk
    chocolate, cut into rectangles

1. Preheat oven to 350°F.

2. Combine cake mix, oats, ½ cup of the coconut, the melted butter, eggs and vanilla extract in large bowl. Cover and chill 15 minutes.

3. Shape dough into 1-inch balls. Place balls 2 inches apart on ungreased cookie sheets. Bake 12 minutes or until tops are slightly cracked. Remove from oven. Press one milk chocolate rectangle into center of each cookie. Sprinkle with remaining ½ cup coconut. Remove to cooling racks.

Makes about 4½ dozen cookies

Oatmeal Lemon-Cheese Cookies

1 cup BUTTER FLAVOR CRISCO®
1 package (3 ounces) cream cheese, softened
1¼ cups sugar
1 egg, separated
1 teaspoon lemon extract
2 teaspoons grated lemon peel
1¼ cups all-purpose flour
1¼ cups quick oats (not instant or old fashioned), uncooked
½ teaspoon salt
1 egg
Sugar for sprinkling
½ cup sliced almonds

1. Preheat oven to 350°F. Combine BUTTER FLAVOR CRISCO®, cream cheese and 1¼ cups sugar in large bowl. Beat at medium speed of electric mixer until well blended. Beat in egg yolk, lemon extract and lemon peel.

2. Combine flour, oats and salt. Stir into creamed mixture with spoon until blended.

3. Drop rounded teaspoonfuls of dough 2 inches apart onto ungreased cookie sheet. Beat whole egg with egg white. Brush over tops of cookies. Sprinkle lightly with sugar. Press almond slices lightly on top.

4. Bake 10 to 12 minutes or until edges are lightly browned. Cool 2 minutes on cookie sheet. Remove to cooling rack.

Makes about 6 dozen cookies

Nutty Toppers

Peanut Butter Layer
¾ cup BUTTER FLAVOR CRISCO®
1 cup JIF® Creamy Peanut Butter
2 eggs
1 cup sugar
1 teaspoon vanilla
1 teaspoon water
2 cups all-purpose flour
1 teaspoon baking soda
¼ teaspoon salt
Chocolate Layer
½ cup dough from Peanut Butter Layer
1 egg
1 tablespoon unsweetened cocoa powder
48 pecans or walnut halves

1. Preheat oven to 375°F. For Peanut Butter Layer, combine BUTTER FLAVOR CRISCO®, JIF® Creamy Peanut Butter, eggs, sugar, vanilla and water in large bowl. Beat at medium speed of electric mixer until well blended.

2. Combine flour, baking soda and salt. Mix into creamed mixture at low speed until blended.

3. For Chocolate Layer, combine ½ cup of dough for Peanut Butter Layer, egg and cocoa. Beat at low speed until blended.

4. Form Peanut Butter Layer dough into 1-inch balls. Place 2 inches apart on ungreased cookie sheet. Flatten slightly with bottom of greased and sugared glass. Place leveled ½ teaspoonful of Chocolate Layer on flattened dough. Press nut into each center. Repeat with remaining dough.

5. Bake 10 minutes or until edges are lightly browned. Cool 2 minutes on cookie sheet. Remove to cooling rack.

Makes about 4 dozen cookies

Left to right:
Double Peanut Butter Supremes (page 106),
Nutty Toppers, Oatmeal Lemon-Cheese Cookies

Double Peanut Butter Supremes

Cookies
- ½ cup BUTTER FLAVOR CRISCO®
- 1 cup JIF® Creamy Peanut Butter
- ½ cup firmly packed brown sugar
- ½ cup granulated sugar
- ⅓ cup dairy sour cream
- 1 egg
- 1 teaspoon vanilla
- 2 cups all-purpose flour
- ¾ teaspoon baking soda
- ½ teaspoon baking powder
- ½ teaspoon salt
- Granulated sugar for rolling

Filling
- 1 package (8 ounces) cream cheese, softened
- ½ cup JIF® Creamy Peanut Butter
- 1 egg, slightly beaten
- ⅓ cup granulated sugar
- Dash salt
- 1 cup semi-sweet miniature chocolate chips

1. For Cookies, combine BUTTER FLAVOR CRISCO®, JIF® Creamy Peanut Butter, sugars, sour cream, egg and vanilla in large bowl. Beat at medium speed of electric mixer until well blended.

2. Combine flour, baking soda, baking powder and salt. Mix into creamed mixture at low speed until blended. Cover and refrigerate 1 hour.

3. For Filling, combine cream cheese, JIF® Creamy Peanut Butter, egg, sugar and salt. Beat at medium speed of electric mixer until blended. Stir in miniature chips.

4. Preheat oven to 350°F. Form dough into 1-inch balls. Roll in granulated sugar. Place 2 inches apart on ungreased cookie sheet. Press thumb gently in center of each cookie. Fill center with rounded teaspoonful of filling.

5. Bake 12 to 13 minutes or until lightly browned. Cool 2 minutes on cookie sheet. Remove to cooling rack.

Makes about 4 dozen cookies

Wheat Germ Cookies

- 1 package DUNCAN HINES® Moist Deluxe Yellow Cake Mix
- 1 large egg
- 3 tablespoons brown sugar
- ¼ cup CRISCO® Oil or PURITAN® Oil
- 2 tablespoons butter or margarine, melted
- ½ cup wheat germ
- 2 tablespoons water
- ½ cup chopped nuts

1. Preheat oven to 375°F. Combine cake mix, egg, brown sugar, oil, butter, wheat germ and water in large bowl. Mix with spoon. (Dough will be stiff.) Stir in nuts.

2. Drop teaspoonfuls of dough 2 inches apart onto ungreased cookie sheets.

3. Bake 10 minutes for chewy cookies, 12 minutes for crispy cookies. Cool 1 minute on cookie sheets; then remove to wire racks to finish cooling.

Makes about 3 dozen cookies

Spicy Oatmeal Raisin Cookies

- 1 package DUNCAN HINES® Moist Deluxe Spice Cake Mix
- 4 egg whites
- 1 cup quick-cooking oats (not instant or old-fashioned), uncooked
- ½ cup CRISCO® Oil or PURITAN® Oil
- ½ cup raisins

1. Preheat oven to 350°F. Grease cookie sheets.

2. Combine cake mix, egg whites, oats and oil in large bowl. Beat on low speed with electric mixer until blended. Stir in raisins. Drop by rounded teaspoons onto cookie sheets. Bake 7 to 9 minutes or until lightly browned. Cool 1 minute on cookie sheets. Remove to cooling racks.

Makes about 4 dozen cookies

Oatmeal Apple Cookies

¾ **cup BUTTER FLAVOR CRISCO®**
1¼ **cups firmly packed brown sugar**
 1 **egg**
¼ **cup milk**
1½ **teaspoons vanilla**
 1 **cup all-purpose flour**
1¼ **teaspoons cinnamon**
½ **teaspoon salt**
¼ **teaspoon baking soda**
¼ **teaspoon nutmeg**
 3 **cups quick oats (not instant or old fashioned), uncooked**
 1 **cup diced, peeled apples**
¾ **cup raisins (optional)**
¾ **cup coarsely chopped walnuts (optional)**

1. Preheat oven to 375°F. Grease cookie sheet with BUTTER FLAVOR CRISCO®.

2. Combine BUTTER FLAVOR CRISCO®, brown sugar, egg, milk and vanilla in large bowl. Beat at medium speed of electric mixer until well blended.

3. Combine flour, cinnamon, salt, baking soda and nutmeg. Mix into creamed mixture at low speed until just blended. Stir in, one at a time, oats, apples, raisins and nuts with spoon.

4. Drop rounded tablespoonfuls of dough 2 inches apart onto cookie sheet.

5. Bake 13 minutes or until set. Cool 2 minutes on cookie sheet. Remove to cooling rack.

Makes about 2½ dozen cookies

Chocolate-Coconut Cookies

 2 **squares (1 ounce each) unsweetened chocolate**
½ **cup butter or margarine, softened**
 1 **cup packed light brown sugar**
 1 **egg**
1¼ **cups all-purpose flour**
¼ **teaspoon baking powder**
⅛ **teaspoon baking soda**
   Dash salt
½ **cup chopped walnuts or pecans**
½ **cup flaked coconut**
   Pecan halves or halved red candied cherries

Preheat oven to 350°F. Lightly grease cookie sheets or line with parchment paper. Melt chocolate in top of double boiler over hot, not boiling, water. Remove from heat; cool. Cream butter and sugar in large bowl until blended. Add egg and melted chocolate; beat until light. Combine flour, baking powder, baking soda and salt in small bowl. Stir into creamed mixture until blended. Mix in nuts and coconut. Drop dough by teaspoonfuls 2 inches apart onto prepared cookie sheets. Press pecan or cherry half into center of each cookie. Bake 10 to 12 minutes or until firm. Remove to wire racks to cool.

Makes about 4 dozen cookies

Oatmeal Apple Cookies

Double Chocolate Cherry Cookies,
Double Chocolate Pecan Cookies

Double Chocolate Cherry Cookies

1¼ cups margarine or butter, softened
1¾ cups sugar
  2 eggs
  1 tablespoon vanilla extract
3½ cups unsifted flour
  ¾ cup unsweetened cocoa
  ½ teaspoon baking powder
  ½ teaspoon baking soda
  ¼ teaspoon salt
  2 (6-ounce) jars maraschino cherries, well drained and halved (about 60 cherries)
  1 (6-ounce) package semi-sweet chocolate chips (1 cup)
  1 (14-ounce) can EAGLE® Brand Sweetened Condensed Milk (NOT evaporated milk)

Preheat oven to 350°F. In large mixer bowl, beat margarine and sugar until fluffy; add eggs and vanilla. Mix well. Combine dry ingredients; stir into margarine mixture (dough will be stiff). Shape into 1-inch balls. Place 1 inch apart on ungreased cookie sheets. Press cherry half into center of each cookie. Bake 8 to 10 minutes. Cool.

In heavy saucepan, over medium heat, melt chips with sweetened condensed milk; cook until mixture thickens, about 3 minutes. Frost each cookie, covering cherry. Store loosely covered at room temperature.
Makes about 10 dozen cookies

Double Chocolate Pecan Cookies: Prepare cookies as above, omitting cherries. Flatten. Bake and frost as directed. Garnish each cookie with a pecan half.

Famous Oatmeal Cookies

3 cups QUAKER® Oats (quick or old fashioned, uncooked)
1 cup all-purpose flour
1 teaspoon salt (optional)
½ teaspoon baking soda
¾ cup vegetable shortening
1 cup firmly packed brown sugar
½ cup granulated sugar
1 egg
¼ cup water
1 teaspoon vanilla

Preheat oven to 350°F. Combine oats, flour, salt and baking soda; set aside. In large bowl, beat shortening, sugars, egg, water and vanilla until fluffy. Add dry ingredients; mix well. Drop dough by rounded teaspoonfuls onto ungreased cookie sheet.

Bake 12 to 15 minutes. Remove to cooling rack; cool completely. Store tightly covered.   *Makes about 5 dozen cookies*

Variations: Add 1 cup of any or a combination of the following ingredients to basic cookie dough: raisins, chopped nuts, chocolate chips or coconut. Proceed as above.

Large Cookies: Preheat oven to 375°F. Prepare dough as above. Drop dough by rounded measuring tablespoonfuls onto ungreased cookie sheet. Bake 12 to 14 minutes. Remove to cooling rack; cool completely.

Makes about 2½ dozen cookies

Black Walnut Refrigerator Cookies

3 cups all-purpose flour
1 cup firmly packed brown sugar
1 cup LAND O LAKES® Butter, softened
2 eggs
1 teaspoon baking soda
1 teaspoon cream of tartar
¼ teaspoon salt
1 teaspoon vanilla
1 cup chopped black walnuts

In large mixer bowl, combine flour, sugar, butter, eggs, baking soda, cream of tartar, salt and vanilla. Beat at low speed, scraping bowl often, until well mixed, 3 to 4 minutes. Stir in nuts. Divide dough into halves. Shape each half into a 12×2-inch roll. Wrap in waxed paper; refrigerate until firm, at least 2 hours.

Preheat oven to 350°F. Cut rolls into ¼-inch slices. Place 1 inch apart on ungreased cookie sheets. Bake for 9 to 12 minutes, or until lightly browned. Remove from cookie sheets immediately; cool on wire racks. *Makes about 8 dozen cookies*

Santa Fe Sun Crisps

½ cup BUTTER FLAVOR CRISCO®
1 cup firmly packed brown sugar
½ cup granulated sugar
1 egg
1 tablespoon water
1 cup all-purpose flour
½ teaspoon baking powder
½ teaspoon baking soda
⅛ teaspoon ground red pepper or to taste
2 cups quick oats (not instant or old fashioned), uncooked
½ cup (about) shelled sunflower seeds

1. Preheat oven to 375°F. Combine BUTTER FLAVOR CRISCO®, brown sugar and granulated sugar in large bowl. Beat at medium speed of electric mixer until well blended. Beat in egg and water.

2. Combine flour, baking powder, baking soda and red pepper. Mix into creamed mixture at low speed until just blended. Stir in oats with spoon.

3. Form rounded teaspoonfuls of dough into balls. Roll dough in sunflower seeds. Place 2 inches apart on ungreased cookie sheet.

4. Bake 7 to 8 minutes or until golden brown. Cool 2 minutes on cookie sheet. Remove to cooling rack.
Makes about 3 dozen cookies

Chocolate Pixies

¼ cup LAND O LAKES® Butter
4 squares (1 ounce each) unsweetened chocolate
2 cups all-purpose flour, divided
2 cups granulated sugar
4 eggs
2 teaspoons baking powder
½ teaspoon salt
½ cup chopped walnuts or pecans
Powdered sugar for rolling

In small saucepan, melt butter and chocolate over low heat, 8 to 10 minutes. Cool. In large mixer bowl, combine melted chocolate mixture, 1 cup of the flour, the granulated sugar, eggs, baking powder and salt. Beat at medium speed, scraping bowl often, until well mixed, 2 to 3 minutes. Stir in remaining 1 cup flour and the nuts. Cover; refrigerate until firm, at least 2 hours.

Preheat oven to 300°F. Shape rounded teaspoonfuls of dough into 1-inch balls; roll in powdered sugar. Place 2 inches apart on greased cookie sheets. Bake for 12 to 15 minutes, or until firm to the touch. Remove immediately; cool on wire racks. *Makes about 4 dozen cookies*

Cream Cheese Cookies

½ cup BUTTER FLAVOR CRISCO®
1 package (3 ounces) cream cheese, softened
1 tablespoon milk
1 cup sugar
½ teaspoon vanilla
1 cup all-purpose flour
½ cup chopped pecans

1. Preheat oven to 375°F. Cream BUTTER FLAVOR CRISCO®, cream cheese and milk in medium bowl at medium speed of electric mixer until well blended. Beat in sugar and vanilla. Mix in flour. Stir in nuts. Drop level measuring tablespoonfuls of dough 2 inches apart onto ungreased cookie sheet.

2. Bake 10 minutes. Remove to cooling rack.   *Makes about 3 dozen cookies*

Lemon or orange variation: Add ½ teaspoon grated lemon or orange peel to dough.

Banana Orange Softies

Cookies
2 cups QUAKER® Oats (quick or old fashioned, uncooked)
2 cups all-purpose flour
¾ teaspoon baking soda
½ teaspoon salt (optional)
1⅔ cups mashed, ripe bananas (about 3 large bananas)
¾ cup (1½ sticks) margarine or butter, softened
½ cup orange juice
2 eggs
2 tespons vanilla
1 teaspoon grated orange peel
¾ cup raisins

Icing
¾ cup powdered sugar
2 to 3 teaspoons orange juice
1 teaspoon grated orange peel

Preheat oven to 350°F. For Cookies, in medium bowl, combine oats, flour, baking soda and salt. Set aside. In large bowl, beat bananas, margarine and orange juice until smooth. Blend in eggs, vanilla and orange peel. Add dry ingredients; mix well. Stir in raisins. Drop dough by rounded tablespoonfuls onto ungreased cookie sheet.

Bake 20 to 22 minutes or until light golden brown. Cool 2 minutes on cookie sheet; remove to wire rack. Cool completely.

For Icing, combine all ingredients; drizzle over cookies. Store tightly covered.
           Makes about 2½ dozen cookies

Chocolate-Dipped Oat Cookies

2 cups uncooked rolled oats
¾ cup packed brown sugar
½ cup vegetable oil
½ cup finely chopped walnuts
1 egg
2 teaspoons grated orange rind
¼ teaspoon salt
1 package (11½ ounces) milk chocolate chips

Combine oats, brown sugar, oil, walnuts, egg, orange rind and salt in large bowl until blended. Cover; refrigerate overnight.

Preheat oven to 350°F. Lightly grease cookie sheets or line with parchment paper. Melt milk chocolate chips in top of double boiler over hot, not boiling, water; set aside. Shape oat mixture into large marble-sized balls. Place 2 inches apart on prepared cookie sheets.

Bake 10 to 12 minutes or until golden and crisp. Cool 10 minutes on wire racks. Dip tops of cookies, one at a time, into melted chocolate. Place on waxed paper; cool until chocolate is set.
           Makes about 6 dozen cookies

Lemon Cookies

1 package DUNCAN HINES® Lemon
    Supreme Cake Mix
2 eggs
⅓ cup CRISCO® Oil or
    PURITAN® Oil
1 tablespoon lemon juice
¾ cup chopped nuts or flaked coconut
    Confectioners sugar

1. Preheat oven to 375°F. Grease cookie
sheets.

2. Combine cake mix, eggs, oil and lemon
juice in large bowl. Beat at low speed with
electric mixer until well blended. Add
nuts. Shape into 1-inch balls. Place on
cookie sheets, 1 inch apart. Bake 6 to 7
minutes or until lightly browned. Cool 1
minute on cookie sheets. Remove to
cooling racks. Dust with confectioners
sugar.

Tip: You can frost cookies with 1 cup
confectioners sugar mixed with 1
tablespoon lemon juice in place of dusting
cookies with confectioners sugar.

Prized Peanut Butter Crunch Cookies

1 cup BUTTER FLAVOR CRISCO®
2 cups firmly packed brown sugar
1 cup JIF® Extra Crunchy Peanut
    Butter
4 egg whites, slightly beaten
1 teaspoon vanilla
2 cups all-purpose flour
1 teaspoon baking soda
½ teaspoon baking powder
2 cups crisp rice cereal
1½ cups chopped peanuts
1 cup quick oats (not instant or old
    fashioned), uncooked
1 cup flake coconut

Lemon Cookies

1. Preheat oven to 350°F. Combine
BUTTER FLAVOR CRISCO®, brown sugar
and JIF® Extra Crunchy Peanut Butter in
large bowl. Beat at medium speed of
electric mixer until blended. Beat in egg
whites and vanilla.

2. Combine flour, baking soda and baking
powder. Mix into creamed mixture at low
speed until just blended. Stir in, one at a
time, rice cereal, nuts, oats and coconut
with spoon.

3. Drop dough by rounded measuring
tablespoonfuls 2 inches apart onto
ungreased cookie sheet.

4. Bake 8 to 10 minutes or until set.
Remove immediately to cooling rack.
                    Makes about 4 dozen cookies

Apple Spice Cookies

¾ cup margarine, softened
¾ cup firmly packed brown sugar
1 egg
1¼ cups flour
1 cup ROMAN MEAL® Apple
    Cinnamon Multi-Bran Hot
    Cereal, uncooked
½ teaspoon baking soda
¼ teaspoon salt
1 teaspoon cinnamon

Preheat oven to 350°F. In large bowl,
cream margarine, sugar and egg. Add
remaining ingredients; mix well. Drop by
rounded teaspoons onto ungreased cookie
sheet. Bake 12 to 14 minutes. Cool on wire
rack.   *Makes about 3 dozen cookies*

Almond Cream Cheese Cookies

1 (3-ounce) package cream cheese,
    softened
1 cup butter, softened
1 cup sugar
1 egg yolk
1 tablespoon milk
⅛ teaspoon almond extract
2½ cups sifted cake flour
1 cup BLUE DIAMOND® Sliced
    Natural Amonds, toasted

Beat cream cheese with butter and sugar
until fluffy. Blend in egg yolk, milk and
almond extract. Gradually mix in flour.
Gently stir in almonds. (Dough will be
sticky.) Divide dough in half; place each
half on large sheet of waxed paper.
Working through waxed paper, shape
each half into 12 × 1½-inch roll. Chill until
very firm.

Preheat oven to 325°F. Cut rolls into
¼-inch slices. Bake on ungreased cookie
sheets 10 to 15 minutes or until edges are
golden. (Cookies will not brown.) Cool on
wire racks.   *Makes about 4 dozen cookies*

Cinnamon-Apricot Tart Oatmeal Cookies

½ cup water
1 package (8 ounces) dried apricot
    halves, diced
1 cup BUTTER FLAVOR CRISCO®
1 cup firmly packed brown sugar
¼ cup granulated sugar
1 egg
2 teaspoons vanilla
1½ cups all-purpose flour
2 teaspoons cinnamon
1 teaspoon baking soda
1 teaspoon salt
1 cup plus 2 tablespoons chopped
    pecans
3 cups quick oats (not instant or old-
    fashioned), uncooked

1. Place ½ cup water in small saucepan.
Heat to boiling. Place diced apricots in
strainer over boiling water. Reduce heat to
warm. Cover; steam for 15 minutes. Cool.
Reserve liquid.

2. Preheat oven to 375°F. Grease cookie
sheet with BUTTER FLAVOR CRISCO®.
Combine BUTTER FLAVOR CRISCO®,
brown sugar, granulated sugar, egg and
vanilla in large bowl. Beat at medium
speed of electric mixer until well blended.

3. Combine flour, cinnamon, baking soda
and salt. Mix into creamed mixture at low
speed until just blended. Stir in nuts,
apricots and reserved liquid from apricots.
Stir in oats with spoon. Drop rounded
tablespoonfuls of dough 2 inches apart
onto cookie sheet.

4. Bake 10 to 11 minutes. Cool 2 minutes
on cookie sheet. Remove to cooling rack.
            Makes 3½ to 4 dozen cookies

Top to bottom:
Chocolate-Orange Chip Cookies (page 22),
Cinnamon-Apricot Tart Oatmeal Cookies

Health Nut Almond Oaties

Health Nut Almond Oaties

¾ cup whole natural almonds
6 tablespoons margarine, softened
1 cup packed brown sugar
½ cup granulated sugar
1 egg
1 teaspoon vanilla extract
¾ cup flour
1 teaspoon baking soda
1 teaspoon cinnamon
3½ cups old-fashioned rolled oats, uncooked
1 can (8 ounces) crushed pineapple in juice
1 cup raisins

Preheat oven to 350°F. Spread almonds in single layer on baking sheet. Bake 12 to 15 minutes, stirring occasionally, until lightly toasted. Cool. Chop almonds and set aside.

Beat margarine with brown sugar and granulated sugar until light and fluffy. Beat in egg and vanilla. Combine flour, baking soda and cinnamon; stir into creamed mixture. Mix in oats, pineapple, raisins and reserved almonds. Drop dough by heaping tablespoonfuls onto lightly greased cookie sheet. Flatten mounds with back of fork. Bake 10 to 12 minutes, or until lightly browned. Remove to wire rack to cool.   *Makes about 3 dozen cookies*

Favorite recipe from **Almond Board of California**

Mocha Mint Crisps

1 cup butter or margarine, softened
1 cup sugar
1 egg
¼ cup light corn syrup
¼ teaspoon peppermint extract
1 teaspoon powdered instant coffee
1 teaspoon hot water
2 cups all-purpose flour
6 tablespoons HERSHEY'S® Cocoa
2 teaspoons baking soda
¼ teaspoon salt
Mocha Mint Sugar (recipe follows)

Preheat oven to 350°F. In large mixer bowl, beat butter and sugar until light and fluffy. Add egg, corn syrup and peppermint extract; mix thoroughly. Dissolve instant coffee in water; stir into butter mixture. Stir together flour, cocoa, baking soda and salt; gradually add to butter mixture, blending thoroughly. Shape dough into 1-inch balls. (Dough may be refrigerated for a short time for easier handling.) Prepare Mocha Mint Sugar. Roll dough balls in sugar mixture. Place on ungreased cookie sheet about 2 inches apart.

Bake 8 to 10 minutes or until no imprint remains when touched lightly. Cool slightly; remove from cookie sheet to wire rack. Cool completely.
        Makes about 4 dozen cookies

Mocha Mint Sugar: In small bowl stir together ¼ cup powdered sugar, 2 tablespoons crushed hard peppermint candies (about 6 candies) and 1½ teaspoons powdered instant coffee.

Beth's Chocolate Oatmeal Cookies

3 squares (1 ounce each) unsweetened
   chocolate
½ cup butter or margarine, softened
½ cup shortening
1½ cups sugar
2 eggs
2 teaspoons vanilla
1½ cups all-purpose flour
2 teaspoons baking powder
½ teaspoon salt
3 cups uncooked rolled oats
1 cup chopped walnuts

Preheat oven to 350°F. Lightly grease
cookie sheets or line with parchment
paper. Melt chocolate in top of double
boiler over hot, not boiling, water. Remove
from heat; cool.

Cream butter, shortening and sugar in
large bowl. Add eggs, beating well. Blend
in melted chocolate and vanilla. Combine
flour, baking powder and salt in small
bowl. Add to creamed mixture; blend
well. Mix in oats and nuts. Drop dough by
rounded teaspoonfuls 2 inches apart onto
prepared cookie sheets.

Bake 10 to 12 minutes or until lightly
browned. Remove to wire racks to cool.
Makes about 8 dozen cookies

Peanut Butter Kisses

1 cup BUTTER FLAVOR CRISCO®
1 cup JIF® Creamy Peanut Butter
1 cup firmly packed brown sugar
1 cup granulated sugar
2 eggs
¼ cup milk
2 teaspoons vanilla
3¼ cups all-purpose flour
2 teaspoons baking soda
1 teaspoon salt
   Granulated sugar for rolling
72 to 90 milk chocolate kisses or stars,
   unwrapped

1. Preheat oven to 375°F. Combine
BUTTER FLAVOR CRISCO®, JIF® Creamy
Peanut Butter, brown sugar and 1 cup
granulated sugar in large bowl. Beat at
medium speed of electric mixer until well
blended. Beat in eggs, milk and vanilla.

2. Combine flour, baking soda and salt.
Mix into creamed mixture at low speed
until just blended. (Dough will be stiff.)

3. Form dough into 1-inch balls. Roll in
granulated sugar. Place 2 inches apart on
ungreased cookie sheet.

4. Bake 8 minutes. Press milk chocolate
kiss into center of each cookie. Return to
oven. Bake 3 minutes. Cool 2 minutes on
cookie sheet. Remove to cooling rack.
Makes 6 to 7½ dozen cookies

Jam-Filled Peanut Butter Kisses: Omit
milk chocolate kisses. Prepare recipe as
directed for steps 1 through 3. Bake 8
minutes. Press handle of wooden spoon
gently into center of each cookie. Return
to oven. Bake 3 minutes. Finish as directed.
Fill cooled cookies with favorite jam.

Peanut Butter Kisses

TEA-TIME TREASURES

Kentucky Bourbon Pecan Tarts

Cream Cheese Pastry (recipe
  follows)
2 eggs
½ cup granulated sugar
½ cup KARO® Light or Dark Corn
  Syrup
2 tablespoons bourbon
1 tablespoon MAZOLA® Margarine,
  melted
½ teaspoon vanilla
1 cup chopped pecans
Confectioners' sugar (optional)

Preheat oven to 350°F. Prepare Cream
Cheese Pastry. Divide dough in half; set
aside 1 half. On floured surface roll out
pastry to ⅛-inch thickness. *If necessary, add
small amount of flour to keep pastry from
sticking.* Cut into 12 (2¼-inch) rounds.
Press evenly into bottoms and up sides of
1¾-inch muffin pan cups. Repeat with
remaining pastry. Refrigerate.

In medium bowl beat eggs slightly. Stir in
granulated sugar, corn syrup, bourbon,
margarine and vanilla until well blended.
Spoon 1 heaping teaspoon pecans into
each pastry-lined cup; top with 1
tablespoon corn syrup mixture.

Bake 20 to 25 minutes or until lightly
browned and toothpick inserted into
center comes out clean. Cool in pans 5
minutes. Remove; cool completely on wire
rack. If desired, sprinkle cookies with
confectioners' sugar.
Makes about 2 dozen cookies

Cream Cheese Pastry

1 cup flour
¾ teaspoon baking powder
  Pinch salt
½ cup MAZOLA® Margarine,
  softened
1 package (3 ounces) cream cheese,
  softened
2 teaspoons sugar

In small bowl combine flour, baking
powder and salt. In large bowl mix
margarine, cream cheese and sugar until
well combined. Stir in flour mixture until
well blended. Press firmly into ball with
hands.

Prep Time: 45 minutes
Bake Time: 25 minutes plus cooling

*Top to bottom: Brandy Lace Cookies (page 118),
Kentucky Bourbon Pecan Tarts*

Brandy Lace Cookies

¼ cup sugar
¼ cup MAZOLA® Margarine
¼ cup KARO® Light or Dark Corn Syrup
½ cup flour
¼ cup very finely chopped pecans or walnuts
2 tablespoons brandy
Melted white and/or semisweet chocolate (optional)

Preheat oven to 350°F. Lightly grease and flour cookie sheets.

In small saucepan combine sugar, margarine and corn syrup. Bring to boil over medium heat, stirring constantly. Remove from heat. Stir in flour, pecans and brandy. Drop 12 evenly spaced half teaspoonfuls of batter onto prepared cookie sheets.

Bake 6 minutes or until golden. Cool 1 to 2 minutes or until cookies can be lifted but are still warm and pliable; remove with spatula. Curl around handle of wooden spoon; slide off when crisp. If cookies harden before curling, return to oven to soften. If desired, drizzle with melted chocolate.   *Makes 4 to 5 dozen cookies*

Prep Time: 30 minutes
Bake Time: 6 minutes, plus curling and cooling

Peanut Butter Cut-Out Cookies

½ cup butter or margarine
1 cup REESE'S® Peanut Butter Chips
⅔ cup packed light brown sugar
1 egg
¾ teaspoon vanilla extract
1⅓ cups all-purpose flour
¾ teaspoon baking soda
½ cup finely chopped pecans
Chocolate Chip Glaze (recipe follows)

In medium saucepan place butter and peanut butter chips; cook over low heat, stirring constantly, until melted. Pour into large mixer bowl; add brown sugar, egg and vanilla, beating until well blended. Stir in flour, baking soda and pecans, blending well. Refrigerate 15 to 20 minutes or until firm enough to roll.

Preheat oven to 350°F. Roll a small portion of dough at a time on lightly floured board or between 2 pieces of waxed paper to ¼-inch thickness. (Keep remaining dough in refrigerator.) With cookie cutters cut into desired shapes; place on ungreased cookie sheet. Bake 7 to 8 minutes or until almost set (do not overbake). Cool 1 minute; remove from cookie sheet to wire rack. Cool completely. Drizzle Chocolate Chip Glaze onto each cookie; allow to set.
Makes about 3 dozen cookies

Chocolate Chip Glaze: In top of double boiler over hot, not boiling, water melt 1 cup HERSHEY'S® Semi-Sweet Chocolate Chips with 1 tablespoon shortening; stir until smooth. Remove from heat; cool slightly, stirring occasionally.

Peanut Butter Cut-Out Cookies

Peanut Butter and Oatmeal Sandwiches

Cookies
   3 cups QUAKER® Oats (quick or old fashioned, uncooked)
1¼ cups all-purpose flour
   1 teaspoon baking powder
   1 cup peanut butter
   1 cup sugar
   ¾ cup (1½ sticks) margarine or butter, softened
   ¼ cup light or dark corn syrup
   1 egg
   2 tablespoons water
   1 teaspoon vanilla

Filling
   1 cup peanut butter
   ⅔ cup light corn syrup

For Cookies, preheat oven to 350°F. In medium bowl, combine oats, flour and baking powder; set aside. In large bowl, beat 1 cup peanut butter, sugar and margarine until fluffy. Add ¼ cup corn syrup, egg, water and vanilla; mix until smooth. Stir in dry ingredients. Shape dough into 1-inch balls. Place on ungreased cookie sheet. Using bottom of glass dipped in sugar, press into 2½-inch circles. Bake 9 to 11 minutes or until light golden brown. Cool 1 minute on cookie sheet; remove to wire rack. Cool completely.

For Filling, combine peanut butter and corn syrup; mix until smooth. Spread rounded teaspoonfuls onto flat side of half the cookies; top with remaining cookies. Sprinkle with powdered sugar and drizzle with melted chocolate*, if desired. Store loosely covered.

Makes about 2½ dozen cookies

*Microwave Directions: Place ⅓ cup semi-sweet chocolate pieces and 2 teaspoons vegetable shortening in microwaveable bowl; microwave on HIGH 1 to 2 minutes, stirring well. Microwave on HIGH for an additional 30 to 60 seconds, stirring twice, until smooth.

Lemony Spritz Sticks

Lemony Spritz Sticks

   1 cup butter or margarine, softened
   1 cup confectioners' sugar
   ¼ cup REALEMON® Lemon Juice from Concentrate
2½ cups unsifted flour
   ¼ teaspoon salt
   Fudgy Chocolate Glaze
   Finely chopped nuts

Preheat oven to 375°F. In large mixer bowl, beat butter and sugar until fluffy. Add REALEMON® brand; beat well. Stir in flour and salt; mix well. Place dough in cookie press with star-shaped plate. Press dough into 3-inch strips onto greased cookie sheets.

Bake 5 to 6 minutes or until lightly browned on ends. Cool 1 to 2 minutes; remove from cookie sheets. Cool completely. Dip ends of cookies in Fudgy Chocolate Glaze, then nuts.

Makes about 8½ dozen cookies

Fudgy Chocolate Glaze: In small saucepan over low heat, melt 3 ounces sweet cooking chocolate and 2 tablespoons margarine or butter.

Makes about ⅓ cup glaze

Raspberry-Filled Chocolate Ravioli

2 squares (1 ounce each) bittersweet
    or semisweet chocolate
1 cup butter or margarine, softened
½ cup granulated sugar
1 egg
1 teaspoon vanilla
½ teaspoon chocolate extract
¼ teaspoon baking soda
    Dash salt
2½ cups all-purpose flour
1 to 1¼ cups seedless raspberry jam
    Powdered sugar

Raspberry-Filled Chocolate Ravioli

Melt chocolate in top of double boiler over hot, not boiling, water. Remove from heat; cool. Cream butter and granulated sugar in large bowl until blended. Add egg, vanilla, chocolate extract, baking soda, salt and melted chocolate; beat until light. Blend in flour to make a stiff dough. Divide dough in half. Cover; refrigerate until firm.

Preheat oven to 350°F. Lightly grease cookie sheets or line with parchment paper. Roll out dough, half at a time, ⅛ inch thick between 2 sheets of plastic wrap. Remove top sheet of plastic. (If dough gets too soft and sticks to plastic, refrigerate until firm.) Cut dough into 1½-inch squares. Place half of squares 2 inches apart on prepared cookie sheets. Place about ½ teaspoon jam in center of each square; top with another square. Using fork, press edges of squares together to seal, then pierce center of each square. Bake 10 minutes or just until edges are browned. Remove to wire racks to cool. Dust lightly with powdered sugar.

Makes about 6 dozen cookies

European Kolacky

1 cup butter or margarine, softened
1 package (8 ounces) cream cheese,
    softened
1 tablespoon milk
1 tablespoon sugar
1 egg yolk
1½ cups all-purpose flour
½ teaspoon baking powder
1 can SOLO® or 1 jar BAKER® Filling
    (any flavor)
    Confectioners' sugar

Beat butter, cream cheese, milk and sugar in medium-size bowl with electric mixer until thoroughly blended. Beat in egg yolk. Sift flour and baking powder together; stir into butter mixture to make stiff dough. Cover bowl and refrigerate several hours or overnight.

Preheat oven to 400°F. Roll out dough on lightly floured surface to ¼-inch thickness. Cut dough with floured 2-inch cookie cutter. Place on ungreased cookie sheets about 1 inch apart. Make depressions in center of cookies with thumb or back of spoon. Spoon 1 teaspoon filling into centers of cookies.

Bake 10 to 12 minutes or until lightly browned. Remove from cookie sheets and cool completely on wire racks. Sprinkle with confectioners' sugar just before serving. *Makes about 36 cookies*

Deep Fried Sour Cream Cookies

1⅔ cups all-purpose flour
1 tablespoon granulated sugar
½ teaspoon salt
½ cup sour cream
3 egg yolks, slightly beaten
2 tablespoons CRISCO® Oil
1 teaspoon vanilla
CRISCO® Oil for frying
Confectioners' sugar

1. Combine flour, granulated sugar and salt in medium mixing bowl. Make well in center of mixture.

2. Blend sour cream, egg yolks, CRISCO® Oil and vanilla in small mixing bowl. Pour into well in dry ingredients. Mix with fork.

3. Transfer mixture to lightly floured surface. Knead until blended. Roll dough to ⅛-inch thickness. Cut into diamond shapes, 3 inches long and 2 inches wide.

4. Heat 2 to 3 inches CRISCO® Oil in deep-fryer or large saucepan to 375°F. Fry a few cookies at a time, about 1½ minutes, or until light golden brown, turning over once. Drain on paper towels. Sprinkle with confectioners' sugar.

Makes about 2 dozen cookies

Chocolate-Gilded Danish Sugar Cones

½ cup butter or margarine, softened
½ cup sugar
½ cup all-purpose flour
2 egg whites
1 teaspoon vanilla
3 ounces bittersweet chocolate *or*
    ½ cup semisweet chocolate chips

Preheat oven to 400°F. Generously grease 4 cookie sheets. Cream butter and sugar in large bowl until light and fluffy. Blend in flour. In clean, dry bowl, beat egg whites until frothy. Blend into butter mixture with vanilla. Using teaspoon, place 4 mounds of dough 4 inches apart on each prepared cookie sheet. Spread mounds with small spatula dipped in water to 3-inch diameter.

Bake 1 sheet at a time 5 to 6 minutes or until edges are just barely golden. (Do not overbake or cookies become crisp too quickly and are difficult to shape.) Remove from oven and quickly loosen each cookie from cookie sheet with thin spatula. Shape each into cone; cones will become firm as they cool. (If cookies become too firm to shape, return to oven for a few seconds to soften.)

Melt chocolate in small bowl over hot water. Stir until smooth. When all cookies are baked and cooled, dip flared ends into melted chocolate; let stand until chocolate is set. If desired, serve cones by standing them in a bowl. (Adding about 1 inch of sugar to bottom of bowl may be necessary to hold them upright.)

Makes about 16 cookies

Chocolate-Gilded Danish Sugar Cones

Cut-Out Sugar Cookies

⅔ cup **BUTTER FLAVOR CRISCO®**
¾ cup **sugar**
1 tablespoon plus 1 teaspoon **milk**
1 teaspoon **vanilla**
1 **egg**
2 cups **all-purpose flour**
1½ teaspoons **baking powder**
¼ teaspoon **salt**

1. Combine BUTTER FLAVOR CRISCO®, sugar, milk and vanilla in large bowl. Beat at medium speed of electric mixer until well blended. Beat in egg.

2. Combine flour, baking powder and salt. Mix into creamed mixture at low speed until well blended. Cover and refrigerate several hours or overnight.

3. Preheat oven to 375°F. Roll out dough, half at a time, to about ⅛-inch thickness on floured surface. Cut out with cookie cutters. Place 2 inches apart on ungreased cookie sheet. Sprinkle with colored sugars and decors or leave plain and frost when cooled.

4. Bake 7 to 9 minutes or until set. Remove immediately to cooling rack.

Makes about 3 dozen cookies

Lemon or Orange Cut-Out Sugar Cookies: Add 1 teaspoon grated lemon or orange peel and 1 teaspoon lemon or orange extract to dough in Step 1.

Creamy Vanilla Frosting: Combine ½ cup BUTTER FLAVOR CRISCO®, 1 pound (4 cups) powdered sugar, ⅓ cup milk and 1 teaspoon vanilla in medium bowl. Beat at low speed of electric mixer until well blended. Scrape bowl. Beat at high speed for 2 minutes, or until smooth and creamy. One or two drops food color can be used to tint each cup of frosting, if desired. Frost cooled cookies. This frosting works well in decorating tube.

Lemon or Orange Creamy Frosting: Prepare Creamy Vanilla Frosting, adding ⅓ cup lemon or orange juice in place of milk. Add 1 teaspoon orange peel with orange juice.

Easy Chocolate Frosting: Place ⅓ cup BUTTER FLAVOR CRISCO® in medium microwave-safe bowl. Cover with waxed paper. Microwave at 100% (HIGH) until melted (or melt on rangetop in small saucepan on low heat). Add ¾ cup unsweetened cocoa powder and ¼ teaspoon salt. Beat at low speed of electric mixer until blended. Add ½ cup milk and 2 teaspoons vanilla. Beat at low speed. Add 1 pound (4 cups) powdered sugar, 1 cup at a time. Beat at low speed after each addition until smooth and creamy. Add more sugar to thicken or milk to thin for good spreading consistency.

Chocolate-Dipped: Combine 1 cup semi-sweet chocolate chips and 1 teaspoon BUTTER FLAVOR CRISCO® in microwave-safe measuring cup. Microwave at 50% (MEDIUM). Stir after 1 minute. Repeat until smooth (or melt on rangetop in small saucepan on very low heat). Dip one end of cooled cookie halfway up in chocolate. Place on waxed paper until chocolate is firm.

Chocolate Nut: Dip cookie in melted chocolate as directed. Sprinkle with finely chopped nuts before chocolate hardens.

Almond Stars

Cookie Dough
  ¾ cup BLUE DIAMOND® Blanched
    Almond Paste
  ¼ cup sugar
  1¼ cups flour
  1 teaspoon grated lemon peel
  ¾ cup cold butter, cut into pieces
  1 teaspoon vanilla
  1 egg yolk

Lemon Filling
  3 tablespoons softened butter
  1½ cups powdered sugar, sifted
  2 tablespoons heavy cream
  2 teaspoons lemon juice
  1½ teaspoons grated lemon peel

Chocolate Garnish
  8 ounces semisweet chocolate
  ½ teaspoon solid vegetable shortening
    or butter

To prepare Dough: In food processor, process almond paste and sugar until mixture resembles coarse crumbs. Add flour and lemon peel; process until combined. Add butter and mix with on-off bursts until butter is broken up into small pieces. Add vanilla and yolk; process just until dough forms. (To prepare by hand, in large bowl, mix almond paste and sugar with electric mixer until mixture resembles coarse crumbs. Stir in flour and lemon peel. With fingertips, work butter into flour mixture until mixture resembles coarse crumbs. Add vanilla and yolk just until dough forms.) Do not overmix. Divide dough into 3 balls and chill at least 30 minutes.

Preheat oven to 350°F. Remove 1 ball dough at a time; roll out on lightly floured board to ¼-inch thickness. Dip 2-inch star shaped cookie cutter in flour; cut out cookies. Place on lightly greased cookie sheets. Repeat process with remaining dough. Bake 10 minutes or until barely colored. Cool on wire racks.

To prepare Filling: Beat butter and powdered sugar until smooth. Beat in cream, lemon juice and lemon peel. Spread filling on half the cookies and top with remaining cookies, pressing down gently. Chill briefly to set filling.

To prepare Garnish: In a double boiler over simmering water, melt chocolate and shortening, stirring occasionally, until smooth. Pour into small cup or bowl. Dip cookies in chocolate mixture, coating one-half of each cookie. Let excess chocolate drip off, and place cookie on waxed paper. Chill until set.   *Makes about 30 cookies*

Little Raisin Logs

  1 cup butter or margarine, softened
  ⅓ cup sugar
  2 teaspoons brandy (optional)
  2 teaspoons vanilla
  ½ teaspoon salt
  1 cup SUN-MAID® Raisins, finely
    chopped
  1 cup DIAMOND® Walnuts, finely
    chopped
  2 cups all-purpose flour
  1 package (6 ounces) real semisweet
    chocolate pieces
  3 tablespoons vegetable shortening

Preheat oven to 350°F. In large bowl, cream butter and sugar. Beat in brandy, vanilla and salt. Stir in raisins, walnuts and flour. Pinch off dough and roll with hands on lightly floured board into logs about ½ inch in diameter and 2½ inches long.

Bake on ungreased cookie sheet 15 to 20 minutes. (Cookies do not brown.) Remove to wire rack to cool.

Meanwhile, in top of double boiler, melt chocolate and shortening over simmering water, blending thoroughly. When cookies have cooled, dip one end into melted chocolate. Place on wire rack to set.

Makes about 6 dozen cookies

Almond Rice Madeleines

Almond Rice Madeleines

**1 cup whole blanched almonds,
    lightly toasted
¾ cup flaked coconut
1½ cups sugar
  3 cups cooked rice, chilled
  3 egg whites
    Vegetable cooking spray
    Fresh raspberries
    Frozen non-dairy whipped topping
    (optional)**

Preheat oven to 350°F. Spray madeleine pans* with cooking spray.

Place almonds in food processor fitted with knife blade; process until finely ground. Add coconut and sugar to processor; process until coconut is finely minced. Add rice; pulse to blend. Add egg whites; pulse to blend. Spoon mixture evenly into madeleine pans, filling to tops.

Bake 25 to 30 minutes or until lightly browned. Cool completely in pans on wire racks. Cover and refrigerate 2 hours or until serving time. Run sharp knife around each shell; gently remove from pan. Invert onto serving plates. Serve with raspberries and whipped topping, if desired.

Makes about 3 dozen cookies

*Substitute miniature muffin tins for madeleine pans, if desired.

Favorite recipe from **USA Rice Council**

Choco-Caramel Delights

Milk Chocolate Florentine Cookies

Cookies:
 ⅔ cup butter
 2 cups quick oats, uncooked
 1 cup sugar
 ⅔ cup all-purpose flour
 ¼ cup corn syrup
 ¼ cup milk
 1 teaspoon vanilla extract
 ¼ teaspoon salt

Filling:
One 11½-oz. pkg. (2 cups) NESTLÉ®
 Toll House® Milk Chocolate
 Morsels

Cookies: Preheat oven to 375°F. Melt butter in medium saucepan. Remove from heat. Stir in oats, sugar, flour, corn syrup, milk, vanilla extract and salt; mix well. Drop by level measuring teaspoonfuls about 3 inches apart onto foil-lined cookie sheets. Spread thin with rubber spatula. Bake 5 to 7 minutes. Cool. Peel foil away from cookies.

Filling: Melt over hot (not boiling) water, NESTLÉ® Toll House® Milk Chocolate Morsels; stir until smooth. Spread chocolate on flat side of half the cookies. Top with remaining cookies.
Makes about 3½ dozen sandwich cookies

Choco-Caramel Delights

 ½ cup butter or margarine, softened
 ⅔ cup sugar
 1 egg, separated
 2 tablespoons milk
 1 teaspoon vanilla extract
 1 cup all-purpose flour
 ⅓ cup HERSHEY'S® Cocoa
 ¼ teaspoon salt
 1 cup finely chopped pecans
   Caramel Filling (recipe follows)
 ½ cup HERSHEY'S® Semi-Sweet
   Chocolate Chips or Premium
   Semi-Sweet Chocolate Chunks
 1 teaspoon shortening

In small mixer bowl, beat butter, sugar, egg yolk, milk and vanilla until blended. Stir together flour, cocoa and salt; blend into butter mixture. Refrigerate dough at least 1 hour or until firm enough to handle.

Preheat oven to 350°F. Beat egg white slightly. Shape dough into 1-inch balls. Dip each ball into egg white; roll in pecans to coat. Place on lightly greased cookie sheet. Press thumb gently in center of each ball. Bake 10 to 12 minutes or until set. While cookies are baking, prepare Caramel Filling. Remove cookies from oven; press center of each cookie again with thumb to make indentation. Immediately spoon about ½ teaspoon Caramel Filling in center of each cookie. Carefully remove from cookie sheet; cool on wire rack.

In small microwave-safe bowl, place chocolate chips and shortening. Microwave at HIGH (100%) 1 minute or until softened; stir. Allow to stand several minutes to finish melting; stir until smooth. Place waxed paper under wire rack with cookies. Drizzle chocolate mixture over top of cookies.
Makes about 2 dozen cookies

Caramel Filling: In small saucepan, combine 14 unwrapped light caramels and 3 tablespoons whipping cream. Cook over low heat, stirring frequently, until caramels are melted and mixture is smooth.

Oats 'n' Pumpkin Pinwheels

1½ cups all-purpose flour
1 cup QUAKER® Oats (quick or old
    fashioned, uncooked)
¼ teaspoon baking soda
1½ cups sugar, divided
½ cup (1 stick) margarine or butter,
    softened
2 egg whites
1 cup canned pumpkin
½ teaspoon pumpkin pie spice
¼ cup sesame seeds

In small bowl, combine flour, oats and baking soda; set aside. In large mixing bowl, beat 1 cup sugar and margarine until fluffy; mix in egg whites. Stir in dry ingredients. On waxed paper, press dough into 16×12-inch rectangle. In small bowl, combine pumpkin, remaining ½ cup sugar and the pumpkin pie spice; mix well. Spread mixture over dough to ½-inch of edge. Roll dough, beginning at narrow end. Sprinkle sesame seeds over roll, pressing gently into dough. Wrap in waxed paper; freeze until firm or overnight.

Preheat oven to 400°F. Spray cookie sheet with non-stick cooking spray. Cut frozen dough into ¼-inch slices; place on cookie sheet. Bake 9 to 11 minutes or until golden brown. Remove to wire rack; cool completely. *Makes about 4 dozen cookies*

Apricot-Pecan Tassies

Pastry
1 cup all-purpose flour
½ cup butter, cut into pieces
6 tablespoons light cream cheese
Filling
¾ cup firmly packed light brown
    sugar
1 egg, lightly beaten
1 tablespoon butter, softened
½ teaspoon vanilla
¼ teaspoon salt
⅔ cup California dried apricot halves,
    diced (about 4 ounces)
⅓ cup chopped pecans

Apricot-Pecan Tassies

To prepare Pastry: In food processor, combine flour, butter and cream cheese; process until dough forms a ball and cleans sides of bowl. Wrap in plastic wrap; chill 15 minutes.

To prepare Filling: Preheat oven to 325°F. In large mixing bowl, combine brown sugar, egg, butter, vanilla and salt; beat until smooth. Stir in apricots and nuts.

Shape dough into 2 dozen 1-inch balls and place each in paper-lined or greased miniature (1¾-inch) muffin cup or tart pan. Press dough on bottom and sides of each cup; fill each with 1 teaspoon filling.

Bake 25 minutes or until golden and filling is set. Cool in pans on wire racks. Cookies can be wrapped tightly in plastic and frozen up to six weeks.

Makes 24 cookies

Favorite recipe from **California Apricot Advisory Board**

Half-Hearted Valentine Cookies

Cookies
  ¾ cup sugar
  1 cup LAND O LAKES® Butter, softened
  1 package (3 ounces) cream cheese, softened
  1 egg
  1 teaspoon peppermint extract
  3 cups all-purpose flour

Glaze
  1 cup semi-sweet real chocolate chips
  ¼ cup LAND O LAKES® Butter

For Cookies, in large mixer bowl, combine sugar, butter, cream cheese, egg and peppermint extract. Beat at medium speed, scraping bowl often, until light and fluffy. Add flour; beat until mixed. Divide dough into halves. Wrap in waxed paper. Refrigerate until firm, at least 2 hours.

Preheat oven to 375°F. Roll out dough on lightly floured surface to ¼-inch thickness. Cut out with floured heart-shaped cutters. Place 1 inch apart on ungreased cookie sheets. Bake for 7 to 10 minutes, or until edges are very lightly browned. Remove immediately; cool completely on wire racks.

For Glaze, in small saucepan, melt chocolate and butter, stirring occasionally, over low heat until melted, 4 to 6 minutes. Dip half of each heart into chocolate. Refrigerate on waxed paper-lined cookie sheet until chocolate is firm. Store, covered, in refrigerator.

Makes about 3½ dozen cookies

Spumoni Bars

  ¾ cup butter or margarine, softened
  ⅔ cup sugar
  3 egg yolks
  1 teaspoon vanilla
  ¼ teaspoon baking powder
  ⅛ teaspoon salt
  2 cups all-purpose flour
  12 maraschino cherries, well drained and chopped
  ¼ cup chopped walnuts
  ¼ cup mint-flavored or plain semisweet chocolate chips
  2 teaspoons water, divided

Preheat oven to 350°F. Cream butter and sugar in large bowl until blended. Beat in egg yolks, vanilla, baking powder and salt until light. Stir in flour to make stiff dough. Divide dough into 3 equal parts; place each part in small bowl. Add cherries and walnuts to one part, blending well. Melt chocolate chips in small bowl over hot water. Stir until smooth. Add melted chocolate and 1 teaspoon of the water to second part, blending well. Stir remaining 1 teaspoon water into third part. (If doughs are soft, refrigerate 10 minutes.)

Divide each color dough into 4 equal parts. Shape each part into a 6-inch rope by rolling on lightly floured surface. Place one rope of each color side by side on ungreased cookie sheets. Flatten ropes so they attach together making 1 strip of 3 colors. With rolling pin, roll strip directly on cookie sheet until it measures 12×3 inches. With straight edge of knife, score strip crosswise at 1-inch intervals. Repeat with remaining ropes to make a total of 4 tri-colored strips of dough. Bake 12 to 13 minutes or until set but not completely browned; remove from oven. While cookies are still warm, trim lengthwise edges to make them even and cut into individual cookies along score marks. (Cookies will bake together but are easy to cut apart while still warm.) Cool on cookie sheets. *Makes 4 dozen cookies*

Half-Hearted Valentine Cookies

Chocolate-Dipped Almond Horns

1 can SOLO® Almond Paste
3 egg whites
½ cup superfine sugar
½ teaspoon almond extract
¼ cup plus 2 tablespoons all-purpose flour
½ cup sliced almonds
5 squares (5 ounces) semisweet chocolate, melted and cooled

Preheat oven to 350°F. Grease 2 cookie sheets; set aside. Break almond paste into small pieces; place in medium-size bowl or container of food processor. Add egg whites, sugar and almond extract; beat with electric mixer or process until mixture is very smooth. Add flour and beat or process until blended.

Spoon almond mixture into pastry bag fitted with ½-inch (#8) plain tip. Pipe mixture into 5- or 6-inch crescents on prepared cookie sheets, leaving about 1½ inches between cookies. Sprinkle with sliced almonds.

Bake 13 to 15 minutes or until edges are golden. Cool 2 minutes on cookie sheets set on wire racks. Remove from cookie sheets; cool completely on racks. Dip ends of cookies in melted chocolate and place on sheet of waxed paper. Let stand until chocolate is set.   *Makes about 16 cookies*

Chocolate-Dipped Almond Horns

Chocolate Cookie Pretzels

⅔ cup butter or margarine, softened
1 cup granulated sugar
2 teaspoons vanilla extract
2 eggs
2½ cups all-purpose flour
½ cup HERSHEY'S® Cocoa
½ teaspoon baking soda
¼ teaspoon salt
  Powdered sugar
  Peanut Butter Chip Frosting (recipe follows)
  Satiny Chocolate Glaze (recipe follows)

Preheat oven to 350°F. In large mixer bowl, beat butter, granulated sugar and vanilla until creamy. Add eggs; blend well. Stir together flour, cocoa, baking soda and salt; gradually add to butter mixture, blending thoroughly. Divide dough into 24 pieces. On lightly floured surface, roll each piece with hands into pencil-like strip, about 12 inches long. Place strip on ungreased cookie sheet. Twist into pretzel shape by crossing left side of strip to middle, forming loop. Fold right side up and over first loop. Place about 2 inches apart on cookie sheet.

Bake 8 minutes or until set. Cool 1 minute; remove from cookie sheet to wire rack. Cool completely. Sprinkle with powdered sugar or frost with Peanut Butter Chip Frosting or Satiny Chocolate Glaze.
Makes 2 dozen cookies

Peanut Butter Chip Frosting

1 cup powdered sugar
¼ cup butter or margarine
3 tablespoons milk
1 cup REESE'S® Peanut Butter Chips
½ teaspoon vanilla extract

In small mixer bowl, place powdered sugar; set aside. In small saucepan, over low heat, combine butter, milk and peanut butter chips; cook, stirring constantly, until chips are melted and mixture is smooth. Remove from heat. Add warm mixture to powdered sugar; blend in vanilla. Beat until smooth. Spread while frosting is warm.   *Makes about 1 cup frosting*

Satiny Chocolate Glaze

2 tablespoons butter or margarine
3 tablespoons HERSHEY'S® Cocoa
2 tablespoons water
½ teaspoon vanilla extract
1 cup powdered sugar

In small saucepan, over low heat, melt butter; add cocoa and water. Cook, stirring constantly, until mixture thickens; do not boil. Remove from heat; stir in vanilla. Gradually add powdered sugar, beating with wire whisk until smooth. Add additional water, ½ teaspoon at a time, until glaze is of desired consistency.
                    Makes about ¾ cup glaze

Chocolate Lace Cornucopias

Chocolate Lace Cornucopias

½ cup firmly packed brown sugar
½ cup corn syrup
¼ cup (½ stick) margarine or butter
4 squares BAKER'S® Semi-Sweet
   Chocolate
1 cup all-purpose flour
1 cup finely chopped nuts
   Whipped cream or COOL WHIP®
   Whipped Topping, thawed

Preheat oven to 350°F.

Microwave sugar, corn syrup and margarine in large microwavable bowl on HIGH 2 minutes or until boiling. Stir in chocolate until completely melted. Gradually stir in flour and nuts until well blended.

Drop by level tablespoonfuls, 4 inches apart, onto foil-covered cookie sheets. Bake for 10 minutes. Lift foil and cookies onto wire rack. Cool on wire rack 3 to 4 minutes or until cookies can be easily

peeled off foil. Remove foil; finish cooling cookies on wire rack that has been covered with paper towels.

Place several cookies, lacy side down, on foil-lined cookie sheet. Heat at 350°F for 2 to 3 minutes or until slightly softened. Remove from foil, one at a time, and roll lacy side out to form cones. Cool completely. Just before serving, fill with whipped cream.
                    Makes about 30 cornucopias

Prep time: 20 minutes
Baking time: 12 to 13 minutes

Saucepan preparation: Mix sugar, corn syrup and margarine in 2-quart saucepan. Bring to boil over medium heat, stirring constantly. Remove from heat; stir in chocolate until melted. Continue as above.

Chocolate-Topped Linzer Cookies

3 cups hazelnuts, toasted, skins removed, divided
1 cup unsalted butter, softened
1 cup powdered sugar, sifted
½ teaspoon grated lemon peel
¼ teaspoon salt
½ egg*
3 cups sifted all-purpose flour
½ cup nougat paste**
½ cup seedless red raspberry jam
6 squares (1 ounce each) semisweet chocolate
2 tablespoons shortening

In food processor or blender, process 1½ cups of the hazelnuts until finely ground. (You should have ½ cup ground nuts; if necessary, process more nuts.) Set aside remaining whole nuts for garnish. In large bowl, beat butter, sugar, lemon peel and salt just until thoroughly blended; do not overmix. Add ½ egg; beat until well mixed. Stir in ground hazelnuts. Gradually stir in flour. Divide dough into quarters. Wrap each portion; refrigerate until firm, about 2 hours.

Preheat oven to 350°F. Roll out dough, one quarter at a time, ⅛ to 1⁄16 inch thick on floured pastry cloth. Cut out with 1¼-inch round cutter. Place ¾ inch apart on parchment-paper-lined cookie sheets.

*To measure ½ egg, lightly beat 1 egg in glass measuring cup; remove half for use in recipe.

**Nougat paste, a mixture of ground hazelnuts, sugar and semisweet chocolate is available in specialty candy and gourmet food shops. If unavailable, substitute melted semisweet chocolate to attach cookie layers.

Bake 7 to 8 minutes or until lightly browned. Let cookies cool completely on cookie sheets set on wire racks.

Spoon nougat paste into pastry bag fitted with ¼-inch round tip. Pipe about ¼ teaspoon paste onto centers of one third of cookies. Top with plain cookies; press gently. Spoon raspberry jam into pastry bag fitted with ⅓-inch round tip. Pipe about ⅓ teaspoon jam onto centers of second cookie layers. Top with plain cookies; press gently. Let cookies stand 1 hour to firm up. In small, heavy saucepan over low heat, melt chocolate and shortening; stir to blend. Press cookie layers lightly together. Dip top of each cookie into chocolate mixture just to cover. Shake to remove excess chocolate. Place cookies, chocolate side up, on wire rack; press reserved whole hazelnuts into soft chocolate in centers of cookies. Let stand until chocolate is set.

Makes about 4 dozen cookies

Left to right: Chocolate-Topped Linzer Cookies, Raspberry Pyramids

Raspberry Pyramids

1 cup unsalted butter, softened
1 cup powdered sugar, sifted
½ teaspoon grated lemon peel
¼ teaspoon salt
½ egg*
½ cup sliced blanched almonds, finely
  chopped
3 cups sifted all-purpose flour
½ cup seedless red raspberry jam
  Powdered sugar

In large bowl, beat butter, 1 cup powdered sugar, lemon peel and salt just until thoroughly blended; do not overmix. Add egg; beat until well mixed. Stir in almonds. Gradually stir in flour. Divide dough into quarters. Wrap each portion; refrigerate until firm, about 2 hours.

Preheat oven to 350°F. Roll out dough, one quarter at a time, ⅛ inch thick on lightly floured pastry cloth. Cut out with scalloped round cutters of 3 graduated sizes, cutting equal number of each size. Place 1 inch apart on parchment-paper-lined cookie sheets. Bake 12 to 15 minutes or until centers are firm to the touch and edges just begin to brown. Let cookies cool completely on cookie sheets set on wire racks.

Spoon about ¼ teaspoon raspberry jam in center of each largest size cookie. Top each with middle-size cookie; press gently. Spoon about ⅛ teaspoon jam in center of each middle-size cookie. Top each with smallest size cookie; press gently. Let cookies stand 1 hour to firm up. Press layers gently together. Just before serving, sprinkle with powdered sugar.

Makes about 5 dozen cookies

* To measure ½ egg, lightly beat 1 egg in glass measuring cup; remove half for use in recipe.

Ricotta Crescents

2½ cups all-purpose flour
1 teaspoon salt
¾ cup (1½ sticks) unsalted butter,
  softened
1 cup POLLY-O® Ricotta Cheese
1 cup sugar, divided
1½ teaspoons grated orange peel
2 tablespoons ground cinnamon
¾ cup raspberry or apricot jam

In small bowl, combine flour and salt. In large bowl with electric mixer at medium speed, beat together butter and ricotta cheese until well blended. Beat in ½ cup sugar and the orange peel, scraping sides of bowl with rubber spatula. With mixer on low speed, beat in flour mixture until dough forms. Wrap dough in plastic wrap; chill 2 hours or overnight.

Preheat oven to 375°F. Line 2 large cookie sheets with foil; grease foil. In small bowl, combine remaining ½ cup sugar and the cinnamon. Sprinkle pastry board or countertop with 1 tablespoon of the cinnamon-sugar mixture. Divide dough into 6 pieces; shape each piece into ball.

With rolling pin, roll out 1 ball of dough into 8-inch circle, turning over several times to coat well with cinnamon-sugar. With knife, cut into 8 wedges. Spoon ½ teaspoon jam on wide end of each wedge. Starting at wide ends, tightly roll up wedges; pinch ends to seal. Place on prepared cookie sheets, curving ends slightly to form crescents. Repeat with remaining dough.

Bake 15 to 20 minutes or until golden brown. Immediately transfer to wire racks to cool. *Makes about 50 cookies*

Jam-Up Oatmeal Cookies

1 cup BUTTER FLAVOR CRISCO®
1½ cups firmly packed brown sugar
2 eggs
2 teaspoons almond extract
2 cups all-purpose flour
1 teaspoon baking powder
1 teaspoon salt
½ teaspoon baking soda
2½ cups quick oats (not instant or old fashioned), uncooked
1 cup finely chopped pecans
1 jar (12 ounces) strawberry jam
Sugar for sprinkling

1. Combine BUTTER FLAVOR CRISCO® and brown sugar in large bowl. Beat at medium speed of electric mixer until well blended. Beat in eggs and almond extract.

2. Combine flour, baking powder, salt and baking soda. Mix into creamed mixture at low speed until just blended. Stir in oats and chopped nuts with spoon. Cover and refrigerate at least 1 hour.

3. Preheat oven to 350°F. Grease cookie sheet with BUTTER FLAVOR CRISCO®. Roll out dough, half at a time, to about ¼-inch thickness on floured surface. Cut out with 2½-inch round cookie cutter. Place 1 teaspoonful of jam in center of half of the rounds. Top with remaining rounds. Press edges to seal. Prick centers; sprinkle with sugar. Place 1 inch apart on cookie sheet.

4. Bake 12 to 15 minutes or until lightly browned. Cool 2 minutes on cookie sheet. Remove to cooling rack.

Makes about 2 dozen cookies

Melting Moments

½ cup butter or margarine, softened
⅓ cup sugar
1 egg yolk
¼ teaspoon vanilla
1 cup all-purpose flour
4 squares (1 ounce each) semisweet chocolate
1 tablespoon shortening
Orange Butter Cream (recipe follows)

In medium bowl, beat butter, sugar, egg yolk and vanilla until fluffy. Add flour; beat until well mixed. Wrap dough; refrigerate until firm, 1 hour.

Preheat oven to 375°F. Drop dough by level teaspoonfuls 2 inches apart onto ungreased cookie sheets or pipe through pastry bag fitted with large closed star tip. Bake 8 to 10 minutes or until lightly browned. Let cookies cool 1 minute before removing them from cookie sheets to wire racks; cool completely.

In small, heavy saucepan over low heat, melt chocolate and shortening; stir to blend. Dip half of each cookie in melted chocolate mixture. Place on waxed paper; let stand until chocolate sets. Prepare Orange Butter Cream. Place slightly rounded ½ teaspoon of butter cream on flat side of half the cookies. Top with remaining cookies, flat side down, forming sandwiches.

Makes about 2 dozen sandwich cookies

Orange Butter Cream: In small bowl, mix ½ cup powdered sugar, 2 tablespoons softened butter, 1½ teaspoons orange juice and ½ teaspoon grated orange peel. Stir until smooth.

Chocolate Pistachio Fingers

¾ cup butter or margarine, softened
⅓ cup sugar
3 ounces (about ⅓ cup) almond paste
1 egg yolk
1⅔ cups all-purpose flour
1 cup (6 ounces) semisweet chocolate chips
½ cup finely chopped natural pistachios

Preheat oven to 350°F. Line cookie sheets with parchment paper or lightly grease and dust with flour. Cream butter and sugar in large bowl until blended. Add almond paste and egg yolk; beat until light. Blend in flour to make a smooth dough. (If dough is too soft to handle, cover and refrigerate until firm.) Turn out onto lightly floured board. Divide into 8 equal pieces; divide each piece in half. Roll each half into 12-inch rope; cut each rope into 2-inch lengths. Place 2 inches apart on prepared cookie sheets.

Bake 10 to 12 minutes or until edges just begin to brown. Remove to wire racks to cool. Melt chocolate chips in small bowl over hot water. Stir until smooth. Dip both ends of cookies about ½ inch into melted chocolate, then dip chocolate ends into pistachios. Place on waxed paper; let stand until chocolate is set.

Makes 8 dozen cookies

Chocolate Cherry Cookies

2 squares (1 ounce each) unsweetened chocolate
½ cup butter or margarine, softened
½ cup sugar
1 egg
2 cups cake flour
1 teaspoon vanilla
¼ teaspoon salt
Maraschino cherries, well drained (about 48)
1 cup (6 ounces) semisweet or milk chocolate chips

Melt unsweetened chocolate in top of double boiler over hot, not boiling, water. Remove from heat; cool. Cream butter and sugar in large bowl until light. Add egg and melted chocolate; beat until fluffy. Stir in cake flour, vanilla and salt until well blended. Cover; refrigerate until firm, about 1 hour.

Preheat oven to 400°F. Lightly grease cookie sheets or line with parchment paper. Shape dough into 1-inch balls. Place 2 inches apart on prepared cookie sheets. With knuckle of finger, make deep indentation in center of each ball. Place cherry into each indentation. Bake 8 minutes or just until set. Meanwhile, melt chocolate chips in small bowl over hot water. Stir until melted. Remove cookies to wire racks. Drizzle melted chocolate over tops while still warm. Refrigerate until chocolate is set.

Makes about 4 dozen cookies

Chocolate Spritz

2 squares (1 ounce each) unsweetened chocolate
1 cup butter, softened
½ cup granulated sugar
1 egg
1 teaspoon vanilla
¼ teaspoon salt
2¼ cups all-purpose flour
Powdered sugar

Preheat oven to 400°F. Line cookie sheets with parchment paper or leave ungreased. Melt chocolate in top of double boiler over hot, not boiling, water. Remove from heat; cool. Cream butter, granulated sugar, egg, vanilla and salt in large bowl until light. Blend in melted chocolate and flour until stiff. Fit cookie press with your choice of plate. Load press with dough; press cookies out onto cookie sheets, spacing 2 inches apart.

Bake 5 to 7 minutes or just until very slightly browned around edges. Remove to wire racks to cool. Dust with powdered sugar. *Makes about 5 dozen cookies*

Top left to bottom right: Mocha Pecan Pinwheels, Chocolate Pistachio Fingers, Chocolate Cherry Cookies, Orange & Chocolate Ribbon Cookies (page 138), Chocolate Spritz

Mocha Pecan Pinwheels

1 square (1 ounce) unsweetened
   chocolate
½ cup (1 stick) butter or margarine,
   softened
¾ cup packed brown sugar
1 egg
1 teaspoon vanilla
¼ teaspoon baking soda
1¾ cups all-purpose flour
½ cup chopped pecans
1 teaspoon instant espresso coffee
   powder

Melt chocolate in small bowl over hot water. Stir until smooth. Cream butter, brown sugar, egg, vanilla and baking soda in large bowl, blending well. Stir in flour to make stiff dough. Remove half of dough; place in another bowl. Blend pecans and coffee powder into half of dough. Stir melted chocolate into remaining dough. Cover doughs; refrigerate 30 minutes.

Roll out light-colored dough to a 15×8-inch rectangle between 2 sheets of plastic wrap. Roll chocolate dough out to same dimensions between 2 more sheets of plastic wrap. Remove top sheets of plastic wrap. Place light-colored dough on top of chocolate dough. Remove remaining sheets of plastic wrap. Roll up firmly, jelly-roll fashion, starting with long side. Wrap in plastic; freeze. (Dough can be frozen up to 6 weeks.)

Preheat oven to 350°F. Line cookie sheets with parchment paper or leave ungreased. Cut frozen dough into ¼-inch-thick slices; place 2 inches apart on cookie sheets. Bake 9 to 12 minutes or until set. Remove to wire racks to cool.

Makes about 5 dozen cookies

Orange & Chocolate Ribbon Cookies

1 cup butter or margarine, softened
½ cup sugar
3 egg yolks
2 teaspoons grated orange zest
1 teaspoon orange extract
2¼ cups all-purpose flour, divided
3 tablespoons unsweetened cocoa
1 teaspoon vanilla
1 teaspoon chocolate extract

Cream butter, sugar and egg yolks in large bowl until light and fluffy. Remove half of mixture; place in another bowl. Add orange zest, orange extract and 1¼ cups of the flour to one half of mixture; mix until blended and smooth. Shape into ball. Add cocoa, vanilla and chocolate extract to second half of mixture; beat until smooth. Stir in remaining 1 cup flour; mix until blended and smooth. Shape into ball. Cover doughs; refrigerate 10 minutes.

Roll out each dough separately on lightly floured surface to 12×4-inch rectangle. Pat edges of dough to straighten; use rolling pin to level off thickness. Place one dough on top of the other. Using sharp knife, make lengthwise cut through center of doughs. Lift half of dough onto other to make long, 4-layer strip of dough. With hands, press dough strips together. Wrap in plastic wrap; refrigerate at least 1 hour or up to 3 days. (For longer storage, freeze up to 6 weeks.)

Preheat oven to 350°F. Lightly grease cookie sheets or line with parchment paper. Cut dough crosswise into ¼-inch-thick slices; place 2 inches apart on prepared cookie sheets. Bake 10 to 12 minutes or until very lightly browned. Remove to wire racks to cool.

Makes about 5 dozen cookies

Tea-Time Sandwich Cookies

Tea-Time Sandwich Cookies

Cookies
    2 cups all-purpose flour
    1 cup LAND O LAKES® Butter, softened
    ⅓ cup whipping cream
        Granulated sugar for dipping
Filling
    ¾ cup powdered sugar
    ¼ cup LAND O LAKES® Butter, softened
    1 to 3 teaspoons milk
    1 teaspoon vanilla *or* almond extract
        Food coloring (optional)

For Cookies, in small mixer bowl, combine flour, butter and whipping cream. Beat at low speed, scraping bowl often, until well mixed, 2 to 3 minutes. Divide dough into thirds. Wrap in waxed paper. Refrigerate until firm.

Preheat oven to 375°F. Roll out each third of the dough on well-floured surface to ⅛-inch thickness. Cut out with 1½-inch round cookie cutters. Dip both sides of each cookie in granulated sugar. Place 1 inch apart on ungreased cookie sheets. Prick with fork. Bake for 6 to 9 minutes, or until slightly puffy but not brown. Cool 1 minute on cookie sheets; remove immediately. Cool completely on wire racks.

For Filling, in small mixer bowl, combine powdered sugar, butter, milk and vanilla. Beat at medium speed, scraping bowl often, until smooth, 1 to 2 minutes. Color filling. Spread ½ teaspoon of filling over bottoms of half the cookies. Top with remaining cookies.

Makes about 4½ dozen cookies

Cocoa Sandies

1 cup butter, softened
1¼ cups confectioners' sugar
1½ teaspoons vanilla extract
½ cup HERSHEY'S® Cocoa
1¾ cups all-purpose flour
    Quick Cocoa Glaze (recipe follows)

Preheat oven to 300°F. In large mixer bowl, beat butter, sugar and vanilla until creamy. Add cocoa; blend well. Gradually add flour, blending until smooth. On lightly floured surface or between 2 pieces of waxed paper, roll dough to about ½-inch thickness. Cut dough into heart or star shapes with 2½-inch cookie cutters. (Scraps can be gathered and rerolled.) Place on ungreased cookie sheet.

Bake 20 minutes or just until firm. Cool slightly; remove from cookie sheet to wire rack. Cool completely. Dip about half of each cookie into Quick Cocoa Glaze. Place on wire rack until glaze is set.

Makes about 2 dozen cookies

Quick Cocoa Glaze

3 tablespoons butter or margarine
⅓ cup HERSHEY'S® Cocoa
¼ cup water
1 teaspoon vanilla extract
1½ cups confectioners' sugar

In small saucepan over low heat, melt butter. Stir in cocoa and water. Cook over low heat, stirring constantly, until mixture thickens; do not boil. Remove from heat; stir in vanilla. Gradually add confectioners' sugar, stirring with wire whisk until smooth. Add additional water, 1 teaspoon at a time, if needed for desired consistency.

Rosettes

CRISCO® Oil for frying
1 cup all-purpose flour
2 tablespoons confectioners' sugar
¼ teaspoon salt
1 cup milk
2 eggs
1 teaspoon vanilla
1 teaspoon almond extract
    Confectioners' sugar

1. Heat 2 to 3 inches CRISCO® Oil in deep-fryer or large saucepan to 365°F. Meanwhile, mix flour, 2 tablespoons confectioners' sugar and salt in small mixing bowl. Add milk, eggs, vanilla and almond extract. Stir until smooth.

2. Place rosette iron in hot CRISCO® Oil 1 minute. Tap excess oil from iron onto paper towel. Dip hot iron in batter, making sure batter does not cover top of iron. Place back in hot oil. Fry about 30 seconds, or until rosette is golden brown. Remove rosette immediately. Drain on paper towels. Reheat iron in hot oil 1 minute before frying each rosette. Sprinkle rosettes with confectioners' sugar.

Makes about 3 dozen rosettes

Banana Cream Sandwich Cookies

Cookies
  2⅓ cups all-purpose flour
  1 cup granulated sugar
  1 cup LAND O LAKES® Butter, softened
  ½ cup banana cut into ¼-inch slices (about 1 medium)
  ¼ teaspoon salt
  1 teaspoon vanilla
  ½ cup chopped pecans

Frosting
  3 cups powdered sugar
  ⅓ cup LAND O LAKES® Butter, softened
  3 to 4 tablespoons milk
  1 teaspoon vanilla
  Food coloring (optional)

Preheat oven to 350°F. For Cookies, in large mixer bowl, combine flour, granulated sugar, butter, banana, salt and vanilla. Beat at low speed, scraping bowl often, until well mixed, 2 to 3 minutes. Stir in nuts. Shape rounded teaspoonfuls of dough into 1-inch balls. Place 2 inches apart on greased cookie sheets. Flatten cookies to ¼-inch thickness with bottom of glass dipped in flour. Bake for 12 to 15 minutes, or until edges are lightly browned. Remove immediately; cool completely on wire racks.

For Frosting, in small mixer bowl, combine all frosting ingredients. Beat at medium speed, scraping bowl often, until light and fluffy, 1 to 2 minutes. If desired, tint with food coloring. Spread 1 tablespoon of frosting over bottoms of half of the cookies. Top with remaining cookies.

Makes about 2 dozen sandwich cookies

Filled Almond Crisps

  ⅓ cup plus 1 tablespoon butter, divided
  ½ cup sugar
  3 tablespoons flour
  2 tablespoons milk
  ⅛ teaspoon salt
  ½ cup BLUE DIAMOND® blanched, slivered almonds, toasted and finely chopped
  3 ounces semisweet chocolate
  1 recipe of either Orange Liqueur Filling or Strawberry Filling (recipes follow)

Preheat oven to 350°F. In small saucepan, combine ⅓ cup butter, sugar, flour, milk and salt; cook and stir over medium heat until smooth. Stir in almonds. Drop scant tablespoonfuls of dough 4 inches apart onto greased and floured cookie sheet. Place only 4 to 6 cookies at one time on cookie sheet.

Bake 5 minutes or until lightly browned. Cool 30 seconds on cookie sheet. Carefully lift with wide spatula and curl around wooden spoon handle to form tubes; cool. If cookies harden before curling, return briefly to oven to soften. Meanwhile, melt chocolate with remaining 1 tablespoon butter. Dip each end of cookie into melted chocolate; set on waxed paper to harden. Prepare desired filling. Just before serving, with pastry bag, pipe filling into cookies.

Makes about 18 cookies

Orange Liqueur Filling: Whip 1½ cups heavy cream and 2 tablespoons powdered sugar until stiff peaks form. Gently fold in 2 tablespoons orange liqueur. Pipe filling into cookies; garnish each end with candied orange peel.

Strawberry Filling: Whip 1½ cups heavy cream, 2 teaspoons powdered sugar and ¼ teaspoon vanilla until stiff peaks form. Gently fold 1½ cups whole strawberries, puréed, into whipped cream. Pipe filling into cookies.

Banana Cream Sandwich Cookies

Chocolate Madeleines

Cocoa Frosting

1¼ cups confectioners' sugar
2 tablespoons HERSHEY'S® Cocoa
2 tablespoons butter, softened
2 to 2½ tablespoons milk
½ teaspoon vanilla extract

In small bowl stir together confectioners' sugar and cocoa. In small mixer bowl beat butter and ¼ cup of the cocoa mixture until light and fluffy. Gradually add remaining cocoa mixture with milk, beating to spreading consistency. Stir in vanilla.

Chocolate Madeleines

1¼ cups all-purpose flour
1 cup sugar
⅛ teaspoon salt
¾ cup butter, melted
⅓ cup HERSHEY'S® Cocoa
3 eggs
2 egg yolks
½ teaspoon vanilla extract
Cocoa Frosting (recipe follows)

Preheat oven to 350°F. Lightly grease indentations of madeleine mold pan (each shell is 3×2 inches). In medium saucepan stir together flour, sugar and salt. Combine melted butter and cocoa; stir into dry ingredients. In small bowl lightly beat eggs, egg yolks and vanilla with fork until well blended; stir into chocolate mixture, blending well. Cook over very low heat, stirring constantly, until mixture is warm; *do not simmer or boil.* Remove from heat. Fill each mold half full with batter (do not overfill).

Bake 8 to 10 minutes or until wooden toothpick inserted in center comes out clean. Invert onto wire rack; cool completely. Prepare Cocoa Frosting; frost flat sides of cookies. Press frosted sides together, forming shells.

Makes about 1½ dozen filled cookies

Apricot Pinwheel Slices

2 cups sifted all-purpose flour
1 cup butter or margarine
1 cup sour cream
1 can SOLO® or 1 jar BAKER®
   Apricot, Raspberry or Strawberry
   Filling
1 cup flaked coconut
1 cup finely chopped pecans
   Confectioners' sugar

Place flour in medium-size bowl. Cut in butter until coarse crumbs form. Add sour cream; stir until blended. Divide dough into 4 equal-size pieces. Wrap each piece separately in plastic wrap or waxed paper; refrigerate 2 to 4 hours.

Preheat oven to 350°F. Roll out dough, 1 piece at a time, on lightly floured surface to 12×6-inch rectangle. Spread one-fourth of apricot filling over dough and sprinkle with ¼ cup coconut and ¼ cup pecans. Roll up, jelly-roll style, starting from short side. Pinch seam to seal. Place, seam side down, on ungreased cookie sheet. Repeat with remaining dough, apricot filling, coconut and pecans.

Bake 40 to 45 minutes or until rolls are golden brown. Remove from cookie sheets; place on wire racks. Dust liberally with confectioners' sugar while still warm. Cool completely on racks. Cut into 1-inch slices. *Makes about 24 cookies*

Pinwheel Cookies

½ cup BUTTER FLAVOR CRISCO®
⅓ cup plus 1 tablespoon butter,
    softened and divided
2 egg yolks
½ teaspoon vanilla
1 package DUNCAN HINES® Moist
    Deluxe Fudge Marble Cake Mix

1. Combine BUTTER FLAVOR CRISCO®, ⅓ cup butter, egg yolks and vanilla in large bowl. Mix at low speed of electric mixer until blended. Set aside cocoa packet. Gradually add cake mix. Blend well.

2. Divide dough in half. Add cocoa packet and remaining 1 tablespoon butter to one half of dough. Knead until well blended and chocolate colored.

Pinwheel Cookies

3. Roll out yellow dough between two pieces of waxed paper into 18×12×⅛-inch rectangle. Repeat for chocolate dough. Remove top pieces of waxed paper from chocolate and yellow dough. Lay yellow dough directly on top of chocolate. Remove remaining layers of waxed paper. Roll up jelly roll fashion, beginning at wide side. Refrigerate 2 hours.

4. Preheat oven to 350°F. Grease cookie sheets.

5. Cut dough into ⅛-inch slices. Bake 9 to 11 minutes or until lightly browned. Cool 5 minutes on cookie sheets. Remove to cooling racks.

Makes about 3½ dozen cookies

Old-Fashioned Molasses Cookies

4 cups sifted all-purpose flour
2 teaspoons ARM & HAMMER® Pure
    Baking Soda
1½ teaspoons ground ginger
½ teaspoon ground cinnamon
⅛ teaspoon salt
1½ cups molasses
½ cup lard, melted
¼ cup butter or margarine, melted
⅓ cup boiling water
    Sugar

Sift together flour, baking soda, spices and salt. Combine molasses, lard, butter and water in large bowl. Add dry ingredients to liquid mixture and blend well. Cover and chill several hours or overnight.

Preheat oven to 350°F. Turn dough out onto well-floured board. Using floured rolling pin, roll to ¼-inch thickness. Cut out with 3½-inch floured cookie cutter. Sprinkle with sugar and place on ungreased cookie sheets. Bake 12 minutes. Cool on wire racks.

Makes about 3 dozen cookies

Peanut Butter Secrets

Cookies
   1 cup BUTTER FLAVOR CRISCO®
   ¾ cup firmly packed brown sugar
   ½ cup granulated sugar
   ½ cup JIF® Creamy Peanut Butter
   1 egg
   1 teaspoon vanilla
   2 cups all-purpose flour
   1 teaspoon baking soda
   ½ teaspoon salt
   40 to 45 chocolate-covered miniature peanut butter cups, unwrapped

Glaze
   1 teaspoon BUTTER FLAVOR CRISCO®
   1 cup semi-sweet chocolate chips
   2 tablespoons JIF® Creamy Peanut Butter

1. Preheat oven to 375°F. Grease cookie sheet with BUTTER FLAVOR CRISCO®.

2. For Cookies, combine BUTTER FLAVOR CRISCO®, brown sugar, granulated sugar and JIF® Creamy Peanut Butter in large bowl. Beat at medium speed of electric mixer until well blended. Beat in egg and vanilla.

3. Combine flour, baking soda and salt. Mix into creamed mixture at low speed until just blended.

4. Form rounded teaspoonfuls of dough around each peanut butter cup. Enclose entirely. Place 2 inches apart on cookie sheet.

5. Bake 8 to 10 minutes or until cookies are just browned. Remove immediately to cooling rack.

6. For Glaze, combine BUTTER FLAVOR CRISCO®, chocolate chips and JIF® Creamy Peanut Butter in microwave-safe cup. Microwave at 50% (MEDIUM). Stir after 1 minute. Repeat until smooth (or melt on rangetop in small saucepan on very low heat). Dip cookie tops in glaze.

Makes about 3½ dozen cookies

Austrian Tea Cookies

   1½ cups sugar, divided
   ½ cup butter, softened
   ½ cup vegetable shortening
   1 egg, beaten
   ½ teaspoon vanilla extract
   2 cups all-purpose flour
   2 cups ALMOND DELIGHT® Brand Cereal, crushed to 1 cup
   ½ teaspoon baking powder
   ¼ teaspoon ground cinnamon
   14 ounces almond paste
   2 egg whites
   5 tablespoons raspberry or apricot jam, warmed

In large bowl beat 1 cup of the sugar, the butter and shortening. Add egg and vanilla; mix well. Stir in flour, cereal, baking powder and cinnamon until well combined. Chill 1 to 2 hours or until firm.

Preheat oven to 350°F. Roll out dough on lightly floured surface to ¼-inch thickness; cut into 2-inch circles. Place on ungreased cookie sheet; set aside. In small bowl beat almond paste, egg whites and remaining ½ cup sugar until smooth. With pastry tube fitted with medium-sized star tip, pipe almond paste mixture ½-inch thick on top of each cookie along outside edge. Place ¼ teaspoon jam in center of cookie, spreading out to paste. Bake 8 to 10 minutes or until lightly browned. Let stand 1 minute before removing from cookie sheet. Cool on wire rack.

Makes about 3½ dozen cookies

Greeting Card Cookies

Greeting Card Cookies

½ cup butter or margarine, softened
¾ cup sugar
1 egg
1 teaspoon vanilla extract
1½ cups all-purpose flour
⅓ cup HERSHEY'S® Cocoa
½ teaspoon baking powder
½ teaspoon baking soda
¼ teaspoon salt
    Decorative Frosting (recipe follows)

In large mixer bowl, beat butter, sugar, egg and vanilla until light and fluffy. Stir together flour, cocoa, baking powder, baking soda and salt; add to butter mixture, blending well. Refrigerate about 1 hour or until firm enough to roll. Cut cardboard rectangle for pattern, 2½ × 4 inches; wrap in plastic wrap.

Preheat oven to 350°F. On lightly floured board or between two pieces of waxed paper, roll out half of dough to ¼-inch thickness. Place pattern on dough; cut through dough around pattern with sharp paring knife. (Save dough trimmings and reroll for remaining cookies.) Carefully place cutouts on lightly greased cookie sheet; bake 8 to 10 minutes or until set. Cool 1 minute on cookie sheet. (If cookies

have lost their shape, trim irregular edges while cookies are still hot.) Carefully transfer to cooling rack. Repeat procedure with remaining dough. Prepare Decorative Frosting; spoon into pastry bag fitted with decorating tip. Pipe names or greetings onto cookies; decorate as desired.

Makes about 12 cookies

Decorative Frosting

3 cups confectioners' sugar
⅓ cup shortening
2 to 3 tablespoons milk
    Food color (optional)

In small mixer bowl, beat sugar and shortening; gradually add milk, beating until smooth and slightly thickened. Divide frosting into two bowls; tint with food color, if desired. Cover until ready to use.

Chocolate & Vanilla Sandwich Cookies

¾ cup margarine or butter, softened
1 (14-ounce) can EAGLE® Brand Sweetened Condensed Milk (NOT evaporated milk)
2 eggs
1 tablespoon vanilla extract
1 cup finely chopped nuts
2½ cups unsifted flour
2 teaspoons baking powder
½ teaspoon baking soda
¼ cup unsweetened cocoa
    Vanilla, Chocolate or Mint Frosting*

In large mixer bowl, beat margarine, sweetened condensed milk, eggs, vanilla and nuts. Divide batter in half (about 1½ cups per half). To one half of batter add 1½ *cups* flour, 1 *teaspoon* baking powder and ¼ *teaspoon* baking soda; mix well. To second half of batter add remaining 1 *cup* flour, 1 *teaspoon* baking powder, ¼ *teaspoon* baking soda and cocoa; mix well. Chill doughs at least 3 hours.

Preheat oven to 350°F. On well-floured surface, knead each dough into a ball. Divide each ball in half (keep unused dough refrigerated). On well-floured surface, roll out each portion to ⅛-inch thickness. Cut out with floured round cookie cutter. Reroll as necessary to use all dough. Place 1 inch apart on lightly greased cookie sheets. Bake 8 to 10 minutes or until set. Cool. Sandwich 2 cookies together with frosting. Store tightly covered at room temperature.

Makes about 6½ dozen cookies

*Vanilla Frosting: In large mixer bowl, beat ⅓ cup margarine, softened, 1 pound confectioners' sugar (4 cups), 3 to 4 tablespoons milk, 2 teaspoons vanilla and ¼ teaspoon salt until smooth and of desired consistency. Add additional milk if needed. *Makes about 2 cups frosting*

*Chocolate Frosting: Add ⅓ cup unsweetened cocoa with confectioners' sugar to Vanilla Frosting. Increase milk as needed. *Makes about 2 cups frosting*

*Mint Frosting: Omit vanilla in Vanilla Frosting. Add ½ teaspoon peppermint extract and red or green food coloring if desired. *Makes about 2 cups frosting*

Petite Macaroon Cups

1 cup margarine or butter, softened
2 (3-ounce) packages cream cheese, softened
2 cups unsifted flour
1 (14-ounce) can EAGLE® Brand Sweetened Condensed Milk (NOT evaporated milk)
2 eggs, beaten
1½ teaspoons vanilla extract
½ teaspoon almond extract
1 (3½-ounce) can flaked coconut (1⅓ cups)

In large mixer bowl, beat margarine and cheese until fluffy; stir in flour. Cover; chill 1 hour.

Preheat oven to 375°F. Divide dough into quarters. On floured surface, shape 1 quarter into ball. Divide into 12 balls. Place each ball in 1¾-inch muffin cup; press evenly on bottom and up side of each cup. Repeat wth remaining dough. In medium bowl, combine sweetened condensed milk, eggs and extracts; mix well. Stir in coconut. Fill muffin cups ¾ full.

Bake 16 to 18 minutes or until lightly browned. Cool in pans; remove. Store loosely covered at room temperature.

Makes 4 dozen cookies

Chocolate Macaroon Cups: Beat ¼ cup unsweetened cocoa into egg mixture; proceed as above.

Petite and Chocolate Macaroon Cups

JUST FOR KIDS

Chocolatey Peanut Butter Goodies

Cookies
1 cup BUTTER FLAVOR CRISCO®
4 cups (1 pound) powdered sugar
1½ cups JIF® Extra Crunchy Peanut Butter
1½ cups graham cracker crumbs

Frosting
1 tablespoon BUTTER FLAVOR CRISCO®
1⅓ cups semi-sweet chocolate chips

1. For Cookies, combine BUTTER FLAVOR CRISCO®, powdered sugar, JIF® Extra Crunchy Peanut Butter and crumbs in large bowl with spoon. Spread evenly on bottom of 13×9-inch pan.

2. For Frosting, combine BUTTER FLAVOR CRISCO® and chocolate chips in small microwave-safe bowl. Microwave at 50% (MEDIUM). Stir after 1 minute. Repeat until smooth (or melt on rangetop in small saucepan on very low heat). Spread over top of cookie mixture. Cool at least 1 hour, or until chocolate hardens. Cut into 2×1½-inch bars. *Makes 3 dozen bars*

P. B. Graham Snackers

½ cup BUTTER FLAVOR CRISCO®
2 cups powdered sugar
¾ cup JIF® Creamy Peanut Butter
1 cup graham cracker crumbs
½ cup semi-sweet chocolate chips
½ cup graham cracker crumbs, crushed peanuts or chocolate sprinkles (optional)

1. Combine BUTTER FLAVOR CRISCO®, powdered sugar and JIF® Creamy Peanut Butter in large bowl. Beat at low speed of electric mixer until well blended. Stir in 1 cup crumbs and chocolate chips. Cover and refrigerate 1 hour.

2. Form dough into 1-inch balls. Roll in ½ cup crumbs, peanuts or sprinkles for a fancier cookie. Cover and refrigerate until ready to serve.

Makes about 3 dozen cookies

Top to bottom: P. B. Graham Snackers, Chocolatey Peanut Butter Goodies

Chocolate Teddy Bears

²⁄₃ **cup butter or margarine, softened**
1 **cup sugar**
2 **teaspoons vanilla extract**
2 **eggs**
2½ **cups all-purpose flour**
½ **cup HERSHEY'S® Cocoa**
½ **teaspoon baking soda**
¼ **teaspoon salt**

In large mixer bowl beat butter, sugar and vanilla until light and fluffy. Add eggs; blend well. Stir together flour, cocoa, baking soda and salt; gradually add to butter mixture, blending thoroughly. Refrigerate until dough is firm enough to handle.

Preheat oven to 350°F. To shape teddy bears: For each cookie, form a portion of dough into 1 large ball for body (1 to 1½ inches), 1 medium-size ball for head (¾ to 1 inch), 4 small balls for arms and legs (½ inch), 2 smaller balls for ears, 1 tiny ball for nose and 4 tiny balls for paws (optional). On ungreased cookie sheet flatten large ball slightly for body. Attach medium-size ball for head by overlapping slightly onto body. Place balls for arms, legs and ears, and a tiny ball on head for nose. Arrange other tiny balls atop ends of legs and arms for paws, if desired. With wooden pick, draw eyes and mouth; pierce small hole at top of cookie for use as hanging ornament, if desired.

Bake 6 to 8 minutes or until set. Cool 1 minute; remove from cookie sheet to wire rack. Cool completely. Store in covered container. If cookies will be used as ornaments, allow to dry on wire rack at least 6 hours before hanging. Pull ribbon through hole for hanging, if desired.

Makes about 14 cookies

Chocolate Teddy Bears

Peanut Butter and Chocolate Cookie Sandwich Cookies

½ cup REESE'S® Peanut Butter Chips
3 tablespoons plus ½ cup butter or
     margarine, softened and divided
1¼ cups sugar, divided
¼ cup light corn syrup
1 egg
1 teaspoon vanilla extract
2 cups plus 2 tablespoons all-purpose
     flour, divided
2 teaspoons baking soda
¼ teaspoon salt
½ cup HERSHEY'S® Cocoa
5 tablespoons butter or margarine,
     melted
Sugar
About 2 dozen large marshmallows

Preheat oven to 350°F. In small saucepan over very low heat, melt peanut butter chips and 3 tablespoons of the softened butter. Remove from heat; cool slightly. In large mixer bowl beat remaining ½ cup softened butter and 1 cup sugar until light and fluffy. Add corn syrup, egg and vanilla; blend thoroughly. Stir together 2 cups flour, baking soda and salt; add to butter mixture, blending well. Remove 1¼ cups batter and place in small bowl; with wooden spoon stir in the remaining 2 tablespoons flour and peanut butter chip mixture. Blend cocoa, remaining ¼ cup sugar and 5 tablespoons melted butter into remaining batter. Refrigerate both batters 5 to 10 minutes or until firm enough to handle. Roll dough into 1-inch balls; roll in sugar. Place on ungreased cookie sheet.

Bake 10 to 11 minutes or until set. Cool slightly; remove from cookie sheet to wire rack. Cool completely. Place 1 marshmallow on flat side of 1 chocolate cookie. Microwave at MEDIUM (50%) 10 seconds or until marshmallow is softened; place a peanut butter cookie over marshmallow, pressing down slightly. Repeat for remaining cookies. Serve immediately.

Makes about 2 dozen cookie sandwiches

Peanut Butter and Chocolate Cookie Sandwich Cookies

Granola Apple Bars

2 cups granola with dates and raisins
½ cup all-purpose flour
½ teaspoon baking powder
½ teaspoon baking soda
1 cup MOTT'S® Cinnamon Apple
     Sauce
1 teaspoon vanilla
1 egg, beaten
½ cup sunflower nuts
½ cup coconut

Preheat oven to 350°F. Grease 8- or 9-inch square pan. In large bowl, combine all ingredients; mix well. Pour into prepared pan. Bake 25 to 35 minutes or until wooden toothpick inserted in center comes out clean. Cool on wire rack. Cut into bars.   *Makes about 20 bars*

Cut Out Chocolate Cookies

Cut Out Chocolate Cookies

½ cup butter or margarine, softened
¾ cup sugar
1 egg
1 teaspoon vanilla extract
1½ cups all-purpose flour
⅓ cup HERSHEY'S® Cocoa
½ teaspoon baking powder
½ teaspoon baking soda
¼ teaspoon salt
    Satiny Chocolate Glaze (page 131) or
    Vanilla Glaze (recipe follows)

In large mixer bowl, cream butter, sugar, egg and vanilla until light and fluffy. Combine flour, cocoa, baking powder, baking soda and salt; add to creamed mixture, blending well. Chill dough about 1 hour or until firm enough to roll.

Preheat oven to 325°F. On lightly floured board or between 2 pieces of waxed paper, roll small portion of dough at a time to ¼-inch thickness. Cut into desired shapes with cookie cutters; place on ungreased cookie sheet.

Bake 5 to 7 minutes or until no indentation remains when touched lightly. Cool slightly; remove from cookie sheet to wire rack. Cool completely. Frost with Satiny Chocolate Glaze or Vanilla Glaze. Decorate as desired.   *Makes about 3 dozen cookies*

Vanilla Glaze

3 tablespoons butter or margarine
2 cups confectioners' sugar
1 teaspoon vanilla extract
2 to 3 tablespoons milk
2 to 4 drops food color (optional)

In small saucepan over low heat, melt butter. Remove from heat; blend in confectioners' sugar and vanilla. Add milk gradually, beating with spoon or wire whisk until glaze is of desired consistency. Blend in food color, if desired.

Makes about 1 cup glaze

Chocolate Peanut Buddy Bars

1 cup peanut butter
6 tablespoons (¾ stick) butter or margarine, softened
1¼ cups sugar
3 eggs
1 teaspoon vanilla extract
1 cup all-purpose flour
¼ teaspoon salt
One 11½-oz. pkg. (2 cups) NESTLÉ® Toll House® Milk Chocolate Morsels, divided

Preheat oven to 350°F. In large mixer bowl, beat peanut butter and butter until smooth, about 1 minute. Add sugar, eggs and vanilla extract; beat until creamy. Blend in flour and salt. Stir in 1 cup NESTLÉ® Toll House® Milk Chocolate Morsels. Spread in ungreased 13×9-inch baking pan.

Bake 25 to 30 minutes until edges begin to brown. Immediately sprinkle remaining 1 cup NESTLÉ® Toll House® Milk Chocolate Morsels over cookie layer. Let stand 5 minutes or until morsels become shiny and soft; spread morsels evenly over top. When cool, refrigerate 5 to 10 minutes to set chocolate. Cut into 2×1½-inch bars.

Makes 36 bars

Peanut Butter Cremes

¾ cup BUTTER FLAVOR CRISCO®
1 cup JIF® Creamy Peanut Butter
1 cup firmly packed dark brown sugar
1 cup marshmallow creme
1 egg
2 teaspoons vanilla
1¾ cups all-purpose flour
1 teaspoon baking powder
1 teaspoon salt

1. Preheat oven to 350°F. Combine BUTTER FLAVOR CRISCO®, JIF® Creamy Peanut Butter, brown sugar and marshmallow creme in large bowl. Beat at medium speed of electric mixer until well blended. Beat in egg and vanilla.

2. Combine flour, baking powder and salt. Mix into creamed mixture at low speed until just blended.

3. Drop rounded tablespoonfuls of dough 2 inches apart onto ungreased cookie sheet.

4. Bake 11 minutes or until lightly browned. Cool 2 minutes on cookie sheet. Remove to cooling rack.

Makes about 4 dozen cookies

Banana Chip Bars

1 cup firmly packed brown sugar
¾ cup (1½ sticks) margarine or butter, softened
2 cups QUAKER® 100% Natural Cereal, any flavor, crushed, divided
1½ cups all-purpose flour
½ cup semi-sweet chocolate pieces
½ cup mashed, ripe banana (about 1 large banana)
1 egg
1 teaspoon salt (optional)
1 teaspoon vanilla
¼ teaspoon baking soda

Preheat oven to 375°F. Lightly grease 13×9-inch baking pan. In large bowl, beat brown sugar and margarine until fluffy. Add 1½ cups of the cereal and remaining ingredients; mix well. Spread dough into prepared pan; sprinkle with remaining ½ cup cereal. Bake 25 to 30 minutes or until wooden toothpick inserted in center comes out clean. Cool completely on wire rack; cut into 2×1½-inch bars. Store tightly covered.

Makes 32 bars

Nestlé® Candy Shop Pizza

1½ cups all-purpose flour
½ teaspoon baking soda
½ teaspoon salt
10 tablespoons (1¼ sticks) butter, softened
½ cup granulated sugar
½ cup firmly packed brown sugar
1 egg
½ teaspoon vanilla extract
One 12-oz. pkg. (2 cups) NESTLÉ® Toll House® Semi-Sweet Chocolate Morsels, divided
½ cup peanut butter
  About 1 cup chopped candy bars such as NESTLÉ® Crunch bars, Butterfingers™, Alpine White™ bars, Goobers™, Raisinets™, Baby Ruth™ bars

Preheat oven to 375°F. In small bowl, combine flour, baking soda and salt; set aside.

In large mixer bowl, beat butter, granulated sugar and brown sugar until creamy. Beat in egg and vanilla extract. Gradually beat in flour mixture. Stir in 1 cup of the NESTLÉ® Toll House® Semi-Sweet Chocolate Morsels. Spread batter in lightly greased 12- to 14-inch pizza pan *or* 15½×10½×1-inch jelly-roll pan. Bake 20 to 24 minutes until lightly browned.

Immediately sprinkle remaining 1 cup NESTLÉ® Toll House® Semi-Sweet Chocolate Morsels over crust; drop peanut butter by spoonfuls on morsels. Let stand 5 minutes or until morsels become soft and shiny. Gently spread chocolate and peanut butter evenly over crust. Decorate pizza with candy. Cut into wedges; serve warm. *Makes about 12 servings*

Chocolate Cherry Brownies

One 16-ounce jar maraschino cherries
⅔ cup (1 stick plus 3 tablespoons) margarine
One 6-ounce package (1 cup) semi-sweet chocolate pieces, divided
1 cup sugar
1 teaspoon vanilla
2 eggs
1¼ cups all-purpose flour
¾ cup QUAKER® Oats (quick or old fashioned, uncooked)
1 teaspoon baking powder
¼ teaspoon salt (optional)
½ cup chopped nuts (optional)
2 teaspoons vegetable shortening

Preheat oven to 350°F. Lightly grease 13×9-inch baking pan. Drain cherries; reserve 12 and chop remainder. In large saucepan over low heat, melt margarine and ½ cup of the chocolate pieces, stirring until smooth. Remove from heat; cool slightly. Add sugar and vanilla. Beat in eggs, one at a time. In small bowl, combine flour, oats, baking powder and salt. Stir in chopped cherries and nuts. Add to chocolate mixture; mix well. Spread into prepared pan. Bake about 25 minutes or until brownies pull away from sides of pan. Cool completely on wire rack.

Cut reserved cherries in half; place evenly on top of brownies. In saucepan over low heat, melt remaining ½ cup chocolate pieces and vegetable shortening, stirring constantly until smooth.* Drizzle over brownies. When chocolate is set, cut into 2½-inch squares. Store tightly covered.
Makes 2 dozen brownies

*Microwave Directions: Place chocolate pieces and shortening in microwavable bowl. Microwave at HIGH 1 to 1½ minutes, stirring after 1 minute.

PARTY!

For: THE WHOLE CLASS

Place: SCHOOL GY

Date:

Chocolate Peanut Butter Cookies

In food processor or blender, process bananas until puréed (2 cups). In large bowl, combine oats, sugar, flour, cocoa, baking soda and salt until well mixed. Stir in puréed bananas, eggs and margarine until blended. Stir in nuts and chocolate chips. Refrigerate dough 1 hour or until mixture becomes partially firm (batter runs during baking if too soft).

Preheat oven to 350°F. Drop dough by ¼ cupfuls onto greased cookie sheet, spacing about 4 inches apart. Flatten slightly with spatula into 2½- to 3-inch circles. Bake 15 to 17 minutes. Remove to wire rack to cool. *Makes about 2½ dozen cookies*

Chocolate Peanut Butter Cookies

1 package DUNCAN HINES® Moist Deluxe Devil's Food Cake Mix
¾ cup JIF® Extra Crunchy Peanut Butter
2 eggs
2 tablespoons milk
1 cup candy-coated peanut butter pieces

1. Preheat oven to 350°F. Grease cookie sheet.

2. Combine cake mix, peanut butter, eggs and milk in large bowl. Mix at low speed with electric mixer until blended. Stir in peanut butter pieces.

3. Drop dough by slightly rounded tablespoonfuls onto cookie sheet. Bake 7 to 9 minutes or until lightly browned. Cool 2 minutes on cookie sheet. Remove to cooling rack.
Makes about 3½ dozen cookies

Tip: You can use 1 cup peanut butter chips in place of peanut butter pieces.

Double Chocolate Banana Cookies

3 to 4 extra-ripe, medium DOLE® Bananas, peeled
2 cups rolled oats, uncooked
2 cups sugar
1¾ cups flour
½ cup unsweetened cocoa powder
1 teaspoon baking soda
½ teaspoon salt
2 eggs, slightly beaten
1¼ cups margarine, melted
1 cup DOLE® Chopped Natural Almonds, toasted
1 to 2 cups semisweet chocolate chips

Mini Morsel Granola Cookies

2½ cups all-purpose flour
2 teaspoons baking powder
1 teaspoon baking soda
1 teaspoon cinnamon
1 cup (2 sticks) butter, softened
1¼ cups firmly packed brown sugar
2 eggs
One 12-oz. pkg. (2 cups) NESTLÉ®
    Toll House® Semi-Sweet
    Chocolate Mini Morsels
2 cups granola cereal
1 cup raisins

Preheat oven to 375°F. In small bowl, combine flour, baking powder, baking soda and cinnamon; set aside.

In large mixer bowl, beat butter and brown sugar until creamy. Beat in eggs. Gradually beat in flour mixture. Stir in NESTLÉ® Toll House® Semi-Sweet Chocolate Mini Morsels, granola and raisins. Drop dough by rounded measuring tablespoonfuls onto ungreased cookie sheets.

Bake 9 to 11 minutes until edges are golden brown. Let stand on cookie sheets 5 minutes. Remove from cookie sheets; cool on wire racks.

Makes about 4 dozen cookies

Teentime Dream Bars

Crust
    1 cup all-purpose flour
    ⅓ cup sugar
    ½ cup LAND O LAKES® Butter,
        softened
Filling
    ½ cup sugar
    ¼ cup chunky peanut butter
    ½ cup light corn syrup
    2 eggs
    ¼ teaspoon salt
    ½ teaspoon vanilla
    ½ cup flaked coconut
    ½ cup semi-sweet chocolate chips

Preheat oven to 350°F. For Crust, in small mixer bowl, combine all crust ingredients. Beat at low speed, scraping bowl often, until mixture is crumbly, 1 to 2 minutes. Press on bottom of greased 9-inch square baking pan. Bake for 12 to 17 minutes, or until edges are lightly browned.

For Filling, in small mixer bowl, combine sugar, peanut butter, corn syrup, eggs, salt and vanilla. Beat at low speed, scraping bowl often, until well mixed, 1 to 2 minutes. Stir in coconut and chocolate chips. Pour over crust. Continue baking for 20 to 30 minutes, or until filling is set and lightly browned. Cool completely on wire rack. Cut into bars.

Makes about 3 dozen bars

Peanut Butter Crunchy Surprises

1 cup BUTTER FLAVOR CRISCO®
1 cup JIF® Creamy Peanut Butter
1 cup firmly packed brown sugar
1 cup granulated sugar
1 teaspoon vanilla
2 eggs
2½ cups all-purpose flour
2 teaspoons baking soda
2 cups crushed potato chips

1. Preheat oven to 375°F. Combine BUTTER FLAVOR CRISCO®, JIF® Creamy Peanut Butter, brown sugar, granulated sugar and vanilla in large bowl. Beat at medium speed of electric mixer until well blended. Beat in eggs.

2. Combine flour and baking soda. Mix into creamed mixture at low speed until just blended.

3. Form dough into 1-inch balls. Roll in crushed potato chips. Place 2 inches apart on ungreased cookie sheet. Make crisscross pattern on dough with floured fork.

4. Bake 8 to 10 minutes or until lightly browned. Cool 2 minutes on cookie sheet. Remove to cooling rack.

Makes about 4 dozen cookies

Peanut Butter Bears

1 cup SKIPPY® Creamy Peanut Butter
1 cup MAZOLA® Margarine,
    softened
1 cup packed brown sugar
⅔ cup KARO® Light or Dark
    Corn Syrup
2 eggs
4 cups flour, divided
1 tablespoon baking powder
1 teaspoon cinnamon (optional)
¼ teaspoon salt

In large bowl with mixer at medium speed, beat peanut butter, margarine, brown sugar, corn syrup and eggs until smooth. Reduce speed; beat in 2 cups of the flour, the baking powder, cinnamon and salt. With spoon stir in remaining 2 cups flour. Wrap dough in plastic wrap; refrigerate 2 hours.

Preheat oven to 325°F. Divide dough in half; set aside half. On floured surface roll out half the dough to ⅛-inch thickness. Cut with floured bear cookie cutter. Repeat with remaining dough. Bake on ungreased cookie sheets 10 minutes or until lightly browned. Remove from cookie sheets; cool completely on wire racks. Decorate as desired.

Makes about 3 dozen bears

Prep Time: 35 minutes, plus chilling
Bake Time: 10 minutes, plus cooling

Note: Use scraps of dough to make bear faces. Make one small ball of dough for muzzle. Form 3 smaller balls of dough and press gently to create eyes and nose; bake as directed. If desired, use frosting to create paws, ears and bow ties.

Gaiety Pastel Cookies

1½ cups (3 sticks) PARKAY® Margarine,
    softened
1 cup sugar
1 package (4-serving size) JELL-O®
    Brand Gelatin, any flavor*
1 egg
1 teaspoon vanilla
3½ cups all-purpose flour
1 teaspoon CALUMET® Baking
    Powder
    Additional JELL-O® Brand Gelatin,
    any flavor*

Preheat oven to 400°F. Beat margarine at medium speed of electric mixer until light and fluffy. Gradually beat in sugar and 1 package of the gelatin. Mix in egg and vanilla. Stir in flour and baking powder until well blended.

Force dough through cookie press onto greased cookie sheets. Sprinkle with additional gelatin. Decorate, if desired. Bake 13 minutes for medium cookies (about 2-inch diameter) or 8 minutes for small cookies (about 1-inch diameter) or until golden brown around edges. Remove; cool on racks. Store in loosely covered container.

*Makes about 5 dozen medium cookies
or 10 dozen small cookies*

*For best results, use same flavor gelatin to flavor cookies and for garnish.

Prep time: 40 minutes
Baking time: 40 minutes

Left to right: Marbled Brownies, Honey Brownies

Creamy Brownie Frosting

3 tablespoons butter or margarine, softened
3 tablespoons HERSHEY'S® Cocoa
1 tablespoon light corn syrup or honey
½ teaspoon vanilla extract
1 cup powdered sugar
1 to 2 tablespoons milk

In small bowl, beat butter, cocoa, corn syrup and vanilla. Add powdered sugar and milk; beat to spreading consistency.
Makes about 1 cup frosting

Honey Brownies

½ cup sugar
⅓ cup butter or margarine, softened
⅓ cup honey
2 teaspoons vanilla extract
2 eggs
½ cup all-purpose flour
⅓ cup HERSHEY'S® Cocoa
½ teaspoon salt
⅔ cup chopped nuts
Creamy Brownie Frosting (recipe follows)

Preheat oven to 350°F. Grease 9-inch square baking pan. In small mixer bowl, beat sugar and butter; blend in honey and vanilla. Add eggs; beat well. Stir together flour, cocoa and salt; gradually add to butter mixture. Stir in nuts. Spread batter into prepared pan.

Bake 25 to 30 minutes or until brownies begin to pull away from sides of pan. Cool completely in pan on wire rack; frost with Creamy Brownie Frosting, if desired. Cut into squares. *Makes about 16 brownies*

Marbled Brownies

Nut Cream Filling (recipe follows)
½ cup butter or margarine
⅓ cup HERSHEY'S® Cocoa
2 eggs
1 cup sugar
1 teaspoon vanilla extract
½ cup all-purpose flour
½ teaspoon baking powder
¼ teaspoon salt

Prepare Nut Cream Filling; set aside. Preheat oven to 350°F. Grease 9-inch square baking pan.

In small saucepan melt butter; remove from heat. Blend in cocoa; set aside to cool slightly. In small mixer bowl, beat eggs until foamy. Gradually add sugar and vanilla; blend well. Combine flour, baking powder and salt; blend into egg mixture. Stir in chocolate mixture. Remove ¾ cup batter; set aside. Spread remaining batter into prepared pan. Spread Nut Cream Filling over batter. Drop teaspoonfuls of reserved batter over top. Swirl gently with metal spatula or knife to marble.

Bake 35 to 40 minutes or until brownies begin to pull away from sides of pan. Cool completely on wire rack. Cut into squares.
Makes about 20 brownies

Nut Cream Filling

1 package (3 ounces) cream cheese, softened
2 tablespoons butter or margarine, softened
¼ cup sugar
1 egg
½ teaspoon vanilla extract
¼ to ½ teaspoon almond extract
1 tablespoon all-purpose flour
¼ cup slivered almonds, toasted and chopped*

In small mixer bowl, beat cream cheese, butter and sugar until creamy. Blend in egg, vanilla and almond extract. Stir in flour and almonds.

*To toast almonds: Toast in shallow baking pan in 350°F oven, stirring occasionally, 8 to 10 minutes or until golden brown. Cool.

Crunch Crowned Brownies

1 package (21 to 23 oz.) fudge brownie mix
1 cup chopped nuts
⅔ cup quick oats, uncooked
½ cup firmly packed light brown sugar
¼ cup margarine, melted
1 teaspoon cinnamon
1½ cups "M&M's"® Plain Chocolate Candies

Preheat oven to 350°F. Prepare brownie mix batter according to package directions for cake-like brownies; spread batter into greased 13×9-inch baking pan. Combine nuts, oats, brown sugar, margarine and cinnamon; mix well. Stir candies into nut mixture; sprinkle over batter. Bake 40 to 45 minutes. Cool completely on wire rack. Cut into squares.

Makes about 30 brownies

Chocolate Chunk Cookies

¾ cup firmly packed brown sugar
½ cup granulated sugar
1 cup LAND O LAKES® Butter, softened
1 egg
1½ teaspoons vanilla
2¼ cups all-purpose flour
1 teaspoon baking soda
½ teaspoon salt
1 cup coarsely chopped walnuts
1 milk chocolate candy bar (8 ounces), cut into ½-inch pieces

Preheat oven to 375°F. In large mixer bowl, combine brown sugar, granulated sugar, butter, egg and vanilla. Beat at medium speed, scraping bowl often, until well mixed, 1 to 2 minutes. Add flour, baking soda and salt. Continue beating until well mixed, 1 to 2 minutes. Stir in nuts and chocolate. Drop rounded tablespoonfuls of dough 2 inches apart onto ungreased cookie sheets. Bake for 9 to 11 minutes, or until lightly browned. Cool 1 minute on cookie sheets; remove immediately. Cool completely on wire racks. *Makes about 3 dozen cookies*

Chocolate Chunk Cookies

Ice Cream Cookie Sandwich

2 pints chocolate chip ice cream, softened
1 package DUNCAN HINES® Moist Deluxe Dark Dutch Fudge Cake Mix
½ cup butter or margarine, softened

1. Line bottom of one 9-inch round cake pan with aluminum foil. Spread ice cream in pan; return to freezer until firm. Run knife around edge of pan to loosen ice cream. Remove from pan; wrap in foil and return to freezer.

2. Preheat oven to 350°F. Line bottom of two 9-inch round cake pans with aluminum foil. Place cake mix in large bowl. Add butter; mix thoroughly until crumbs form. Place half the cake mix in each pan; press lightly. Bake 15 minutes or until browned around edges; do not overbake. Cool 10 minutes; remove from pans. Remove foil from cookie layers; cool completely.

3. To assemble, place one cookie layer on serving plate. Top with ice cream. Peel off foil. Place second cookie layer on top. Wrap in foil and freeze 2 hours. To keep longer, store in airtight container. Let stand at room temperature for 5 to 10 minutes before cutting.

Makes 10 to 12 servings

Movietime Crunch Bars

6 cups CAP'N CRUNCH® Cereal, Regular Flavor, divided
1 cup salted peanuts
1 cup raisins
1 cup semi-sweet chocolate pieces
One 14-ounce can sweetened condensed milk

Preheat oven to 350°F. Grease 13×9-inch baking pan. Crush 4 cups of the cereal; spread evenly in bottom of prepared pan. Top with peanuts, raisins, chocolate pieces and remaining 2 cups uncrushed cereal. Drizzle sweetened condensed milk evenly over mixture. Bake 25 to 30 minutes or until golden brown. Cool completely; cut into 2×1½-inch bars. Store tightly covered.

Makes 24 bars

Oatmeal Scotchies

1¼ cups all-purpose flour
1 teaspoon baking soda
½ teaspoon salt
½ teaspoon ground cinnamon
1 cup (2 sticks) margarine or butter, softened
¾ cup granulated sugar
¾ cup firmly packed brown sugar
2 eggs
1 teaspoon vanilla extract *or* grated rind of 1 orange
3 cups QUAKER® Oats (quick or old fashioned, uncooked)
One 12-oz. pkg. (2 cups) NESTLÉ® Toll House® Butterscotch Flavored Morsels

Preheat oven to 375°F. In small bowl, combine flour, baking soda, salt and cinnamon; set aside. In large mixer bowl, beat margarine, granulated sugar, brown sugar, eggs and vanilla extract until creamy. Gradually beat in flour mixture. Stir in oats and butterscotch morsels. Drop by measuring tablespoonfuls onto ungreased cookie sheets.

Bake 7 to 8 minutes for chewy cookies or 9 to 10 minutes for crisp cookies. Let stand on cookie sheets 2 minutes. Remove from cookie sheets; cool completely on wire racks. Store tightly covered.

Makes about 4 dozen cookies

Ice Cream Cookie Sandwich

Peanut Butter Chips and Jelly Bars

1½ cups all-purpose flour
½ cup sugar
¾ teaspoon baking powder
½ cup butter or margarine
1 egg, beaten
¾ cup grape jelly
1⅔ cups (10-ounce package) REESE'S® Peanut Butter Chips, divided

Preheat oven to 375°F. Grease 9-inch square baking pan.

In large bowl, stir together flour, sugar and baking powder; cut in butter with pastry blender or fork until mixture resembles coarse crumbs. Add egg; blend well. Reserve half of mixture; press remaining mixture onto bottom of prepared pan. Spread jelly evenly over crust. Sprinkle with 1 cup chips. Stir together remaining crumb mixture with remaining ⅔ cup chips; sprinkle over top.

Bake 25 to 30 minutes or until lightly browned. Cool completely in pan on wire rack; cut into bars.

Makes about 1½ dozen bars

Polka-Dot Cookies

1 package DUNCAN HINES® Moist Deluxe Yellow Cake Mix
¾ cup BUTTER FLAVOR CRISCO®
2 eggs, separated
1 tablespoon milk
Assorted colored decors

1. Preheat oven to 375°F. Grease cookie sheet.

2. Combine cake mix, BUTTER FLAVOR CRISCO®, egg yolks and milk in large bowl. Shape into 1-inch balls. Beat egg whites slightly in small bowl. Dip balls into egg whites. Roll in colored decors. Bake 8 to 10 minutes or until lightly browned. Cool 1 minute. Remove to cooling rack.   *Makes about 4 dozen cookies*

Spiced Apple-Raisin Cookies

¾ cup butter, softened
1 cup packed brown sugar
1 egg
1 teaspoon vanilla
1½ cups all-purpose flour
1 teaspoon baking powder
½ teaspoon baking soda
½ teaspoon salt
½ teaspoon ground cinnamon
½ teaspoon ground nutmeg
1½ cups quick-cooking oats, uncooked
1 cup finely chopped unpeeled apple
½ cup raisins
½ cup chopped nuts

Preheat oven to 350°F. In large bowl, cream butter. Gradually add brown sugar; beat until light and fluffy. Beat in egg and vanilla. In small bowl, combine flour, baking powder, baking soda, salt and spices. Gradually add flour mixture to creamed mixture; blend well. Stir in oats, apple, raisins and nuts.

Drop dough by rounded teaspoonfuls 2 inches apart onto lightly buttered cookie sheets. Bake 10 to 12 minutes or until lightly browned. Remove to wire racks to cool completely.

Makes 5 dozen cookies

Favorite recipe from **American Dairy Association**

Peanut Butter Chips and Jelly Bars

Lemon Cut-Out Cookies

2¾ cups unsifted flour
1 teaspoon baking powder
½ teaspoon baking soda
¼ teaspoon salt
½ cup margarine or butter, softened
1½ cups sugar
1 egg
⅓ cup REALEMON® Lemon Juice
    from Concentrate
Easy Lemon Icing, optional

Stir together flour, baking powder, baking soda and salt; set aside. In large mixer bowl, beat margarine and sugar until fluffy; beat in egg. Gradually add dry ingredients alternately with REALEMON® brand; mix well (dough will be soft). Chill overnight in refrigerator or 2 hours in freezer.

Preheat oven to 375°F. On well-floured surface, roll out one-third of dough to ⅛-inch thickness; cut with floured cookie cutters. Place 1 inch apart on greased cookie sheets; bake 8 to 10 minutes. Cool. Repeat with remaining dough. Ice and decorate as desired.

Makes 4 to 5 dozen cookies

Easy Lemon Icing: Mix 1¼ cups confectioners' sugar and 2 tablespoons REALEMON® brand until smooth. Add food coloring if desired.

Makes ½ cup icing

Milky Way® Bar Cookies

3 MARS® MILKY WAY® Bars
    (2.15 ounces each), chopped,
    divided
2 tablespoons milk
½ cup butter or margarine, softened
⅓ cup light brown sugar
1 egg
½ teaspoon vanilla extract
1⅔ cups all-purpose flour
½ teaspoon baking soda
¼ teaspoon salt
½ cup chopped walnuts

Lemon Cut-Out Cookies

Preheat oven to 350°F. Stir 1 of the MARS® MILKY WAY® Bars with milk in small saucepan over low heat until melted and smooth; cool. In large mixing bowl, beat butter and brown sugar until creamy. Beat in egg, vanilla and melted MARS® MILKY WAY® Bar mixture. Combine flour, baking soda and salt in small bowl. Stir into chocolate mixture. Add remaining chopped MARS® MILKY WAY® Bars and nuts; stir gently. Drop dough by rounded teaspoonfuls onto ungreased cookie sheets.

Bake 12 to 15 minutes or until cookies are just firm to the touch. Cool on wire racks.

Makes about 2 dozen cookies

Preparation time: 20 minutes
Baking time: 15 minutes

Banana Oatmeal Cookies with Banana Frosting

Cookies
  ¾ cup BUTTER FLAVOR CRISCO®
  1 cup firmly packed brown sugar
  1 egg
  1 cup mashed ripe bananas
     (2 to 3 medium)
 1½ cups all-purpose flour
  1 teaspoon salt
  1 teaspoon cinnamon
  ½ teaspoon baking soda
  ¼ teaspoon nutmeg
 1¾ cups quick oats (not instant or old
     fashioned), uncooked
  ½ cup coarsely chopped walnuts

Banana Frosting
  2 tablespoons BUTTER FLAVOR
     CRISCO®
  ¼ cup mashed ripe banana
  1 teaspoon lemon juice
  2 cups powdered sugar
     Finely chopped walnuts (optional)

1. Preheat oven to 350°F. Grease cookie sheet with BUTTER FLAVOR CRISCO®.

2. For Cookies, combine BUTTER FLAVOR CRISCO® and brown sugar in large bowl. Beat at medium speed of electric mixer until well blended. Beat in egg. Add mashed bananas. Beat until blended.

3. Combine flour, salt, cinnamon, baking soda and nutmeg. Mix into creamed mixture at low speed until blended. Stir in oats and nuts with spoon.

4. Drop 2 level measuring tablespoonfuls of dough into a mound 2 inches apart onto cookie sheet. Repeat with remaining dough.

5. Bake 15 to 17 minutes or until set. Cool 1 minute on cookie sheet. Cool completely on wire rack.

6. For Frosting, combine BUTTER FLAVOR CRISCO®, banana and lemon juice in medium bowl. Beat at medium speed of electric mixer until well blended. Add powdered sugar 1 cup at a time. Beat at low speed after each addition until blended. Frost cooled cookies. Sprinkle with nuts.   *Makes about 5 dozen cookies*

Milk Chocolate Brownies

  ½ cup butter or margarine
  4 MARS® MILKY WAY® Bars
     (2.15 ounces each), sliced
  ¼ cup sugar
  1 teaspoon vanilla extract
  2 eggs
  ¾ cup all-purpose flour
  ¼ teaspoon baking powder
  ¼ teaspoon salt

Preheat oven to 350°F. Stir butter and MARS® MILKY WAY® Bars in medium saucepan over low heat until smooth (use wire whisk if necessary). Remove from heat; stir in sugar and vanilla. Add eggs, one at a time, beating well after each addition. Combine flour, baking powder and salt in small bowl. Stir into chocolate mixture. Spread batter in greased 8×8-inch square pan.

Bake 25 minutes or until edges pull away from sides of pan. Cool completely on wire rack. Sprinkle, if desired, with confectioners' sugar. Cut into squares.
      Makes about 16 brownies

Preparation time: 10 minutes
Baking time: 25 minutes

Buttery Butterscotch Cutouts

Buttery Butterscotch Cutouts

3 cups all-purpose flour
1 cup butterscotch chips, melted
½ cup granulated sugar
½ cup firmly packed brown sugar
1 cup LAND O LAKES® Butter, softened
1 egg
2 tablespoons milk
2 teaspoons vanilla
Powdered sugar for sprinkling

In large mixer bowl, combine flour, melted butterscotch chips, granulated sugar, brown sugar, butter, egg, milk and vanilla. Beat at low speed, scraping bowl often, until well mixed, 1 to 2 minutes. Divide dough into halves. Wrap in waxed paper; refrigerate until firm, 1 to 2 hours.

Preheat oven to 375°F. Roll out dough on well-floured surface to ⅛-inch thickness. Cut out with 2½-inch cookie cutter. Place 1 inch apart on ungreased cookie sheets. Bake for 5 to 8 minutes, or until edges are lightly browned. Remove immediately; cool completely on wire racks. Sprinkle with powdered sugar or decorate as desired.   *Makes about 4 dozen cookies*

Peanut-Butter-Chip Brownies

½ cup butter or margarine
4 squares (1 ounce each) semisweet chocolate
½ cup sugar
2 eggs
1 teaspoon vanilla
½ cup all-purpose flour
1 package (12 ounces) peanut butter chips
1 cup (6 ounces) milk chocolate chips

Preheat oven to 350°F. Butter 8-inch square pan. Melt butter and semisweet chocolate in small heavy saucepan over low heat, stirring just until chocolate melts completely. Remove from heat; cool. Beat sugar and eggs in large bowl until light. Blend in vanilla and chocolate mixture. Stir in flour until blended; fold in peanut butter chips. Spread batter evenly in pan.

Bake 25 to 30 minutes or just until firm and dry in center. Remove from oven; sprinkle milk chocolate chips over top. Place pan on wire rack. When chocolate chips have melted, spread over brownies. Refrigerate until chocolate topping is set. Cut into 2-inch squares.

Makes 16 brownies

Oatmeal Carmelita Bars

¾ cup BUTTER FLAVOR CRISCO®, melted
1½ cups quick oats (not instant or old fashioned), uncooked
¾ cup firmly packed brown sugar
½ cup all-purpose flour
½ cup whole wheat flour
½ teaspoon baking soda
¼ teaspoon cinnamon
1⅓ cups milk chocolate chips
½ cup chopped walnuts
1 jar (12.5 ounces) or ¾ cup caramel ice cream topping
3 tablespoons all-purpose flour

1. Preheat oven to 350°F. Grease bottom and sides of 9×9×2-inch pan with BUTTER FLAVOR CRISCO®.

2. Combine BUTTER FLAVOR CRISCO®, oats, sugar, ½ cup all-purpose flour, whole wheat flour, baking soda and cinnamon in large bowl. Mix at low speed of electric mixer until crumbs form. Reserve ½ cup for topping. Press remaining crumbs into pan.

3. Bake at 350°F for 10 minutes. Sprinkle chocolate chips and nuts over crust.

4. Combine caramel topping and 3 tablespoons all-purpose flour. Stir until well blended. Drizzle over chocolate chips and nuts. Sprinkle reserved crumbs over caramel topping.

5. Return to oven. Bake for 20 to 25 minutes or until golden brown. Run spatula around edge of pan before cooling. Cool completely in pan on wire rack. Cut into 1½×1½-inch squares.

Makes 3 dozen squares

Chewy Fingers

1¼ cups BUTTER FLAVOR CRISCO®
¾ cup firmly packed brown sugar
¾ cup granulated sugar
3 tablespoons maple syrup
1 egg
1 teaspoon vanilla
1¾ cups all-purpose flour
1 teaspoon baking soda
1 teaspoon salt
3 cups quick oats (not instant or old fashioned), uncooked
¾ cup semi-sweet chocolate chips
2 candy bars (2.1 ounces each) Butterfinger™, cut into ¼-inch pieces

1. Preheat oven to 375°F. Grease cookie sheet with BUTTER FLAVOR CRISCO®.

2. Combine BUTTER FLAVOR CRISCO®, brown sugar, granulated sugar, maple syrup, egg and vanilla in large bowl. Beat at medium speed of electric mixer until well blended.

3. Combine flour, baking soda and salt. Mix into creamed mixture at low speed until just blended. Stir in oats, 1 cup at a time, with spoon. Stir in chocolate chips and candy pieces.

4. Form dough into 1-inch balls. Place 2 inches apart on cookie sheet.

5. Bake 7 minutes for chewy cookies, 9 minutes for crisper cookies. Cool 2 minutes on cookie sheet. Remove to cooling rack.

Makes about 6½ dozen cookies

Top to bottom: Oatmeal Carmelita Bars, Chewy Fingers

Granola Bars

Rocky Road Bars

Base

 ⅔ cup **BUTTER FLAVOR CRISCO®**
 4 squares (1 ounce each) **unsweetened chocolate**
 2 cups **granulated sugar**
 4 **eggs**
 1 teaspoon **vanilla**
1¼ cups **all-purpose flour**
 1 teaspoon **baking powder**
 1 teaspoon **salt**

Topping

 ¼ cup **BUTTER FLAVOR CRISCO®**
 1 square (1 ounce) **unsweetened chocolate**
 ⅓ cup **evaporated milk**
 ½ cup **granulated sugar**
1¾ cups **powdered sugar**
 ½ teaspoon **vanilla**
 1 cup **miniature marshmallows**
 ⅓ cup **JIF® Creamy Peanut Butter**

1. Preheat oven to 350°F. Grease 13×9×2-inch baking pan with BUTTER FLAVOR CRISCO®.

2. For Base, combine BUTTER FLAVOR CRISCO® and chocolate in large microwave-safe bowl. Microwave at 50% (MEDIUM). Stir after 1 minute. Repeat until smooth (or melt on rangetop in large saucepan on very low heat). Stir in granulated sugar. Add eggs, one at a time; stirring quickly into hot mixture. Stir in vanilla. Combine flour, baking powder and salt. Stir gradually into chocolate mixture. Spread in prepared pan. Bake 30 minutes or until set.

3. For Topping, start preparation 5 minutes before base is finished baking. Combine BUTTER FLAVOR CRISCO® and chocolate in medium microwave-safe bowl. Microwave at 50% (MEDIUM). Stir after 1 minute. Repeat until smooth (or melt on rangetop in medium saucepan on very low heat). Add evaporated milk and granulated sugar. Beat at low speed of electric mixer until well blended. Add powdered sugar and vanilla; beat until blended.

4. Sprinkle marshmallows over hot baked base. Pour chocolate topping over marshmallows. Drop JIF® Creamy Peanut Butter by teaspoonfuls on top of chocolate mixture. Swirl together using tip of knife. Cover pan immediately with foil. Cool in pan on wire rack. Cut into 2×1½-inch bars. *Makes 36 bars*

Note: If topping becomes too firm to pour, microwave on low to reheat.

Granola Bars

 3 cups **quick-cooking oats, uncooked**
 1 cup **peanuts**
 1 cup **raisins**
 1 cup **sunflower meats**
1½ teaspoons **ground cinnamon**
 1 (14-ounce) can **EAGLE® Brand Sweetened Condensed Milk (NOT evaporated milk)**
 ½ cup **margarine or butter, melted**

Preheat oven to 325°F. Line 15×10-inch pan with foil; grease. In large bowl, combine all ingredients; mix well. Press evenly into prepared pan. Bake 25 to 30 minutes or until golden brown. Cool slightly; remove from pan and peel off foil. Cut into bars. Store loosely covered at room temperature. *Makes 36 to 48 bars*

Lollipop Sugar Cookies

⅔ cup BUTTER FLAVOR CRISCO®
¾ cup sugar
1 tablespoon plus 1 teaspoon milk
1 teaspoon vanilla
1 egg
2 cups all-purpose flour
1½ teaspoons baking powder
¼ teaspoon salt
24 to 30 flat ice cream sticks
   Assorted decorations (baking chips, raisins, red hots, snipped dried fruit, flake coconut, nuts, colored sugar)

1. Combine BUTTER FLAVOR CRISCO®, sugar, milk and vanilla in large bowl. Beat at medium speed of electric mixer until well blended. Beat in egg.

2. Combine flour, baking powder and salt. Mix into creamed mixture at low speed until just blended. Cover and refrigerate for several hours or overnight.

3. Preheat oven to 375°F.

4. Form dough into 1½-inch balls. Push ice cream stick into center of each ball. Place balls 3 inches apart on ungreased cookie sheet. Flatten balls to ½-inch thickness with large, smooth, greased and floured spatula. Decorate as desired. Press decorations into dough.*

5. Bake 8 to 10 minutes or until set. Cool 2 minutes on cookie sheet. Remove to cooling rack.

Makes about 2 dozen cookies

*Cookies can also be painted before baking. Mix 1 egg yolk and ¼ teaspoon water. Divide into 3 small cups. Add 2 to 3 drops food color to each. Stir. Use clean watercolor brushes to paint designs on cookies.

Giant Raisin-Chip Frisbees

1 cup butter or margarine, softened
1 cup packed brown sugar
½ cup granulated sugar
2 eggs
1 teaspoon vanilla
1½ cups all-purpose flour
¼ cup unsweetened cocoa
1 teaspoon baking soda
1 cup (6 ounces) semisweet chocolate chips
¾ cup raisins
¾ cup chopped walnuts

Preheat oven to 350°F. Line cookie sheets with parchment paper or lightly grease and dust with flour.

Cream butter with sugars in large bowl. Add eggs and vanilla; beat until light. Combine flour, cocoa and baking soda in small bowl. Add to creamed mixture with chocolate chips, raisins and walnuts; stir until well blended.

Scoop out about ½ cupful of dough for each cookie. Place on prepared cookie sheets, spacing about 5 inches apart. Using knife dipped in water, smooth balls of dough out to 3½ inches in diameter. Bake 10 to 12 minutes or until golden. Remove to wire racks to cool.

Makes about 16 cookies

Lollipop Sugar Cookies

Graham Peanut Butter Crunchies

1 cup BUTTER FLAVOR CRISCO®
1 cup JIF® Extra Crunchy Peanut
   Butter
1 cup firmly packed brown sugar
1 cup granulated sugar
2 eggs
1 teaspoon vanilla
2 cups all-purpose flour
2 teaspoons baking soda
½ teaspoon salt
1 cup graham cracker crumbs
⅓ cup milk

1. Preheat oven to 350°F. Combine BUTTER FLAVOR CRISCO®, JIF® Extra Crunchy Peanut Butter, brown sugar and granulated sugar in large bowl. Beat at medium speed of electric mixer until well blended. Beat in eggs and vanilla.

2. Combine flour, baking soda and salt. Mix into creamed mixture at low speed until just blended. Stir in crumbs and milk.

3. Form dough into 1-inch balls. Place 2 inches apart on ungreased cookie sheet. Make crisscross pattern on dough with floured fork.

4. Bake 10 to 11 minutes or until edges of cookies are lightly browned. Remove immediately to cooling rack.

Makes about 6 dozen cookies

Crispie Treats

4 cups miniature marshmallows
½ cup peanut butter
¼ cup margarine
⅛ teaspoon salt
4 cups crisp rice cereal
1½ cups "M&M's"® Plain or Peanut
   Chocolate Candies

Melt together marshmallows, peanut butter, margarine and salt in heavy saucepan over low heat, stirring occasionally, until smooth. Pour over combined cereal and candies, tossing lightly until thoroughly coated. With greased fingers, gently shape into 1½-inch balls. Place on waxed paper; cool at room temperature until set.

Makes about 3 dozen cookies

Variation: After cereal mixture is thoroughly coated, press lightly into greased 13×9-inch baking pan. Cool thoroughly; cut into bars.

Makes about 32 bars

Fudgey Microwave Brownies

1¼ cups granulated sugar
½ cup vegetable oil
2 eggs
2 tablespoons light corn syrup
2 teaspoons vanilla extract
1 cup all-purpose flour
½ cup HERSHEY'S® Cocoa
¼ teaspoon baking powder
¼ teaspoon salt
Powdered sugar (optional)

Grease 8-inch square microwave-safe pan. In large bowl stir together granulated sugar, oil, eggs, corn syrup and vanilla. Stir together flour, cocoa, baking powder and salt; add to egg mixture, beating until smooth. Pour batter into prepared pan. Microwave at MEDIUM-HIGH (70%) 3 minutes. Rotate ½ turn; microwave at MEDIUM-HIGH additional 3 minutes. Check for doneness: Brownies begin to pull away from sides of pan and surface has no wet spots. (If brownies are not done, rotate pan ¼ turn; continue to microwave at MEDIUM-HIGH, checking every 30 seconds for doneness. *Do not overcook.*) Place on heatproof surface; allow to stand 20 minutes. Sprinkle powdered sugar over top, if desired. Cut into squares.

Makes about 16 brownies

Fudgey Microwave Brownies

Oatmeal-Chocolate Raisin Cookies

1 cup BUTTER FLAVOR CRISCO®
¾ cup firmly packed dark brown
  sugar
¾ cup granulated sugar
2 eggs
2 tablespoons milk
2 teaspoons vanilla
2 cups all-purpose flour
1 teaspoon baking powder
1 teaspoon baking soda
1 teaspoon salt
2 cups quick oats (not instant or old
  fashioned), uncooked
2 cups chocolate-covered raisins
1 cup coarsely chopped pecans

1. Preheat oven to 350°F. Grease cookie sheet with BUTTER FLAVOR CRISCO®.

2. Combine BUTTER FLAVOR CRISCO®, brown sugar, granulated sugar, eggs, milk and vanilla in large bowl. Beat at medium speed of electric mixer until well blended.

3. Combine flour, baking powder, baking soda and salt. Mix into creamed mixture at low speed until just blended. Stir in oats, raisins and nuts with spoon.

4. Drop rounded teaspoonfuls of dough 2 inches apart onto cookie sheet.

5. Bake 10 to 12 minutes or until set. Remove immediately to cooling rack.

Makes about 6 dozen cookies

Cowboy Macaroons

1 cup BUTTER FLAVOR CRISCO®
1 cup firmly packed brown sugar
1 cup granulated sugar
2 eggs
1 teaspoon vanilla
2 cups all-purpose flour
1 teaspoon baking powder
1 teaspoon salt
½ teaspoon baking soda
2 cups quick oats (not instant or old
  fashioned), uncooked
2 cups corn flakes
1 cup finely chopped pecans
1 cup flake coconut
½ cup maraschino cherries, cut into
  quarters (optional)

1. Preheat oven to 350°F. Grease cookie sheet with BUTTER FLAVOR CRISCO®.

2. Combine BUTTER FLAVOR CRISCO®, brown sugar and granulated sugar in large bowl. Beat at medium speed of electric mixer until well blended. Beat in eggs and vanilla.

3. Combine flour, baking powder, salt and baking soda. Mix into creamed mixture at low speed until just blended. Stir in oats, corn flakes and nuts with spoon. Stir in coconut and cherries.

4. Form dough into 1-inch balls. Place 2 inches apart on cookie sheet.

5. Bake 12 to 14 minutes or until set. Cool 1 minute on cookie sheet. Remove to cooling rack.

Makes about 4 dozen cookies

Buttery Jam Tarts

Buttery Jam Tarts

2½ cups all-purpose flour
½ cup sugar
⅔ cup LAND O LAKES® Butter,
  softened
1 egg
¼ teaspoon baking soda
¼ teaspoon salt
2 tablespoons milk
1 teaspoon almond extract
¾ cup cherry preserves
  Sugar for sprinkling

Preheat oven to 350°F. In large mixer bowl, combine flour, sugar, butter, egg, baking soda, salt, milk and almond extract. Beat at low speed, scraping bowl often, until well mixed, 3 to 4 minutes. Roll out dough, half at a time, on well-floured surface, to ⅛-inch thickness. Cut out with 2½-inch round cookie cutter. Place half the cookies 2 inches apart on ungreased cookie sheets. Make small X or a cutout with a very small cookie cutter in top of each remaining cookie. Place level teaspoonfuls of cherry preserves in center of each cookie. Top each with another cookie; press together around edges with fork. Sprinkle with sugar. Bake for 11 to 13 minutes, or until edges are very lightly browned. Remove immediately; cool on wire racks.   *Makes about 2 dozen cookies*

Granola & Chocolate Chip Cookies

½ cup BUTTER FLAVOR CRISCO®
½ cup firmly packed brown sugar
¼ cup granulated sugar
1 egg
2 tablespoons milk
½ teaspoon vanilla
1¼ cups all-purpose flour
½ teaspoon baking soda
½ teaspoon cinnamon
¼ teaspoon salt
2 cups granola cereal
1 cup semi-sweet chocolate chips

1. Preheat oven to 350°F. Grease cookie sheet with BUTTER FLAVOR CRISCO®.

2. Combine BUTTER FLAVOR CRISCO®, brown sugar, granulated sugar, egg, milk and vanilla in large bowl. Beat at medium speed of electric mixer until well blended.

3. Combine flour, baking soda, cinnamon and salt. Mix into creamed mixture at low speed until just blended. Stir in granola and chocolate chips with spoon. Drop rounded tablespoonfuls of dough 2 inches apart onto cookie sheet.

4. Bake 10 to 12 minutes or until lightly browned but soft in center. Cool 3 minutes on cookie sheet. Remove to cooling rack.
    Makes about 4 dozen cookies

FESTIVE HOLIDAY COOKIES

Chocolate Raspberry Linzer Cookies

2⅓ cups all-purpose flour
1 teaspoon baking powder
½ teaspoon salt
½ teaspoon cinnamon
1 cup granulated sugar
¾ cup (1½ sticks) butter, softened
2 eggs
½ teaspoon almond extract
One 12-oz. pkg. (2 cups) NESTLÉ®
    Toll House® Semi-Sweet
    Chocolate Morsels
6 tablespoons raspberry jam or
    preserves
    Confectioners' sugar

In small bowl, combine flour, baking powder, salt and cinnamon; set aside. In large mixer bowl, beat granulated sugar and butter until creamy. Beat in eggs and almond extract. Gradually beat in flour mixture. Divide dough in half. Wrap in plastic wrap; refrigerate until firm.

Preheat oven to 350°F. On lightly floured board, roll half of dough ⅛ inch thick. Cut with 2½-inch fluted round cookie cutter. Repeat with remaining dough. Cut 1-inch round centers from half of unbaked cookies. Place cookies on ungreased cookie sheets. Reroll dough trimmings.

Bake 8 to 10 minutes or just until set. Let stand on cookie sheets 2 minutes. Remove from cookie sheets; cool completely on wire racks.

Over hot (not boiling) water, melt NESTLÉ® Toll House® Semi-Sweet Chocolate Morsels, stirring until smooth. Spread 1 measuring teaspoonful chocolate on flat side of each whole cookie. Top with ½ measuring teaspoonful raspberry jam. Sprinkle confectioners' sugar on cookies with center holes; place sugar-side up on top of chocolate-jam cookies to form sandwiches.

Makes about 3 dozen cookies

Clockwise from top right:
Chocolate Mint Pinwheels (page 178),
Chocolate Raspberry Linzer Cookies,
New Wave Chocolate Spritz Cookies (page 178)

Chocolate Mint Pinwheels

One 10-oz. pkg. (1½ cups) NESTLÉ®
   Toll House® Mint Flavored Semi-
   Sweet Chocolate Morsels, divided
¾ cup (1½ sticks) butter, softened
⅓ cup sugar
½ teaspoon salt
1 egg
1 teaspoon vanilla extract
2¼ cups all-purpose flour

Over hot (not boiling) water, melt ½ cup NESTLÉ® Toll House® Mint Flavored Semi-Sweet Chocolate Morsels, stirring until smooth. Cool to room temperature; set aside.

In large mixer bowl, beat butter, sugar and salt until creamy. Beat in egg and vanilla extract (mixture may look curdled). Gradually beat in flour. Place 1 cup dough in bowl; blend in melted morsels. Shape each dough into a ball; flatten and wrap with plastic wrap. Refrigerate until firm, about 1½ hours.

Preheat oven to 375°F. Between sheets of waxed paper, roll each ball of dough into a 13×9-inch rectangle. Remove top layers of waxed paper. Invert chocolate dough onto plain dough. Peel off waxed paper. Starting with 13-inch side, roll up jelly-roll style. Cut into ¼-inch-thick slices; place on ungreased cookie sheets.

Bake 7 to 10 minutes. Let stand on cookie sheets 2 minutes. Remove from cookie sheets; cool completely on wire racks.

Over hot (not boiling) water, melt remaining 1 cup NESTLÉ® Toll House® Mint Flavored Semi-Sweet Chocolate Morsels, stirring until smooth. Spread flat side of each cookie with slightly rounded ½ teaspoonful chocolate. Refrigerate 10 minutes to set chocolate.

Makes about 3½ dozen cookies

New Wave Chocolate Spritz Cookies

One 6-oz. pkg. (1 cup) NESTLÉ®
   Toll House® Semi-Sweet
   Chocolate Morsels
1 cup (2 sticks) butter, softened
⅔ cup sugar
1 teaspoon vanilla extract
2 eggs
2½ cups all-purpose flour
One 4-oz. jar cinnamon candies

Over hot (not boiling) water, melt NESTLÉ® Toll House® Semi-Sweet Chocolate Morsels, stirring until smooth; set aside. In large mixer bowl, beat butter, sugar and vanilla extract until creamy. Beat in eggs. Stir in melted morsels. Gradually beat in flour. Cover dough; refrigerate 30 to 45 minutes.

Preheat oven to 400°F. Place dough in cookie press fitted with star tip. Press dough into 2-inch circles on ungreased cookie sheets; decorate with cinnamon candies.

Bake 5 minutes or just until set. Let stand on cookie sheets 2 minutes. Remove from cookie sheets; cool completely on wire racks.   *Makes about 7½ dozen cookies*

Applesauce Fruitcake Bars

Applesauce Fruitcake Bars

1 (14-ounce) can EAGLE® Brand
  Sweetened Condensed Milk
  (NOT evaporated milk)
2 eggs
¼ cup margarine or butter, melted
2 teaspoons vanilla extract
3 cups biscuit baking mix
1 (15-ounce) jar applesauce
1 cup chopped dates
1 (6-ounce) container green candied
  cherries, chopped
1 (6-ounce) container red candied
  cherries, chopped
1 cup chopped nuts
1 cup raisins
  Confectioners' sugar

Preheat oven to 325°F. In large mixer
bowl, beat sweetened condensed milk,
eggs, margarine and vanilla. Stir in
remaining ingredients except
confectioners' sugar; mix well. Spread
evenly into well-greased and floured
15×10-inch baking pan.

Bake 35 to 40 minutes or until wooden
toothpick inserted in center comes out
clean. Cool. Sprinkle with confectioners'
sugar. Cut into bars. Store tightly covered
at room temperature.

Makes 36 to 48 bars

Walnut Christmas Balls

Walnut Christmas Balls

1 cup California walnuts
⅔ cup powdered sugar, divided
1 cup butter or margarine, softened
1 teaspoon vanilla
1¾ cups all-purpose flour
    Chocolate Filling (recipe follows)

Preheat oven to 350°F. In food processor or blender, process walnuts with 2 tablespoons of the sugar until finely ground; set aside. In large bowl, cream butter and remaining sugar. Beat in vanilla. Add flour and ¾ cup of the walnut mixture; beat until blended. Roll dough into about 3 dozen walnut-size balls. Place 2 inches apart on ungreased cookie sheets.

Bake 10 to 12 minutes or until just golden around edges. Remove to wire racks to cool completely. Prepare Chocolate Filling. Place generous teaspoonful of filling on flat side of half the cookies. Top with remaining cookies, flat side down, forming sandwiches. Roll chocolate edges of cookies in remaining ground walnuts.
Makes about 1½ dozen sandwich cookies

Chocolate Filling: Chop 3 squares (1 ounce each) semisweet chocolate into small pieces; place in food processor or blender with ½ teaspoon vanilla. In small saucepan, heat 2 tablespoons *each* butter or margarine and whipping cream over medium heat until hot; pour over chocolate. Process until chocolate is melted, turning machine off and scraping sides as needed. With machine running, gradually add 1 cup powdered sugar; process until smooth.

Favorite recipe from **Walnut Marketing Board**

Holiday Pineapple Cheese Bars

¼ cup PARKAY® Margarine
¼ cup packed brown sugar
¾ cup flour
¾ cup finely chopped macadamia nuts
1 (8 oz.) can crushed pineapple, undrained
1 (8 oz.) pkg. PHILADELPHIA BRAND® Cream Cheese, softened
¼ cup granulated sugar
1 egg
1 cup BAKER'S® ANGEL FLAKE® Coconut
½ cup coarsely chopped macadamia nuts
1 tablespoon PARKAY® Margarine, melted

- Preheat oven to 350°F.
- Beat ¼ cup margarine and brown sugar in small mixing bowl at medium speed with electric mixer until well blended. Add flour and ¾ cup finely chopped nuts; mix well. Press onto bottom of 9-inch square baking pan. Bake 10 minutes. Cool.
- Drain pineapple, reserving 2 tablespoons liquid.
- Beat cream cheese, reserved liquid, granulated sugar and egg in small mixing bowl at medium speed with electric mixer until well blended. Stir in pineapple. Pour over crust.
- Sprinkle with combined coconut, ½ cup coarsely chopped nuts and 1 tablespoon margarine.
- Bake 18 minutes. Cool completely. Cut into bars. *Makes about 1½ dozen bars*

Prep time: 20 minutes
Cooking time: 18 minutes

Slice 'n Bake Pumpkin Cookies

Slice 'n Bake Pumpkin Cookies

3 cups all-purpose flour
1 tablespoon pumpkin pie spice
1 tablespoon ground ginger
½ teaspoon salt
1 cup butter, softened
2 cups granulated sugar
1 cup LIBBY'S® Solid Pack Pumpkin
1 egg yolk

In medium bowl, combine flour, pumpkin pie spice, ginger and salt; set aside. In large mixer bowl, cream butter and sugar, beating until light and fluffy. Add pumpkin and egg yolk; mix well. Blend in dry ingredients; mix well. Cover. Chill dough until firm. Divide dough into 4 parts. Place each part on 14×10-inch sheet of plastic wrap. Wrap loosely around dough. Shape dough into roll 1½ inches in diameter; wrap securely. Freeze 4 hours or until firm.

Preheat oven to 350°F. Grease cookie sheet. Cut rolls into ¼-inch-thick slices. Place on cookie sheet; pat to spread slightly. Reserve some slices to make stems; cut into fourths. Shape and press into top of cookie slice to form stem. Bake 16 to 18 minutes, or until lightly browned.

Cool on wire racks. Decorate in pumpkin design with orange and green frosting.
Makes about 5 dozen cookies

Hint: Spread orange frosting with small spatula; use pastry bag to pipe leaves using leaf frosting tip; vines with smallest frosting tip.

Lebkuchen Spice Spritz Cookies

Cookies
⅔ cup granulated sugar
1 cup LAND O LAKES® Butter, softened
1 egg
1 teaspoon ground cinnamon
1 teaspoon ground nutmeg
½ teaspoon ground allspice
¼ teaspoon ground cloves
2 teaspoons lemon juice
2 cups all-purpose flour

Glaze
1 cup powdered sugar
1 tablespoon milk
½ teaspoon vanilla

For Cookies, in large mixer bowl, combine granulated sugar, butter, egg, cinnamon, nutmeg, allspice, cloves and lemon juice. Beat at medium speed, scraping bowl often, until mixture is light and fluffy. Stir in flour until well mixed. If dough is too soft, cover; refrigerate until firm enough to form cookies.

Preheat oven to 400°F. Place dough into cookie press; form desired shapes 1 inch apart on greased cookie sheets. Bake for 8 to 12 minutes, or until cookie edges are lightly browned. Remove immediately.

For Glaze, in small bowl, stir together all glaze ingredients until smooth. Drizzle glaze on warm cookies.

Makes about 5 dozen cookies

Brandied Buttery Wreaths

Cookies
2¼ cups all-purpose flour
⅓ cup granulated sugar
⅔ cup LAND O LAKES® Butter, softened
1 egg
1 teaspoon ground nutmeg
¼ teaspoon salt
2 tablespoons grated orange peel
2 tablespoons brandy*
⅓ cup chopped maraschino cherries, drained

Glaze
1¼ cups powdered sugar
1 to 2 tablespoons milk
1 tablespoon brandy**
⅛ teaspoon ground nutmeg
Red and green maraschino cherries, cut into pieces or eighths and drained

Preheat oven to 350°F. For Cookies, in large mixer bowl, combine flour, granulated sugar, butter, egg, nutmeg, salt, orange peel and brandy. Beat at low speed, scraping bowl often, until well mixed, 1 to 2 minutes. Stir in cherries. Shape rounded teaspoonfuls of dough into 1-inch balls; form into 5-inch long strips. Shape strips into circles (wreaths), candy canes or leave as strips. Place 2 inches apart on greased cookie sheets. Bake for 8 to 12 minutes, or until edges are lightly browned. Remove immediately.

For Glaze, in small bowl, stir together powdered sugar, milk, brandy and nutmeg until smooth. Frost warm cookies with glaze. Decorate with maraschino cherries.

Makes about 2 dozen cookies

*You may substitute 1 teaspoon brandy extract plus 2 tablespoons water for the 2 tablespoons brandy.

**You may substitute ½ teaspoon brandy extract plus 1 tablespoon water for the 1 tablespoon brandy.

Lebkuchen Spice Spritz Cookies,
Brandied Buttery Wreaths

Peanut Butter Crackles

1½ cups all-purpose flour
1 teaspoon baking soda
⅛ teaspoon salt
½ cup MAZOLA® Margarine,
   softened
½ cup SKIPPY® Creamy or Super
   Chunk Peanut Butter
½ cup granulated sugar
½ cup packed brown sugar
1 egg
1 teaspoon vanilla
   Granulated sugar
   Chocolate candy stars

Preheat oven to 375°F. In small bowl, combine flour, baking soda and salt; set aside. In large bowl, beat margarine and peanut butter until well blended. Beat in sugars until blended. Beat in egg and vanilla. Gradually beat in flour mixture until well mixed. Shape dough into 1-inch balls. Roll in granulated sugar. Place 2 inches apart on ungreased cookie sheets.

Bake 10 minutes or until lightly browned. Remove from oven and quickly press chocolate star firmly into top of each cookie (cookie will crack around edges). Remove to wire racks to cool completely.

Makes about 5 dozen cookies

Crisp Peanut Butter Cookies

2½ cups all-purpose flour
1 teaspoon baking powder
1 teaspoon baking soda
¼ teaspoon salt
1 cup MAZOLA® Margarine,
   softened
1 cup SKIPPY® Creamy or Super
   Chunk Peanut Butter
1 cup granulated sugar
1 cup packed brown sugar
2 eggs
1 teaspoon vanilla
   Granulated sugar

Preheat oven to 350°F. In small bowl, combine flour, baking powder, baking soda and salt; set aside. In large bowl, beat margarine and peanut butter until well blended. Beat in sugars until blended. Beat in eggs and vanilla. Add flour mixture; beat until well blended. If dough is too soft to handle, cover and refrigerate until firm. Shape dough into 1-inch balls. Place 2 inches apart on ungreased cookie sheets. Using back of fork dipped in granulated sugar, flatten balls making crisscross pattern. Bake 12 minutes or until lightly browned. Remove to wire racks to cool completely.

Makes about 6 dozen cookies

Cherry-Coconut Peanut Butter Cookies:
Prepare cookie dough as directed; shape into 1-inch balls. Roll balls in 2⅔ cups (2 3½-ounce cans) flaked coconut. *Do not flatten.* Place red or green candied cherry half in center of each cookie. Bake as directed for 15 minutes.

Makes about 6 dozen cookies

Cloverleaf Cookies: Prepare cookie dough as directed; divide into 3 parts. Stir ⅓ cup miniature semisweet chocolate chips into first part. Stir ⅔ cup miniature semisweet chocolate chips, melted, into second part. Leave third part plain. To form each cookie, shape ½ teaspoon of each dough into a ball. Place balls cloverleaf-style on ungreased cookie sheets, leaving 2 inches between clusters. Bake as directed for 12 minutes. Let cookies cool on cookie sheets for 1 minute. Carefully remove to wire racks; cool completely. *Makes about 5 dozen cookies*

Clockwise from top left: Peanut Butter Cutouts (page 186), Peanut Butter Gingerbread Men, Peanut Butter Chocolate Chip Cookies (page 187), Crisp Peanut Butter Cookies, Santa Lollipop Cookies (page 186), Cherry-Coconut Peanut Butter Cookies, Peanut Butter Crackles, Cloverleaf Cookies, Wreath Cookies (page 186)

Peanut Butter Gingerbread Men

5 cups all-purpose flour
1½ teaspoons ground cinnamon
1 teaspoon baking soda
½ teaspoon ground ginger
¼ teaspoon salt
¾ cup MAZOLA® Margarine, softened
¾ cup SKIPPY® Creamy Peanut Butter
1 cup packed brown sugar
1 cup KARO® Dark Corn Syrup
2 eggs
Frosting for decorating (optional)

In large bowl, combine flour, cinnamon, baking soda, ginger and salt; set aside. In separate large bowl, beat margarine and peanut butter until well blended. Add brown sugar, corn syrup and eggs; beat until smooth. Gradually beat in 2 cups of the dry ingredients. With wooden spoon, beat in remaining dry ingredients, 1 cup at a time, until well blended. Divide dough into thirds. Wrap each portion; refrigerate until firm, at least 1 hour.

Preheat oven to 300°F. Roll out dough, one third at a time, ⅛ inch thick on lightly floured surface. Cut out with 5½-inch gingerbread cutter. Place 2 inches apart on ungreased cookie sheets. Bake 10 to 12 minutes or until very lightly browned. Remove to wire racks to cool completely. If desired, pipe frosting on cookies to make eyes and buttons.

Makes about 2½ dozen cookies

Fruit Burst Cookies

Peanut Butter Cutouts

1½ cups all-purpose flour
¾ teaspoon baking soda
⅛ teaspoon salt
½ cup MAZOLA® Margarine, softened
½ cup SKIPPY® Creamy Peanut Butter
½ cup granulated sugar
½ cup packed brown sugar
1 egg
Colored sugars (optional)

In small bowl, combine flour, baking soda and salt; set aside. In large bowl, beat margarine and peanut butter until well blended. Beat in granulated and brown sugars until blended. Beat in egg. Gradually beat in flour mixture until well mixed. Divide dough into thirds. Wrap each portion; refrigerate until firm, about 3 hours.

Preheat oven to 350°F. Roll out dough, one third at a time, ¼ inch thick on lightly floured surface. Cut out with cookie cutters. Place 2 inches apart on ungreased cookie sheets. If desired, sprinkle cookies with colored sugars. Bake 8 to 10 minutes or until lightly browned. Remove to wire racks to cool.

Makes about 4 dozen cookies

Santa Lollipop Cookies: Prepare cookie dough as above. Place lollipop sticks 3 inches apart on ungreased cookie sheets. Roll out dough ⅛ inch thick. Cut out with 4-inch Santa cookie cutter; place over 1 end of each lollipop stick. Bake as above. Decorate as desired.

Makes about 3 dozen cookies

Wreath Cookies: Prepare cookie dough as above. Roll out dough ⅛-inch thick. Cut out with 2½-inch round cookie cutter with scalloped edge. Using ¾-inch round cookie cutter with scalloped edge, cut out center of cookies. Bake as above. Decorate with red and green candied cherry pieces to form bows.

Makes about 6 dozen cookies

Fruit Burst Cookies

1 cup margarine or butter, softened
¼ cup sugar
1 teaspoon almond extract
2 cups all-purpose flour
½ teaspoon salt
1 cup finely chopped nuts
SMUCKER'S® Simply Fruit

Preheat oven to 400°F. Cream margarine and sugar until light and fluffy. Blend in almond extract. Combine flour and salt; add to margarine mixture and blend well. Shape level tablespoons of dough into balls; roll in nuts. Place 2 inches apart on ungreased cookie sheets; flatten slightly. Indent centers; fill with fruit spread.

Bake 10 to 12 minutes or just until lightly browned. Cool on wire racks.

Makes about 2½ dozen cookies

Cranberry Orange Ricotta Cheese Brownies

Filling
- 1 cup ricotta cheese
- 3 tablespoons whole-berry cranberry sauce
- ¼ cup sugar
- 1 egg
- 2 tablespoons cornstarch
- ¼ to ½ teaspoon grated orange peel
- 4 drops red food color (optional)

Brownie
- ½ cup butter or margarine, melted
- ¾ cup sugar
- 1 teaspoon vanilla extract
- 2 eggs
- ¾ cup all-purpose flour
- ½ cup HERSHEY'S® Cocoa
- ½ teaspoon baking powder
- ½ teaspoon salt

Preheat oven to 350°F. Grease 9-inch square baking pan.

To prepare Filling, in small mixer bowl, beat ricotta cheese, cranberry sauce, sugar, egg and cornstarch until smooth. Stir in orange peel and food color, if desired.

To prepare Brownie, in small bowl, stir together melted butter, sugar and vanilla; add eggs, beating well. Stir together flour, cocoa, baking powder and salt; add to butter mixture, mixing thoroughly. Spread half of chocolate batter in prepared pan. Spread cheese mixture over top. Drop remaining chocolate batter by teaspoonfuls onto cheese mixture.

Bake 40 to 45 minutes or until wooden toothpick inserted in center comes out clean. Cool completely in pan on wire rack. Cut into squares. Refrigerate leftovers. *Makes about 16 brownies*

Cranberry Orange Ricotta Cheese Brownies

Peanut Butter Chocolate Chip Cookies

- 1 cup sugar
- ½ cup SKIPPY® Creamy or Super Chunk Peanut Butter
- ½ cup *undiluted* evaporated milk
- 1 package (6 ounces) semisweet chocolate chips
- 1 cup coarsely chopped nuts

Preheat oven to 325°F. In medium bowl, combine sugar and peanut butter until well blended. Stir in evaporated milk, chips and nuts until well mixed. Drop batter by heaping teaspoonfuls 1½ inches apart onto foil-lined cookie sheets. Spread batter evenly into 2-inch rounds. Bake 18 to 20 minutes or until golden. Cool completely on foil on wire racks. Peel foil from cookies.

Makes about 3½ dozen cookies

Cream Cheese Cutout Cookies

1 cup butter, softened
1 8-ounce package cream cheese, softened
1½ cups sugar
1 egg
1 teaspoon vanilla
½ teaspoon almond extract
3½ cups all-purpose flour
1 teaspoon baking powder
Almond Frosting (recipe follows)
Assorted candies and colored sugars for decoration (optional)

In large bowl, beat butter and cream cheese until well combined. Add sugar; beat until fluffy. Add egg, vanilla and almond extract; beat well. In small bowl, combine flour and baking powder. Add dry ingredients to cream cheese mixture; beat until well mixed. Divide dough in half. Wrap each portion; refrigerate until easy to handle, about 1½ hours.

Preheat oven to 375°F. Roll out dough, half at a time, ⅛ inch thick on lightly floured surface. Cut out with desired cookie cutters. Place 2 inches apart on ungreased cookie sheet. Bake 8 to 10 minutes or until edges are lightly browned. Remove to wire racks; cool completely. Pipe or spread Almond Frosting onto cooled cookies. Garnish with assorted candies and colored sugars, if desired.   *Makes about 7 dozen cookies*

Almond Frosting: In small bowl, beat 2 cups sifted confectioners' sugar, 2 tablespoons softened butter and ¼ teaspoon almond extract until smooth. For piping consistency, beat in 4 to 5 teaspoons milk. For spreading consistency, add a little more milk. If desired, tint with food coloring.

Favorite recipe from **Wisconsin Milk Marketing Board**
© 1992

Lebkuchen Jewels

¾ cup packed brown sugar
1 egg
1 cup honey
1 tablespoon grated lemon peel
1 teaspoon lemon juice
2¾ cups all-purpose flour
1 teaspoon ground nutmeg
1 teaspoon ground cinnamon
1 teaspoon ground cloves
½ teaspoon baking soda
½ teaspoon salt
1 cup SUN-MAID® Golden Raisins
½ cup *each* mixed candied fruits and citron
1 cup chopped DIAMOND® Walnuts
Lemon Glaze (recipe follows)
Candied cherries and citron, for garnish

Preheat oven to 375°F. In large bowl, beat brown sugar and egg until smooth and fluffy. Add honey, lemon peel and juice; beat well. In medium bowl, sift flour with nutmeg, cinnamon, cloves, baking soda and salt; gradually mix into egg-sugar mixture on low speed of electric mixer. Stir in fruits and nuts. Spread batter into greased 15×10-inch jelly-roll pan.

Bake 20 minutes or until lightly browned. Cool slightly in pan; brush with Lemon Glaze. Cool; cut into diamonds. Decorate with candied cherries and slivers of citron, if desired. Store in covered container up to 1 month.   *Makes about 4 dozen cookies*

Lemon Glaze: In small bowl, combine 1 cup sifted powdered sugar with enough lemon juice (1½ to 2 tablespoons) to make thin glaze.

Honey 'n' Spice Cookies

Cookies
- 2 cups all-purpose flour
- ¾ cup granulated sugar
- ¾ cup LAND O LAKES® Butter, softened
- ¼ cup honey
- 1 egg
- ½ teaspoon salt
- ½ teaspoon baking soda
- ½ teaspoon ground nutmeg
- ¼ teaspoon ground cloves
- ½ teaspoon orange extract or vanilla

Glaze
- 1 cup powdered sugar
- 2 tablespoons milk
- 2 teaspoons grated orange peel

Preheat oven to 375°F. For Cookies, in large mixer bowl, combine all cookie ingredients. Beat at low speed, scraping bowl often, until well mixed, 1 to 2 minutes. Drop rounded teaspoonfuls of dough 2 inches apart onto ungreased cookie sheets. Bake for 7 to 10 minutes, or until edges are lightly browned. Remove immediately.

For Glaze, in small bowl, stir together all glaze ingredients. Frost warm cookies with glaze. *Makes about 3 dozen cookies*

Kahlúa® Kisses

- ¾ teaspoon instant coffee powder
- ⅓ cup water
- 1 cup plus 2 tablespoons sugar
- ¼ cup KAHLÚA®
- 3 egg whites
- ¼ teaspoon cream of tartar
- Dash salt

Set oven rack in center of oven. Preheat oven to 200°F. In heavy 2-quart saucepan, dissolve coffee powder in water. Add 1 cup sugar; stir over low heat until sugar dissolves. Do not allow to boil. Stir in KAHLÚA®. Brush down sides of pan with pastry brush dipped frequently into cold water. Bring mixture to a boil over medium heat. Boil until candy thermometer registers about 240° to 242°F, about 15 minutes, adjusting heat if necessary to prevent boiling over. Mixture will be very thick. Remove from heat (temperature will continue to rise).

Immediately beat egg whites with cream of tartar and salt until soft peaks form. Add remaining 2 tablespoons sugar; continue beating until stiff peaks form. Gradually beat hot KAHLÚA® syrup into egg whites, beating after each addition to thoroughly mix. Continue beating 4 to 5 minutes or until meringue is very thick, firm and cooled to lukewarm.

Line baking sheet with foil, shiny side down. Using pastry bag fitted with large (#6) star tip, pipe meringue into kisses about 1½ inches wide at base and 1½ inches high onto baking sheet. Bake 4 hours. Without opening door, turn heat off and let kisses dry in oven about 2 more hours or until crisp. Remove from oven; cool completely on cookie sheet. Store in airtight container up to 1 week.

Makes about 30 cookies

Kahlúa® Kisses

Cherry Oatmeal Cookies

1¼ cups flour
½ teaspoon ground cinnamon
¼ teaspoon salt
¼ teaspoon baking soda
½ cup butter or margarine, softened
1 cup packed dark brown sugar
1 egg
½ teaspoon vanilla
¼ cup milk
1 teaspoon vinegar
1 cup quick-cooking oats, uncooked
½ cup red maraschino cherries,
    chopped
    Red maraschino cherry halves, if
    desired

Preheat oven to 375°F. In small bowl, combine flour, cinnamon, salt and baking soda; set aside. In large mixer bowl, beat butter and brown sugar until creamy. Add egg and vanilla; beat until fluffy. Combine milk and vinegar; add to creamed mixture, beating until blended. Beat in flour mixture until blended. Stir in oats; mix well. Gently fold in chopped cherries.

Drop teaspoonfuls of dough 2 inches apart onto ungreased cookie sheets. Press cherry half into center of each cookie if desired. Bake 10 to 12 minutes or until lightly browned around edges. Cool on wire racks. *Makes about 3 dozen cookies*

Favorite recipe from **National Cherry Foundation**

Fa-La-La-La-Las

1 cup BUTTER FLAVOR CRISCO®
½ cup sugar
1 egg
¾ teaspoon salt
¾ teaspoon vanilla
½ teaspoon almond extract
2¼ cups all-purpose flour
    Assorted colored sugars, decors and
    red cinnamon candies for garnish

Preheat oven to 400°F. Cream BUTTER FLAVOR CRISCO® and sugar in large bowl at medium speed of electric mixer until well blended. Beat in egg, salt, vanilla and almond extract. Stir in flour. Place dough in cookie press. Press into desired shapes 2 inches apart on ungreased cookie sheet. Garnish as desired.

Bake 5 to 7 minutes or until set but not brown. Cool on cookie sheet 1 minute. Remove to cooling rack.
    Makes 4 to 4½ dozen cookies

Note: Dough may be tinted using a few drops of food color. Cookies may also be frosted.

Eggnog Snickerdoodles

Cookies
2¾ cups all-purpose flour
1½ cups sugar
1 cup LAND O LAKES® Butter,
    softened
2 eggs
2 teaspoons cream of tartar
1 teaspoon baking soda
¼ teaspoon salt
½ teaspoon brandy extract
½ teaspoon rum extract

Sugar Mixture
¼ cup sugar or colored sugar
1 teaspoon nutmeg

Preheat oven to 400°F. For Cookies, in large mixer bowl, combine all cookie ingredients. Beat at low speed, scraping bowl often, until well mixed, 2 to 4 minutes.

For Sugar Mixture, in small bowl, stir together sugar and nutmeg. Shape rounded teaspoonfuls of dough into 1-inch balls; roll in sugar mixture. Place 2 inches apart on ungreased cookie sheets. Bake for 8 to 10 minutes, or until edges are lightly browned. Remove; cool on wire racks. *Makes about 4 dozen cookies*

Philly Cream Cheese Cookie Dough

1 (8 oz.) pkg. PHILADELPHIA
  BRAND® Cream Cheese,
  softened
¾ cup butter, softened
1 cup powdered sugar
2¼ cups flour
½ teaspoon baking soda

- Beat cream cheese, butter and sugar in large mixing bowl at medium speed with electric mixer until well blended.
- Add flour and baking soda; mix well.
  Makes 3 cups dough

Chocolate Mint Cutouts:

- Preheat oven to 325°F.
- Add ¼ teaspoon mint extract and few drops green food coloring to 1½ cups Cookie Dough; mix well. Chill 30 minutes.
- On lightly floured surface, roll dough to ⅛-inch thickness; cut with assorted 3-inch cookie cutters. Place on ungreased cookie sheet.
- Bake 10 to 12 minutes or until edges begin to brown. Cool on wire rack.
- Melt ¼ cup mint flavored semi-sweet chocolate chips in small saucepan over low heat, stirring until smooth. Drizzle over cookies.
  Makes about 3 dozen cookies

Prep time: 20 minutes plus chilling
Cooking time: 12 minutes per batch

Snowmen:

- Preheat oven to 325°F.
- Add ¼ teaspoon vanilla to 1½ cups Basic Cookie Dough; mix well. Chill 30 minutes.
- For each snowman, shape dough into two small balls, one slightly larger than the other. Place balls, slightly overlapping, on ungreased cookie sheet; flatten with bottom of glass. Repeat with remaining dough.

- Bake 18 to 20 minutes or until light golden brown. Cool on wire rack.
- Sprinkle each snowman with sifted powdered sugar. Decorate with icing as desired. Cut miniature peanut butter cups in half for hats.
  Makes about 2 dozen cookies

Prep time: 15 minutes plus chilling and decorating
Cooking time: 20 minutes per batch

Choco-Orange Slices:

- Preheat oven to 325°F.
- Add 1½ teaspoons grated orange peel to 1½ cups Cookie Dough; mix well. Shape into 8 × 1½-inch log. Chill 30 minutes.
- Cut log into ¼-inch slices. Place on ungreased cookie sheet.
- Bake 15 to 18 minutes or until edges begin to brown. Cool on wire rack.
- Melt ⅓ cup BAKER'S® Semi-Sweet Real Chocolate Chips with 1 tablespoon orange juice and 1 tablespoon orange flavored liqueur in small saucepan over low heat, stirring until smooth. Dip cookies halfway up into chocolate mixture. *Makes about 2½ dozen cookies*

Prep time: 20 minutes plus chilling
Cooking time: 18 minutes per batch

Preserve Thumbprints:

- Preheat oven to 325°F.
- Add ½ cup chopped pecans and ½ teaspoon vanilla to 1½ cups Cookie Dough; mix well. Chill 30 minutes.
- Shape dough into 1-inch balls. Place on ungreased cookie sheet.
- Indent centers; fill each with 1 teaspoon KRAFT® Preserves.
- Bake 14 to 16 minutes or until light golden brown.
- Cool on wire rack.
  Makes about 3½ dozen cookies

Prep time: 15 minutes plus chilling
Cooking time: 16 minutes per batch

Clockwise from top left:
Preserve Thumbprints, Snowmen,
Choco-Orange Slices, Chocolate Mint Cutouts

Chocolate Candy Thumbprints:

- Preheat oven to 325°F.
- Add ½ cup chopped pecans and ½ teaspoon vanilla to 1½ cups Cookie Dough; mix well. Chill 30 minutes.
- Shape dough into 1-inch balls. Place on ungreased cookie sheet. Indent centers.
- Bake 14 to 16 minutes or until light golden brown.
- Immediately place milk chocolate candy kiss in center of each cookie. Let stand 1 to 2 minutes or until chocolate is slightly softened; spread over top of cookies. Cool on wire rack.

Makes about 3½ dozen cookies

Prep time: 15 minutes plus chilling
Cooking time: 16 minutes per batch

Chocolate Mint Snow-Top Cookies

1½ cups all-purpose flour
1½ teaspoons baking powder
¼ teaspoon salt
One 10-oz. pkg. (1½ cups) NESTLÉ® Toll House® Mint Flavored Semi-Sweet Chocolate Morsels, divided
1 cup granulated sugar
6 tablespoons (¾ stick) butter, softened
1½ teaspoons vanilla extract
2 eggs
Confectioners' sugar

In small bowl, combine flour, baking powder and salt; set aside. Over hot (not boiling) water, melt 1 cup NESTLÉ® Toll House® Mint Flavored Semi-Sweet Chocolate Morsels, stirring until smooth.*

In large mixer bowl, beat granulated sugar and butter until creamy. Add melted NESTLÉ® Toll House® Mint Flavored Semi-Sweet Chocolate Morsels and vanilla extract. Beat in eggs. Gradually beat in flour mixture. Stir in remaining ½ cup NESTLÉ® Toll House® Mint Flavored Semi-Sweet Chocolate Morsels. Wrap dough in plastic wrap; freeze until firm, about 20 minutes.

Preheat oven to 350°F. Shape dough into 1-inch balls; coat with confectioners' sugar. Place on ungreased cookie sheet.

Bake 10 to 12 minutes until tops appear cracked. Let stand 5 minutes on cookie sheet. Remove to wire rack; cool completely. *Makes about 36 cookies*

*Or, microwave morsels in bowl on HIGH power 1 minute; stir. Microwave on HIGH power 30 seconds longer; stir until smooth.

Cookie Cutouts

1 cup margarine, softened
½ cup granulated sugar
½ cup packed light brown sugar
1 egg
1 teaspoon vanilla extract
3 cups all-purpose flour
1 teaspoon baking soda
  Assorted SUNKIST® FUN FRUITS®

In large bowl, with electric mixer, beat margarine with sugars until light and fluffy. Beat in egg and vanilla until smooth. Combine flour with baking soda. Gradually add to margarine mixture, blending well after each addition. Chill at least 2 hours.

Preheat oven to 375°F. On lightly floured board, roll dough ⅛ inch thick; cut into assorted shapes. Decorate with fun fruit snacks. Place on lightly greased cookie sheets; bake 8 to 9 minutes. Cool completely on wire racks. Decorate, if desired, with decorative icing.

Makes about 4½ dozen cookies

For Spicy Cookie Cutouts, increase brown sugar to ¾ cup and add 1½ teaspoons ground cinnamon and 1 teaspoon ground ginger to flour mixture.

For Chocolate Cookie Cutouts, decrease flour to 2¾ cups, increase granulated sugar to 1 cup and add ½ cup unsweetened cocoa powder to flour mixture.

Favorite recipe from **Thomas J. Lipton Company**

Frost on the Pumpkin Cookies

2 cups all-purpose flour
1 teaspoon baking powder
1 teaspoon ground cinnamon
½ teaspoon baking soda
½ teaspoon ground nutmeg
1 cup butter, softened
¾ cup JACK FROST® Granulated Sugar
¾ cup JACK FROST® Brown Sugar (packed)
1 egg
1 cup canned pumpkin
2 teaspoons vanilla
½ cup raisins
½ cup chopped walnuts
  Cream Cheese Frosting (recipe follows)

Preheat oven to 350°F. In small mixing bowl, combine flour, baking powder, cinnamon, baking soda and nutmeg. Set aside. In large mixer bowl, beat butter for 1 minute. Add granulated sugar and brown sugar; beat until fluffy. Add egg, pumpkin and vanilla; beat well. Add dry ingredients to pumpkin mixture; mix until well blended. Stir in raisins and walnuts. Drop dough by teaspoonfuls 2 inches apart onto greased cookie sheet.

Bake 10 to 12 minutes. Cool on cookie sheet 2 minutes; transfer to wire rack to finish cooling. Frost with Cream Cheese Frosting. Garnish with chopped nuts, if desired.   *Makes about 48 cookies*

Cream Cheese Frosting: In medium mixing bowl, beat 3 ounces softened cream cheese, ¼ cup softened butter and 1 teaspoon vanilla until light and fluffy. Gradually add 2 cups JACK FROST® Powdered Sugar, beating until smooth.

Snow Covered Almond Crescents

1 cup (2 sticks) margarine or butter, softened
¾ cup powdered sugar
½ teaspoon almond extract *or* 2 teaspoons vanilla
2 cups all-purpose flour
¼ teaspoon salt (optional)
1 cup QUAKER® Oats (quick or old fashioned, uncooked)
½ cup finely chopped almonds
Powdered sugar

Preheat oven to 325°F. Beat margarine, ¾ cup powdered sugar and almond extract until fluffy. Add flour and salt; mix until well blended. Stir in oats and almonds. Using level measuring tablespoonfuls, shape dough into crescents.

Bake on ungreased cookie sheet 14 to 17 minutes or until bottoms are light golden brown. Remove to wire rack. Generously sift additional powdered sugar over warm cookies. Cool completely. Store tightly covered. *Makes about 4 dozen cookies*

Fruit & Nut Snack Bars

½ cup margarine or butter, softened
1¼ cups granulated sugar
3 eggs
1⅓ cups (one-half jar) NONE SUCH® Ready-to-Use Mincemeat (Regular *or* Brandy & Rum)
½ cup chopped pecans
2 (1-ounce) squares unsweetened chocolate, melted
¼ teaspoon salt
1½ cups unsifted flour
Confectioners' sugar
Pecan halves, optional

Preheat oven to 350°F. In large mixer bowl, beat margarine and granulated sugar until fluffy. Add eggs; beat well. Stir in mincemeat, chopped pecans, chocolate and salt; mix well. Stir in flour. Spread evenly into lightly greased 13×9-inch baking pan. Bake 30 minutes or until wooden toothpick inserted near center comes out clean. Cool. Sprinkle with confectioners' sugar. Cut into bars. Garnish with pecan halves if desired. *Makes 24 to 36 bars*

Crumbly-Topped Lemon Mince Bars

1¼ cups unsifted flour
1 cup firmly packed light brown sugar
1 cup flaked coconut
1 cup finely crushed saltines (about 28)
½ cup margarine or butter, melted
2 teaspoons grated lemon rind
½ teaspoon baking soda
1⅓ cups (one-half jar) NONE SUCH® Ready-to-Use Mincemeat
½ cup chopped nuts, optional

Preheat oven to 350°F. In large bowl, combine all ingredients except mincemeat and nuts; blend well. Reserving *1 cup* crumb mixture, press remainder firmly on bottom of 13×9-inch baking dish. Spoon mincemeat over crust; top with reserved crumbs and nuts if desired. Press down gently. Bake 30 minutes or until edges are lightly browned. Cool completely; cut into bars. *Makes 24 to 36 bars*

Left to right: Fruit & Nut Snack Bars, Crumbly-Topped Lemon Mince Bars, Chocolate Fruit Truffles, Chocolate Spice Cookies

Chocolate Fruit Truffles

2½ cups vanilla wafer crumbs (about 65 wafers)
1 (14-ounce) can EAGLE® Brand Sweetened Condensed Milk (NOT evaporated milk)
1 (9-ounce) package NONE SUCH® Condensed Mincemeat, crumbled
1 cup chopped cashews *or* almonds
½ cup chopped candied cherries
2 tablespoons unsweetened cocoa
½ teaspoon almond extract
  Confectioners' sugar
  Additional candied cherries, optional

In large bowl, combine all ingredients except confectioners' sugar and additional candied cherries until well blended. Chill 4 hours or overnight. Dip hands in confectioners' sugar; shape mixture into 1-inch balls. (Rechill if mixture becomes too soft.) Roll in confectioners' sugar. Place on wax paper-lined baking sheets; chill 2 hours or until firm. Store tightly covered in refrigerator. Garnish with additional candied cherries if desired.

Makes about 6 dozen truffles

Tip: Flavor of these truffles improves after 24 hours. They can be made ahead and stored in refrigerator for several weeks.

Chocolate Spice Cookies

2 cups unsifted flour
½ cup unsweetened cocoa
1 teaspoon baking soda
½ teaspoon salt
1¼ cups sugar
¾ cup shortening
¼ cup margarine or butter, softened
2 eggs
2 teaspoons vanilla extract
1 (9-ounce) package NONE SUCH® Condensed Mincemeat, crumbled
1 cup chopped nuts, optional

Preheat oven to 350°F. Stir together flour, cocoa, baking soda and salt; set aside. In large mixer bowl, beat sugar, shortening and margarine until fluffy. Beat in eggs and vanilla. Add flour mixture; mix well. Stir in mincemeat and nuts if desired. Roll into 1¼-inch balls; place 2 inches apart on ungreased cookie sheets. Flatten slightly.

Bake 8 to 10 minutes or until almost no imprint remains when lightly touched (*do not overbake*). Store tightly covered at room temperature.

Makes about 4 dozen cookies

Brownie Bon Bons

4 squares BAKER'S® Unsweetened
  Chocolate
¾ cup (1½ sticks) margarine or butter
2 cups granulated sugar
4 eggs
1 teaspoon vanilla
1 cup all-purpose flour
  Chocolate Fudge Filling
    (recipe follows)
2 jars (10 ounces each) maraschino
    cherries with stems
  Cherry liqueur (optional)*
½ cup powdered sugar

Preheat oven to 350°F.

Microwave chocolate and margarine in
large microwave-safe bowl on HIGH 2
minutes or until margarine is melted. **Stir
until chocolate is completely melted.**

Stir granulated sugar into melted chocolate
mixture. Mix in eggs and vanilla until well
blended. Stir in flour. Fill greased 1¾×1-
inch miniature muffin cups ⅔ full with
batter.

Bake for 20 minutes or until wooden
toothpick inserted into center comes out
with fudgy crumbs. **Do not overbake.**

Brownie Bon Bons

Cool slightly in muffin pans; loosen edges
with tip of knife. Remove from pans. Turn
each brownie onto waxed-paper-lined tray
while warm. Make ½-inch indentation
into top of each brownie with end of
wooden spoon. Cool completely.

Prepare Chocolate Fudge Filling. Drain
cherries, reserving liquid or liqueur. Let
cherries stand on paper towels to dry.
Combine powdered sugar with enough
reserved liquid to form a thin glaze.

Spoon or pipe about 1 teaspoon Chocolate
Fudge Filling into indentation of each
brownie. Gently press cherry into filling.
Drizzle with powdered sugar glaze.
Makes about 48 bon bons

Prep time: 1 hour
Baking time: 20 minutes

*For liqueur-flavored cherries, drain liquid
from cherries. Do not remove cherries
from jars. Refill jars with liqueur to
completely cover cherries; cover tightly.
Let stand at least 24 hours for best flavor.

Chocolate Fudge Filling

1 package (3 ounces) PHILADELPHIA
    BRAND® Cream Cheese,
    softened
1 teaspoon vanilla
¼ cup light corn syrup
3 squares BAKER'S® Unsweetened
    Chocolate, melted and cooled*
1 cup powdered sugar

Beat cream cheese and vanilla in small
bowl until smooth. Slowly pour in corn
syrup, beating until well blended. Add
chocolate; beat until smooth. Gradually
add powdered sugar, beating until well
blended and smooth.
Makes about 1 cup filling

*Place unwrapped chocolate in microwave-
safe dish. Microwave on HIGH 1½ to 2½
minutes or until almost melted, stirring
after each minute. Stir until completely
melted. *Or*, place chocolate, unwrapped, in
heavy saucepan over very low heat,
stirring constantly, until chocolate is just
melted.

Chocolate Kahlúa® Bears

¼ cup KAHLÚA®
2 squares (1 ounce each) unsweetened chocolate
⅔ cup shortening
1⅔ cups sugar
2 eggs
2 teaspoons vanilla
2 cups sifted all-purpose flour
2 teaspoons baking powder
¾ teaspoon salt
½ teaspoon ground cinnamon
Chocolate Icing (recipe follows)

Add enough water to KAHLÚA® in measuring cup to make ⅓ cup liquid. In small saucepan, melt chocolate over low heat; cool. In large bowl, beat shortening, sugar, eggs and vanilla until light and fluffy. Stir in chocolate. In small bowl, combine flour, baking powder, salt and cinnamon. Add dry ingredients to egg mixture alternately with ⅓ cup liquid. Cover; refrigerate until firm.

Preheat oven to 350°F. Roll out dough, one fourth at a time, about ¼ inch thick on well-floured surface. Cut out with bear-shaped or other cookie cutters. Place 2 inches apart on ungreased cookie sheets.

Bake 8 to 10 minutes. Remove to wire racks to cool. Spread Chocolate Icing in thin, even layer on cookies. Let stand until set; decorate as desired.

Makes about 2½ dozen cookies

Chocolate Icing: In medium saucepan, combine 6 squares (1 ounce each) semisweet chocolate, ⅓ cup butter or margarine, ¼ cup KAHLÚA® and 1 tablespoon light corn syrup. Cook over low heat until chocolate melts, stirring to blend. Add ¾ cup sifted powdered sugar; beat until smooth. If necessary, beat in additional KAHLÚA® to make icing of spreading consistency.

Holiday Chocolate Cookies

½ cup butter or margarine, softened
¾ cup sugar
1 egg
1 teaspoon vanilla
1½ cups unsifted all-purpose flour
⅓ cup HERSHEY'S® Cocoa
½ teaspoon baking powder
½ teaspoon baking soda
¼ teaspoon salt
Decorator's Frosting (recipe follows)

Preheat oven to 325°F. Cream butter, sugar, egg and vanilla in large mixer bowl until light and fluffy. Combine remaining ingredients except Decorator's Frosting; add to creamed mixture, blending well.

Roll small portion of dough at a time on lightly floured surface to ¼-inch thickness. (If too soft, chill dough until firm enough to roll.) Cut out with 2½-inch cutter; place on ungreased cookie sheet. Bake 5 to 7 minutes or until only a slight indentation remains when touched lightly. Cool 1 minute on cookie sheet; cool completely on wire rack. Prepare Decorator's Frosting and decorate with holiday designs or messages.

Makes about 3 dozen cookies

Decorator's Frosting

1½ cups confectioners' sugar
2 tablespoons shortening
2 tablespoons milk
½ teaspoon vanilla
Red, green or yellow food color

Combine all ingredients except food color in small mixer bowl; beat until smooth and of spreading consistency. Tint with drops of food color, blending well.

Pecan Date Bars

Crust
- 1 package DUNCAN HINES® Moist Deluxe White Cake Mix
- 1/3 cup butter or margarine
- 1 egg

Topping
- 1 package (8 ounces) chopped dates
- 1¼ cups chopped pecans
- 1 cup water
- ½ teaspoon vanilla extract
- Confectioners sugar

1. Preheat oven to 350°F. Grease and flour 13×9×2-inch pan.

2. For Crust, cut butter into cake mix with pastry blender or 2 knives until mixture is crumbly. Add egg; stir well (mixture will be crumbly). Pat mixture into bottom of prepared pan.

3. For Topping, combine dates, pecans and water in medium saucepan; bring to a boil. Reduce heat and simmer until mixture thickens, stirring constantly. Remove from heat; stir in vanilla extract. Spread date mixture evenly over crust. Bake 25 to 30 minutes. Cool completely in pan on wire rack. Dust with confectioners sugar.

Makes about 32 bars

Tip: Pecan Date Bars are moist and store well in airtight containers. Dust with confectioners sugar to freshen before serving.

Chocolate Rum Balls

- ½ cup butter or margarine, softened
- 1/3 cup granulated sugar
- 1 egg yolk
- 1 tablespoon dark rum
- 1 teaspoon vanilla
- 1 cup all-purpose flour
- ¼ cup unsweetened cocoa
- 1 cup finely chopped walnuts or pecans
- Powdered sugar

Cream butter, granulated sugar and egg yolk in large bowl until light and fluffy. Blend in rum and vanilla. Stir in flour, cocoa and nuts; mix well. Cover; refrigerate until firm, about 1 hour.

Preheat oven to 350°F. Lightly grease cookie sheets or line with parchment paper. Shape dough into 1-inch balls. Place 2 inches apart on prepared cookie sheets. Bake 15 to 20 minutes or until firm. Remove to wire racks to cool. Roll in powdered sugar.

Makes about 3 dozen cookies

Linzer Bars

- ¾ cup butter or margarine, softened
- ½ cup sugar
- 1 egg
- ½ teaspoon grated lemon peel
- ¼ teaspoon salt
- ½ teaspoon ground cinnamon
- ⅛ teaspoon ground cloves
- 2 cups all-purpose flour
- 1 cup DIAMOND® Walnuts, finely chopped or ground
- 1 cup raspberry or apricot jam

Preheat oven to 325°F. In large bowl, cream butter, sugar, egg, lemon peel, salt and spices. Blend in flour and walnuts. Set aside about ¼ of the dough for lattice top. Pat remaining dough into bottom and about ½ inch up sides of greased 9-inch square pan. Spread with jam. Make pencil-shaped strips of remaining dough, rolling against floured board with palms of hands. Arrange in lattice pattern over top, pressing ends against dough on sides.

Bake 45 minutes or until lightly browned. Cool in pan on wire rack. Cut into bars.

Makes about 2 dozen bars

Preheat ov
mix flour,
orange pe
blender or
orange jui
Knead a fe

Shape dou
each on fl
strip. Twis
Pinch end
wreath; pl
sheets.

In a shallo
remaining
orange pe
egg white
sugar mix

Bake 8 to
browned.
completel
small leaf
wreaths w

1 cup
2 table
so
1 to 2 t
Few

In small b
butter, 1 t
green food
necessary
spreadabl

Favorite recipe

Black Forest Brownies

1 (12-ounce) package semi-sweet
  chocolate chips
¼ cup margarine or butter
2 cups biscuit baking mix
1 (14-ounce) can EAGLE® Brand
  Sweetened Condensed Milk
  (NOT evaporated milk)
1 egg, beaten
1 teaspoon almond extract
½ cup chopped candied cherries
½ cup sliced almonds, toasted

Preheat oven to 350°F. In large saucepan,
over low heat, melt *1 cup* chips with
margarine; remove from heat. Add biscuit
mix, sweetened condensed milk, egg and
extract. Stir in remaining chips and
cherries. Turn into well-greased 13×9-
inch baking pan. Top with almonds.

Bake 20 to 25 minutes or until brownies
begin to pull away from sides of pan.
Cool. Cut into bars. Store tightly covered
at room temperature.

Makes 24 to 36 brownies

*Left to right: Sparkly Cookie Stars,
Black Forest Brownies*

Sparkly Cookie Stars

3½ cups unsifted flour
1 tablespoon baking powder
½ teaspoon salt
1 (14-ounce) can EAGLE® Brand
  Sweetened Condensed Milk
  (NOT evaporated milk)
¾ cup margarine or butter, softened
2 eggs
1 tablespoon vanilla *or* 2 teaspoons
  almond or lemon extract
1 egg white, slightly beaten
  Red and green colored sugars *or*
  colored sprinkles

In small bowl, combine flour, baking
powder and salt. In large mixer bowl, beat
sweetened condensed milk, margarine,
eggs and vanilla until well blended. Add
dry ingredients; mix well. Chill 2 hours.

Preheat oven to 350°F. On floured surface,
knead dough to form smooth ball. Divide
into thirds. On well-floured surface, roll
out each portion to ⅛-inch thickness. Cut
out with floured star cookie cutter. Reroll
as necessary to use all dough. Place 1 inch
apart on greased cookie sheets. Brush with
egg white; sprinkle with sugar.

Bake 7 to 9 minutes or until lightly
browned around edges (*do not overbake*).
Cool completely on wire racks. Store
loosely covered at room temperature.

Makes about 6½ dozen cookies

Note: If desired, cut small stars from
dough and place on top of larger stars.
Proceed as above.

Cocoa Gingerbread Cookies

¼ cup butter or margarine, softened
2 tablespoons shortening
⅓ cup packed brown sugar
¼ cup dark molasses
1 egg
1½ cups all-purpose flour
¼ cup unsweetened cocoa
½ teaspoon baking soda
½ teaspoon ground ginger
½ teaspoon ground cinnamon
¼ teaspoon salt
¼ teaspoon ground nutmeg
⅛ teaspoon ground cloves
Decorator Icing (recipe follows)

Preheat oven to 400°F. Lightly grease cookie sheets or line with parchment paper.

Cream butter, shortening, brown sugar and molasses in large bowl. Add egg; beat until light. Combine flour, cocoa, baking soda, ginger, cinnamon, salt, nutmeg and cloves in small bowl. Blend into creamed mixture until smooth. (If dough is too soft to handle, cover and refrigerate until firm.) Roll out dough ¼ inch thick on lightly floured surface. Cut out with cookie cutters. Place 2 inches apart on prepared cookie sheets.

Bake 8 to 10 minutes or until firm. Remove to wire racks to cool. Prepare Decorator Icing. Spoon into pastry bag fitted with small tip. Decorate cookies with icing.

Makes about 6 dozen cookies

Decorator Icing

1 egg white*
3½ cups powdered sugar
1 teaspoon almond or lemon extract
2 to 3 tablespoons water

Beat egg white in large bowl until frothy. Gradually beat in powdered sugar until blended. Add almond extract and enough water to moisten. Beat until smooth and glossy.

*Use clean, uncracked egg.

Old-Fashioned Harvest Cookies

¾ cup BUTTER FLAVOR CRISCO®
1 cup firmly packed dark brown sugar
1 egg
¾ cup canned solid packed pumpkin (not pumpkin pie filling)
2 tablespoons molasses
1½ cups all-purpose flour
1 teaspoon nutmeg
½ teaspoon baking powder
½ teaspoon baking soda
¼ teaspoon salt
¼ teaspoon cinnamon
2½ cups quick oats (not instant or old fashioned), uncooked
1½ cups finely chopped dates
½ cup chopped walnuts

1. Preheat oven to 350°F. Grease cookie sheet with BUTTER FLAVOR CRISCO®.

2. Combine BUTTER FLAVOR CRISCO® and brown sugar in large bowl. Beat at medium speed of electric mixer until well blended. Beat in egg, pumpkin and molasses.

3. Combine flour, nutmeg, baking powder, baking soda, salt and cinnamon. Mix into creamed mixture at low speed until just blended. Stir in, one at a time, oats, dates and nuts with spoon.

4. Drop rounded tablespoons of dough 2 inches apart onto cookie sheet.

5. Bake 10 to 12 minutes or until bottoms are lightly browned. Cool 2 minutes on cookie sheet. Remove to cooling rack.

Makes about 4 dozen cookies

Choco-Coco Pecan Crisps

½ cup butter or margarine, softened
1 cup packed light brown sugar
1 egg
1 teaspoon vanilla
1½ cups all-purpose flour
⅓ cup unsweetened cocoa
½ teaspoon baking soda
1 cup chopped pecans
1 cup flaked coconut

Cream butter and brown sugar in large bowl until blended. Beat in egg and vanilla. Combine flour, cocoa, baking soda and pecans in small bowl until well blended. Add to creamed mixture, blending until stiff dough is formed.

Sprinkle coconut on work surface. Divide dough into 4 parts. Shape each part into a roll, about 1½ inches in diameter; roll in coconut until thickly coated. Wrap in plastic wrap; refrigerate until firm, at least 1 hour or up to 2 weeks. (For longer storage, freeze up to 6 weeks.)

Preheat oven to 350°F. Line cookie sheets with parchment paper or leave ungreased. Cut rolls into ⅛-inch-thick slices; place 2 inches apart on ungreased cookie sheets. Bake 10 to 13 minutes or until firm, but not overly browned. Remove to wire racks to cool.   *Makes about 6 dozen cookies*

Snowball Cookies

2 cups all-purpose flour
2 cups finely chopped pecans
¼ cup granulated sugar
1 cup LAND O LAKES® Butter, softened
1 teaspoon vanilla
    Powdered sugar for rolling

Preheat oven to 325°F. In large mixer bowl, combine flour, nuts, granulated sugar, butter and vanilla. Beat at low speed, scraping bowl often, until well mixed, 3 to 4 minutes. Shape rounded teaspoonfuls of dough into 1-inch balls. Place on ungreased cookie sheets.

Bake for 18 to 25 minutes, or until very lightly browned. Remove immediately. Roll in powdered sugar while still warm and again when cool.

Makes about 3 dozen cookies

Holiday Fruit Drops

½ cup butter, softened
¾ cup packed brown sugar
1 egg
1¼ cups all-purpose flour
1 teaspoon vanilla
½ teaspoon baking soda
½ teaspoon cinnamon
    Pinch salt
1 cup (8 ounces) diced candied pineapple
1 cup (8 ounces) red and green candied cherries
8 ounces chopped pitted dates
1 cup (6 ounces) semisweet chocolate chips
½ cup whole hazelnuts
½ cup pecan halves
½ cup coarsely chopped walnuts

Preheat oven to 325°F. Lightly grease cookie sheets or line with parchment paper.

Cream butter and brown sugar in large bowl. Beat in egg until light. Mix in flour, vanilla, baking soda, cinnamon and salt. Stir in pineapple, cherries, dates, chocolate chips, hazelnuts, pecans and walnuts. Drop dough by rounded teaspoonfuls 2 inches apart onto prepared cookie sheets.

Bake 15 to 20 minutes or until firm and lightly browned around edges. Remove to wire racks to cool.

Makes about 8 dozen cookies

Note: The hazelnuts, pecans and cherries are not chopped, but left whole.

Left to right: Choco-Coco Pecan Crisps, Holiday Fruit Drops

Nutcracker Sweets

Base
   ⅓ cup BUTTER FLAVOR CRISCO®
   ½ cup JIF® Creamy Peanut Butter
   1½ cups firmly packed brown sugar
   2 eggs
   1½ cups all-purpose flour
   1½ teaspoons baking powder
   ½ teaspoon salt
   ¼ cup milk
   1 teaspoon vanilla

Frosting and Drizzle
   ¼ cup BUTTER FLAVOR CRISCO®
   ⅔ cup JIF® Creamy Peanut Butter
   4 cups (1 pound) confectioners' sugar
   ½ cup milk
   ½ cup semi-sweet chocolate pieces

Preheat oven to 350°F. Grease 15×10×1-inch baking pan.

For Base, cream BUTTER FLAVOR CRISCO® and JIF® Creamy Peanut Butter in large bowl at medium speed of electric mixer. Blend in brown sugar. Beat in eggs one at a time. Beat until creamy. Combine flour, baking powder and salt in small bowl; set aside. Combine milk and vanilla in measuring cup. Add dry ingredients and milk mixture alternately to creamed mixture. Mix at low speed of mixer, scraping sides of bowl frequently. Beat until blended. Spread batter in prepared pan. Bake 18 to 20 minutes. Cool on wire rack.

For Frosting, cream BUTTER FLAVOR CRISCO® and JIF® Creamy Peanut Butter in large bowl at medium speed of electric mixer. Add sugar and milk; beat until fluffy. Spread frosting on cooled cookie base. For Drizzle, melt chocolate pieces on *very* low heat in small saucepan. Drizzle chocolate from end of spoon back and forth over frosting. Cut into 2-inch squares. Refrigerate 15 to 20 minutes until chocolate is firm.

Makes 3 dozen squares

Nutcracker Sweets

Holiday Chocolate Chip Squares

   2¼ cups all-purpose flour
   1¼ teaspoons baking powder
   ¼ teaspoon salt
   1 cup (2 sticks) butter, softened
   1¼ cups sugar
   1 egg
   1 teaspoon vanilla extract
One 12-oz. pkg. (2 cups) NESTLÉ®
      Toll House® Semi-Sweet
      Chocolate Morsels
   1 cup nuts, chopped
   3 6-oz. jars (30) maraschino cherries,
      drained, patted dry
   8 small candy spearmint leaves, cut
      into quarters lengthwise and
      halved

Preheat oven to 350°F. In small bowl, combine flour, baking powder and salt; set aside.

In large mixer bowl, beat butter and sugar until creamy. Beat in egg and vanilla extract. Gradually blend in flour mixture. Stir in NESTLÉ® Toll House® Semi-Sweet Chocolate Morsels and nuts. Spread in greased 13×9-inch baking dish. Press 30 maraschino cherries into dough, spacing them to form 6 rows, 5 cherries per row. Place 2 spearmint ''leaves'' at base of each cherry; press into dough.

Bake 25 to 30 minutes. Cool completely in pan on wire rack. Cut into 2-inch squares.

Makes 30 squares

Orange Pumpkin Bars

Bars
- 1½ cups all-purpose flour
- 1 teaspoon baking powder
- 1 teaspoon pumpkin pie spice
- ½ teaspoon baking soda
- ½ teaspoon salt
- 1 cup solid pack canned pumpkin (not pumpkin pie filling)
- ¾ cup granulated sugar
- ⅔ cup CRISCO® Oil
- 2 eggs
- ¼ cup firmly packed light brown sugar
- 2 tablespoons orange juice
- ½ cup chopped nuts
- ½ cup raisins

Icing
- 1½ cups confectioners' sugar
- 2 tablespoons orange juice
- 2 tablespoons butter or margarine, softened
- ½ teaspoon grated orange peel

1. Preheat oven to 350°F. Grease and flour 12×8-inch baking dish; set aside.

2. For Bars, combine flour, baking powder, pumpkin pie spice, baking soda and salt in medium mixing bowl; set aside.

3. Combine pumpkin, granulated sugar, CRISCO® Oil, eggs, brown sugar and orange juice in large mixing bowl. Beat at low speed of electric mixer until blended, scraping bowl constantly. Add flour mixture. Beat at medium speed until smooth, scraping bowl frequently. Stir in nuts and raisins. Pour into prepared pan.

4. Bake 35 minutes or until center springs back when touched lightly. Cool bars completely in pan on wire rack.

5. For Icing, combine all ingredients. Beat at medium speed of electric mixer until smooth. Spread over cooled base. Cut into bars. *Makes about 24 bars*

Chocolate Biscotti

- 1½ cups all-purpose flour
- ½ cup NESTLÉ® Cocoa
- 1½ teaspoons baking powder
- ½ teaspoon baking soda
- ⅔ cup sugar
- 3 tablespoons butter, softened
- 2 eggs
- ½ teaspoon almond extract
- ½ cup almonds, coarsely chopped

Preheat oven to 350°F. In small bowl, combine flour, NESTLÉ® Cocoa, baking powder and baking soda; set aside. In large mixer bowl, beat sugar, butter, eggs and almond extract until creamy. Gradually beat in flour mixture; stir in almonds. Divide dough in half. Shape into two 12-inch long rolls; flatten slightly. Place in greased 15½×10½-inch baking pan.

Bake 25 minutes. Cool on wire rack 5 minutes. Cut in ½-inch thick slices; return to baking pan, cut-sides down. Bake 20 minutes longer. Cool completely on wire rack. *Makes about 48 cookies*

Chocolate Biscotti

Meringue Kisses

2 egg whites
¼ teaspoon cream of tartar
½ cup sugar
Variation Ingredients* (optional)

Preheat oven to 225°F. In small mixer bowl, beat egg whites with cream of tartar at high speed until foamy. Add sugar, 2 tablespoons at a time, beating constantly until sugar is dissolved and whites are glossy and stand in stiff peaks. If desired, beat or fold in Variation Ingredients. Drop meringue by rounded teaspoonfuls or pipe through pastry tube 1 inch apart onto greased or waxed-paper-lined cookie sheets.

Bake until firm, about 1 hour. Turn off oven. Let cookies stand in oven with door closed until cool, dry and crisp, at least 1 additional hour. Store in tightly sealed container. *Makes 4 to 5 dozen cookies*

*Variation Ingredients: Amounts listed are for 1 batch of cookies. To make 2 variations at a time, divide meringue mixture equally between 2 bowls. Beat or fold into each bowl half of the amounts listed for each variation.

Chocolate: Beat in ¼ cup unsweetened cocoa and 1 teaspoon vanilla.

Citrus: Beat in 1 tablespoon grated orange peel, ¼ teaspoon lemon extract and a few drops yellow food coloring.

Mint: Beat in ¼ teaspoon mint extract and a few drops green food coloring.

Rocky Road: Beat in 1 teaspoon vanilla. Fold in ½ cup semisweet chocolate chips and ½ cup chopped nuts.

Cherry-Almond: Fold in ½ cup chopped, drained maraschino cherries and ½ cup chopped almonds.

Favorite recipe from **American Egg Board**

Chocolate-Frosted Lebkuchen

4 eggs
1 cup sugar
1½ cups all-purpose flour
1 cup (6 ounces) pulverized almonds*
⅓ cup candied lemon peel, finely chopped
⅓ cup candied orange peel, finely chopped
1½ teaspoons ground cinnamon
1 teaspoon grated lemon rind
½ teaspoon ground cardamom
½ teaspoon ground nutmeg
¼ teaspoon ground cloves
Bittersweet Glaze (recipe follows)

In large bowl of electric mixer, combine eggs and sugar. Beat at high speed for 10 minutes. Meanwhile, in separate bowl, combine flour, almonds, lemon and orange peels, cinnamon, lemon rind, cardamom, nutmeg and cloves. Blend in egg mixture, stirring until evenly mixed. Cover; refrigerate 12 hours or overnight.

Preheat oven to 350°F. Grease cookie sheets and dust with flour or line with parchment paper. Drop dough by rounded teaspoonfuls 2 inches apart onto prepared cookie sheets. Bake 8 to 10 minutes or until just barely browned. Do not overbake. Remove to wire racks. While cookies bake, prepare Bittersweet Glaze. Spread over tops of warm cookies using pastry brush. Cool until glaze is set. Store in airtight container.
Makes about 5 dozen cookies

*To pulverize almonds, place in food processor or blender. Process until thoroughly ground with a dry, not pasty, texture.

Bittersweet Glaze

3 squares (1 ounce each) bittersweet or semisweet chocolate, chopped
1 tablespoon butter or margarine

Melt chocolate and butter in small bowl over hot water. Stir until smooth.

Gingerbread Men

Gingerbread Men

1 package DUNCAN HINES® Moist
　　Deluxe Spice Cake Mix
½ cup all-purpose flour
2 eggs
⅓ cup CRISCO® Oil or
　　PURITAN® Oil
⅓ cup dark molasses
2 teaspoons ground ginger
　　Raisins for decorations

1. Combine cake mix, flour, eggs, oil,
molasses and ginger in large bowl
(mixture will be soft). Refrigerate 2 hours.

2. Preheat oven to 375°F.

3. Roll dough to ¼-inch thickness on
lightly floured surface. Cut out with
gingerbread man cookie cutter. Place on
ungreased cookie sheet 3 inches apart.
Decorate with raisins.

4. Bake 8 to 10 minutes or until edges start
to brown. Remove immediately to cooling
rack.

Makes 12 to 14 six-inch tall gingerbread men

Tip: To make holes for hanging cookie
ornaments, push straw or meat skewer in
head section of cookies before baking.

Cranberry Walnut Bars

Bar Cookie Crust (recipe follows)
4 eggs
1⅓ cups KARO® Light or Dark Corn
　　Syrup
1 cup sugar
3 tablespoons MAZOLA® Margarine,
　　melted
2 cups coarsely chopped fresh or
　　frozen cranberries
1 cup chopped walnuts

Preheat oven to 350°F. Prepare Bar Cookie
Crust according to recipe directions. In
large bowl beat eggs, corn syrup, sugar
and margarine until well blended. Stir in
cranberries and walnuts. Pour over hot
crust; spread evenly. Bake 25 to 30
minutes or until set. Cool completely on
wire rack before cutting.

Makes about 48 bars

Prep Time: 30 minutes
Bake Time: 30 minutes, plus cooling

Bar Cookie Crust

MAZOLA® No Stick cooking spray
2½ cups flour
1 cup cold MAZOLA® Margarine, cut
　　in pieces
½ cup confectioners sugar
¼ teaspoon salt

Preheat oven to 350°F. Spray 15×10×1-
inch baking pan with cooking spray. In
large bowl with mixer at medium speed,
beat flour, margarine, sugar and salt until
mixture resembles coarse crumbs; press
firmly and evenly into prepared pan. Bake
20 minutes or until golden brown.

Star Christmas Tree Cookies

Cookies
- 1 package DUNCAN HINES® Moist Deluxe Yellow or Devil's Food Cake Mix
- ½ cup CRISCO® Shortening
- ⅓ cup butter or margarine, softened
- 2 egg yolks
- 1 teaspoon vanilla extract
- 1 tablespoon water

Frosting
- 1 container (16 ounces) DUNCAN HINES® Vanilla Frosting
- Green food coloring
- Red and green sugar crystals, for garnish
- Assorted colored candies and decors, for garnish

1. Preheat oven to 375°F.

2. For Cookies, combine shortening, butter, egg yolks and vanilla extract. Blend in cake mix gradually. Add 1 teaspoonful water at a time until dough is rolling consistency. Divide dough into 4 balls. Flatten one ball with hand; roll to ⅛-inch thickness on lightly floured surface. Cut with graduated sized star cookie cutters. Repeat using remaining dough. Bake large cookies together on ungreased cookie sheet 6 to 8 minutes or until edges are light golden brown. Cool cookies 1 minute; remove from cookie sheet. Repeat with smaller cookies, testing for doneness at minimum bake time.

3. For Frosting, tint vanilla frosting with green food coloring. Frost cookies and stack beginning with largest cookies on bottom and ending with smallest cookies on top. Rotate cookies when stacking to alternate corners. Decorate as desired with sugar crystals, colored candies and decors.

Makes 2 to 3 dozen cookies

Tip: If assorted star cookie cutters are not available, use your favorite assorted cookie cutters. Stack cookies into one large "tree" or stack into smaller trees using 3 to 5 cookies per tree.

Oatmeal Cranberry-Nut Cookies

- ¾ cup BUTTER FLAVOR CRISCO®
- 1 cup firmly packed dark brown sugar
- ¼ cup dark molasses
- 1 egg
- 2 tablespoons milk
- 1½ teaspoons vanilla
- 1 cup all-purpose flour
- 1¼ teaspoons cinnamon
- ½ teaspoon baking soda
- ½ teaspoon salt
- ¼ teaspoon allspice
- 1 cup crushed berry cranberry sauce
- ½ cup sliced almonds, broken into pieces
- 3 cups quick oats (not instant or old fashioned), uncooked

1. Preheat oven to 375°F. Grease cookie sheet with BUTTER FLAVOR CRISCO®

2. Combine BUTTER FLAVOR CRISCO® and brown sugar in large bowl. Beat at medium speed of electric mixer until well blended. Beat in molasses, egg, milk and vanilla.

3. Combine flour, cinnamon, baking soda, salt and allspice. Mix into creamed mixture at low speed until just blended. Stir in cranberry sauce and nuts. Stir in oats with spoon.

4. Drop tablespoonfuls of dough 2 inches apart onto cookie sheet.

5. Bake for 12 minutes or until set. Cool 2 minutes on cookie sheet. Remove to cooling rack.

Makes about 4 dozen cookies

Star Christmas Tree Cookies

Acknowledgments

*The publishers would like to thank the companies
and organizations listed below for the use
of their recipes in this book.*

Almond Board of California
American Dairy Association
American Egg Board
Arm & Hammer Division,
    Church & Dwight Co., Inc.
Best Foods, a division of CPC International
Blue Diamond Growers
Borden Kitchens, Borden, Inc.
California Apricot Advisory Board
Carnation Company
Checkerboard Kitchens,
    Ralston Purina Company
Diamond Walnut Growers, Inc.
Dole Food Company
Florida Department of Citrus
Hershey Chocolate U.S.A.
Kahlúa Liqueur
Kraft General Foods, Inc.
Land O'Lakes, Inc.
Leaf, Inc.
Libby's, Nestlé Food Company

M & M/Mars through Mateer Marketing
    Communication
Mott's U.S.A., a division of Cadbury
    Beverages Inc.
Nabisco Foods Company
National Cherry Foundation
Nestlé Chocolate and Confection Company
Oregon Washington California Pear Bureau
Pollio Dairy Products Corporation
The Procter & Gamble Company, Inc.
The Quaker Oats Company
Refined Sugars Incorporated
Roman Meal Hot Cereals
The J.M. Smucker Company
Sokol and Company
Sunkist Growers, Inc.
Sun-Maid Growers of California
Thomas J. Lipton Company
USA Rice Council
Walnut Marketing Board
Wisconsin Milk Marketing Board

Photo Credits

*The publishers would like to thank the companies
and organizations listed below for the use
of their photographs in this book.*

Almond Board of California
Best Foods, a division of CPC International
Blue Diamond Growers
Borden Kitchens, Borden, Inc.
California Apricot Advisory Board
Dole Food Company
Hershey Chocolate U.S.A.
Kahlúa Liqueur
Kraft General Foods, Inc.
Land O'Lakes, Inc.
Leaf, Inc.
Libby's, Nestlé Food Company

Mott's U.S.A., a division of Cadbury
    Beverages Inc.
Nabisco Foods Company
Nestlé Chocolate and Confection Company
The Procter & Gamble Company, Inc.
The J.M. Smucker Company
Sokol and Company
Thomas J. Lipton Company
USA Rice Council
Walnut Marketing Board
Wisconsin Milk Marketing Board

INDEX

A

Almonds
Almond Chinese Chews, 62
Almond Chocolate Chip Cookies, 29
Almond Cream Cheese Cookies, 112
Almond Frosting, 188
Almond Macaroon Brownies, 40
Almond Raspberry Thumbprint
    Cookies, 92
Almond Rice Madeleines, 125
Almond Shortbread Bars, 66
Almond Stars, 124
Austrian Tea Cookies, 144
Black Forest Brownies, 204
Buttery Caramel Crisps, 75
Chocolate Almond Brownies, 43
Chocolate Almond Buttons, 98
Chocolate-Dipped Almond Horns,
    130
Chocolate-Frosted Almond
    Shortbread, 72
Chocolate-Frosted Lebkuchen, 210
Crisp 'n' Crunchy Almond Coconut
    Bars, 79
Double Almond Butter Cookies, 92
Double Chocolate Banana Cookies,
    156
Double Chocolate Raspberry Bars, 50
Double Nut Chocolate Chip Cookies,
    20
Filled Almond Crisps, 141
Health Nut Almond Oaties, 114
Macaroon Almond Crumb Bars, 64
Mocha Almond Bars, 55
Nut Cream Filling, 161
Oatmeal Cranberry-Nut Cookies, 213
Pineapple Raisin Jumbles, 94
Snow Covered Almond Crescents, 196
White Chocolate & Almond Brownies,
    32
Any-Way-You-Like 'em Cookies, 100
Apples
Apple Pie Bars, 53
Applesauce Fruitcake Bars, 179
Apple Spice Cookies, 112

Apples (*continued*)
Breakfast Bars to Go, 70
Granola Apple Bars, 151
Granola Apple Cookies, 90
Oatmeal Apple Cookies, 107
Spice 'n' Easy Apple Raisin Bars, 75
Spiced Apple-Raisin Cookies, 164
Apricots
Apricot Oatmeal Bars, 80
Apricot-Pecan Tassies, 127
Apricot Pinwheel Slices, 142
California Apricot Power Bars, 76
Chocolate Chip Whole Wheat
    Cookies, 22
Cinnamon-Apricot Tart Oatmeal
    Cookies, 112
Scrumptious Chocolate Fruit and Nut
    Cookies, 29
Austrian Tea Cookies, 144

B

Bananas
Banana Chip Bars, 153
Banana Cream Sandwich Cookies,
    141
Banana Oatmeal Cookies with Banana
    Frosting, 166
Banana Orange Softies, 110
Banana Split Bars, 60
Double Chocolate Banana Cookies,
    156
San Francisco Cookies, 17
Bar Cookie Crust, 211
Bar Cookies (*see also* **Brownies**)
Almond Chinese Chews, 62
Almond Shortbread Bars, 66
Apple Pie Bars, 53
Applesauce Fruitcake Bars, 179
Apricot Oatmeal Bars, 80
baking, 7
Banana Chip Bars, 153
Banana Split Bars, 60
Breakfast Bars to Go, 70

Bar Cookies (*continued*)
Butterscotch Bars, 78
Butterscotch Peanut Bars, 50
Buttery Caramel Crisps, 75
California Apricot Power Bars, 76
Caramel Chocolate Pecan Bars, 56
Caramel Granola Bars, 56
Cherry Date Sparkle Bars, 77
Chewy Bar Cookies, 46
Choco-Coconut Layer Bars, 76
Chocolate Caramel Nut Bars, 76
Chocolate Cheese Ripple Bars, 49
Chocolate-Frosted Almond
    Shortbread, 72
Chocolate Macadamia Bars, 54
Chocolate Meringue Peanut Squares,
    73
Chocolate Mint Bars, 61
Chocolate Peanut Buddy Bars, 153
Chocolate Peanut Butter Bars, 58
Chocolate Pecan Pie Bars, 48
Chocolatey Peanut Butter Goodies,
    148
Cocoa Shortbread, 71
"Cordially Yours" Chocolate Chip
    Bars, 70
Cranberry Walnut Bars, 211
Creative Pan Cookies, 62
Crisp 'n' Crunchy Almond Coconut
    Bars, 79
Crispy Chocolate Logs, 57
Crumbly-Topped Lemon Mince Bars,
    196
Crunchy Peanut Brickle Bars, 67
Double Chocolate Crispy Bars, 54
Double Chocolate Fantasy Bars, 65
Double Chocolate Raspberry Bars, 50
Double Peanut-Choco Bars, 60
Frosted Honey Bars, 80
Fruit and Chocolate Dream Bars, 48
Fruit & Nut Snack Bars, 196
Fudgy Cookie Wedges, 53
Glazed Rum Raisin Bars, 81
Granola Apple Bars, 151
Granola Bars, 170
Heath® Bars, 71

Bar Cookies (*continued*)

Holiday Chocolate Chip Squares, 208
Holiday Pineapple Cheese Bars, 180
Kahlúa® Chocolate Nut Squares, 72
Layered Chocolate Cheese Bars, 58
Layered Lemon Crumb Bars, 61
Lebkuchen Jewels, 188
Lemon Chocolate Bars, 75
Lemon Iced Ambrosia Bars, 57
Linzer Bars, 200
Macaroon Almond Crumb Bars, 64
Magic Rainbow Cookie Bars, 51
Mississippi Mud Bars, 66
Mocha Almond Bars, 55
Movietime Crunch Bars, 163
Naomi's Revel Bars, 55
Nutcracker Sweets, 208
Oatmeal Caramel Bars, 73
Oatmeal Carmelita Bars, 168
Orange Butter Cream Squares, 63
Orange Pumpkin Bars, 209
Pan Cookies, 10
Peanut Butter Bars, 68
Peanut Butter Chips and Jelly Bars, 164
Pear Blondies, 51
Pecan Date Bars, 200
Pecan Pie Bars, 71
Pineapple Walnut Bars, 67
preparation, 5
Prune Bars, 63
Quick and Easy Nutty Cheese Bars, 49
Raspberry Meringue Bars, 64
Rocky Road Bars, 170
Sour Cream Cherry Bars, 77
Spice 'n' Easy Apple Raisin Bars, 75
storing, 7
Strawberry Wonders, 78
Teentime Dream Bars, 157
Toffee Bars, 64
Toffee-Bran Bars, 46
Zesty Fresh Lemon Bars, 81
Bavarian Cookie Wreaths, 202
Beth's Chocolate Oatmeal Cookies, 115
Bittersweet Brownies, 35
Bittersweet Glaze, 210
Black Forest Brownies, 204
Black Forest Oatmeal Fancies, 21
Black Walnut Refrigerator Cookies, 109
Blonde Brickle Brownies, 41
Brandied Buttery Wreaths, 183
Brandy Lace Cookies, 118
Breakfast Bars to Go, 70
Brown Butter Icing, 72
Brownie Cookie Bites, 25
Brownies
Almond Macaroon Brownies, 40
Bittersweet Brownies, 35
Black Forest Brownies, 204
Blonde Brickle Brownies, 41
Brownie Bon Bons, 198
Brownie Fudge, 32
Cappucino Bon Bons, 33
Caramel-Layered Brownies, 44
Cheesecake Topped Brownies, 42

Brownies (*continued*)

Chewy Chocolate Brownies, 35
Chocolate Almond Brownies, 43
Chocolate Cherry Brownies, 154
Chocolate-Mint Brownies, 36
Cranberry Orange Ricotta Cheese
Brownies, 187
Crunch Crowned Brownies, 161
Deep Dish Brownies, 36
Double Fudge Saucepan Brownies, 40
Fudgey Microwave Brownies, 173
Fudgy Brownie Bars, 41
Honey Brownies, 160
Madison Avenue Mocha Brownies, 37
Marbled Brownies, 160
Milk Chocolate Brownies, 166
One Bowl Brownies, 30
Our Best Bran Brownies, 43
Peanut-Butter-Chip Brownies, 167
Peanut Butter Swirl Brownies, 30
Peanut-Layered Brownies, 38
Raspberry Fudge Brownies, 37
Rocky Road Brownies, 30
Rocky Road Fudge Brownies, 44
Semi-Sweet Chocolate Brownies, 43
Sour Cream Brownies, 33
Toffee Brownie Bars, 35
Ultimate Chocolate Brownies, 45
Walnut Crunch Brownies, 38
White Chocolate & Almond Brownies,
32
Buttermilk
Double Mint Chocolate Cookies, 91
Ivory Chip Strawberry Fudge Drops,
25
Kentucky Oatmeal-Jam Cookies, 102
Nutty Clusters, 93
Butterscotch
Butterscotch Bars, 78
Butterscotch Frosting, 50
Butterscotch Peanut Bars, 50
Buttery Butterscotch Cutouts, 167
Oatmeal Scotch Chippers, 16
Oatmeal Scotchies, 163
Peanut Butter Sunshine Cookies, 20
Buttery Butterscotch Cutouts, 167
Buttery Caramel Crisps, 75
Buttery Jam Tarts, 175

C

California Apricot Power Bars, 76
Cappucino Bon Bons, 33
Caramel
Caramel-Chocolate Delights, 18
Caramel Chocolate Pecan Bars, 56
Caramel Filling, 126
Caramel Granola Bars, 56
Caramel-Layered Brownies, 44
Choco-Caramel Delights, 126
Chocolate Caramel Nut Bars, 76
Chocolate-Caramel Sugar Cookies, 96

Caramel (*continued*)

Oatmeal Caramel Bars, 73
Oatmeal Carmelita Bars, 168
Cheesecake Topped Brownies, 42
Cherries
Applesauce Fruitcake Bars, 179
Banana Split Bars, 60
Black Forest Brownies, 204
Black Forest Oatmeal Fancies, 21
Brandied Buttery Wreaths, 183
Brownie Bon Bons, 198
Cherry-Coconut Peanut Butter
Cookies, 184
Cherry Date Sparkle Bars, 77
Cherry Oatmeal Cookies, 191
Chewy Cherry Chocolate Chip
Cookies, 16
Chocolate Cherry Brownies, 154
Chocolate Cherry Cookies, 136
"Cordially Yours" Chocolate Chip
Bars, 70
Double Chocolate Cherry Cookies,
108
Holiday Chocolate Chip Squares, 208
Holiday Fruit Drops, 206
Holiday Hideaways, 202
Sour Cream Cherry Bars, 77
Spumoni Bars, 129
Chewy Bar Cookies, 46
Chewy Cherry Chocolate Chip Cookies,
16
Chewy Chocolate Brownies, 35
Chewy Fingers, 168
Choco-Caramel Delights, 126
Choco-Coconut Layer Bars, 57
Choco-Coco Pecan Crisps, 206
Chocolate (*see also* **Brownies; Chocolate
Chips; Cocoa**)
Almond Stars, 124
Beth's Chocolate Oatmeal Cookies,
115
Bittersweet Glaze, 210
Brownie Cookie Bites, 25
Brown-Sugar Icing, 101
Butterscotch Bars, 78
Caramel Chocolate Pecan Bars, 56
Choco-Caramel Delights, 126
Choco-Coconut Layer Bars, 57
Chocolate Almond Buttons, 98
Chocolate Candy Thumbprints, 193
Chocolate Caramel Nut Bars, 76
Chocolate-Caramel Sugar Cookies, 96
Chocolate Cheese Ripple Bars, 49
Chocolate Cherry Cookies, 136
Chocolate Chip Glaze, 118
Chocolate-Coconut Cookies, 107
Chocolate-Dipped Almond Horns,
130
Chocolate-Dipped Oat Cookies, 110
Chocolate Dream Frosting, 68
Chocolate Filling, 180
Chocolate-Frosted Marshmallow
Cookies, 99
Chocolate Fudge Filling, 198

Chocolate (*continued*)
Chocolate Glaze, 36
Chocolate Icing, 199
Chocolate Kahlúa® Bears, 199
Chocolate Kiss Cookies, 89
Chocolate Lace Cornucopias, 131
Chocolate Macadamia Bars, 54
Chocolate Mint Bars, 61
Chocolate Mint Cutouts, 192
Chocolate Mint Pinwheels, 178
Chocolate Oat Chewies, 103
Chocolate-Orange Chip Cookies, 22
Chocolate Peanut Butter Bars, 58
Chocolate Peanut Butter Cookies, 156
Chocolate-Peanut Cookies, 82
Chocolate Pecan Pie Bars, 48
Chocolate Pistachio Fingers, 136
Chocolate Pixies, 109
Chocolate Raspberry Linzer Cookies, 176
Chocolate Spritz, 136
Chocolate Sugar Cookies, 96
Chocolate-Topped Linzer Cookies, 132
Chocolatey Peanut Butter Goodies, 148
Choco-Orange Slices, 192
Cloverleaf Cookies, 184
Crispy Chocolate Logs, 57
Date Fudge Cookies, 101
Double Chocolate Cookies, 22
Double Chocolate Crispy Bars, 54
Double Chocolate Fantasy Bars, 65
Easy Chocolate Icing, 93
Fruit and Chocolate Dream Bars, 48
Fruit & Nut Snack Bars, 196
Fudge Topping, 32
Fudgy Chocolate Glaze, 119
Fudgy Cookie Wedges, 53
German Chocolate Oatmeal Cookies, 85
Half-Hearted Valentine Cookies, 129
Holiday Hideaways, 202
Ice Cream Cookie Sandwich, 163
Ice Cream Sandwiches, 100
Jam-Filled Chocolate Sugar Cookies, 96
Layered Chocolate Cheese Bars, 58
Macaroon Almond Crumb Bars, 64
Macaroon Kiss Cookies, 102
melting, 4
Melting Moments, 134
Microwave Chocolate Chip Glaze, 68
Milk Chocolate Florentine Cookies, 126
Milky Way® Bar Cookies, 165
Mocha Pecan Pinwheels, 137
Naomi's Revel Bars, 55
New Wave Chocolate Spritz Cookies, 178
Nutty Clusters, 93
Orange Butter Cream Squares, 63
Peanut Blossoms, 100
Peanut Butter Crackles, 184
Peanut Butter Kisses, 115

Chocolate (*continued*)
Pinwheel Cookies, 143
Quick Chocolate Drizzle, 75
Raspberry-Filled Chocolate Ravioli, 120
Rocky Road Bars, 170
Swiss Chocolate Crispies, 86
Toffee Bars, 64
Toffee-Bran Bars, 46
Triple Chocolate Cookies, 10
Chocolate Almond Brownies, 43
Chocolate & Vanilla Sandwich Cookies, 146
Chocolate Biscotti, 209
Chocolate Cherry Brownies, 154
Chocolate Chips (*see also* **Chocolate**)
Almond Chocolate Chip Cookies, 29
Banana Chip Bars, 153
Banana Split Bars, 60
Black Forest Brownies, 204
Black Forest Oatmeal Fancies, 21
Brownie Cookie Bites, 25
Caramel-Chocolate Delights, 18
Caramel Granola Bars, 56
Caramel-Layered Brownies, 44
Chewy Cherry Chocolate Chip Cookies, 16
Chewy Fingers, 168
Chocolate Chip 'n Oatmeal Cookies, 18
Chocolate Chip Rugalach, 203
Chocolate Chip Whole Wheat Cookies, 22
Chocolate Chunk Cookies, 161
Chocolate Meringue Peanut Squares, 73
Chocolate Mint Snow-Top Cookies, 193
Chocolate-Orange Chip Cookies, 22
Chocolate Peanut Buddy Bars, 153
Chunky Fruit Chews, 26
"Cordially Yours" Chocolate Chip Bars, 70
Cowboy Cookies, 23
Creative Pan Cookies, 62
Crispie Treats, 173
Crunch Crowned Brownies, 161
Crunchy Chocolate Chipsters, 29
Double Chocolate Banana Cookies, 156
Double Chocolate Black-Eyed Susans, 26
Double Chocolate Raspberry Bars, 50
Double Fudge Saucepan Brownies, 40
Double Nut Chocolate Chip Cookies, 20
Double Peanut Butter Supremes, 106
Double Peanut-Choco Bars, 60
Fudgy Brownie Bars, 41
Giant Raisin-Chip Frisbees, 171
Giant Toll House® Cookies, 10
Granola & Chocolate Chip Cookies, 175

Chocolate Chips (*continued*)
Hershey's® More Chips Chocolate Chip Cookies, 16
Holiday Chocolate Chip Squares, 208
Holiday Fruit Drops, 206
Island Treasure Cookies, 23
Kahlúa® Chocolate Nut Squares, 72
Magic Rainbow Cookie Bars, 51
Mini Morsel Granola Cookies, 157
Mississippi Mud Bars, 66
Movietime Crunch Bars, 163
Nestlé® Candy Shop Pizza, 154
Oatmeal Carmelita Bars, 168
Oatmeal Chocolate Chip Cookies, 13
Oatmeal Scotch Chippers, 16
Original Toll House® Chocolate Chip Cookies, 10
Pan Cookies, 10
Party Cookies, 17
P.B. Graham Snackers, 148
Peanut Butter Chocolate Chip Cookies, 187
Peanut Butter Jumbos, 12
Pear Blondies, 51
Pistachio Chip Cookies, 15
Pudding Chip Cookies, 20
Quick Peanut Butter Chocolate Chip Cookies, 28
Ricotta Cookies with Chocolate and Pecans, 26
Rocky Road Brownies, 30
San Francisco Cookies, 17
Scrumptious Chocolate Fruit and Nut Cookies, 29
Simply Delicious Minty Cookies, 15
Sour Cream Chocolate Chip Cookies, 28
Teentime Dream Bars, 157
Tracy's Pizza-Pan Cookies, 15
Triple Chocolate Cookies, 10
Ultimate Chocolate Brownies, 45
Whole Grain Chippers, 27
Chocolate Cookie Pretzels, 130
Chocolate-Frosted Almond Shortbread, 72
Chocolate-Frosted Lebkuchen, 210
Chocolate Frosting, 147
Chocolate Fruit Truffles, 197
Chocolate-Gilded Danish Sugar Cones, 121
Chocolate Macaroon Cups, 147
Chocolate Madeleines, 142
Chocolate-Mint Brownies, 36
Chocolate Rum Balls, 200
Chocolate Spice Cookies, 197
Chocolate Teddy Bears, 150
Choco-Orange Slices, 192
Chunky Fruit Chews, 26
Cinnamon-Apricot Tart Oatmeal Cookies, 112
Cloverleaf Cookies, 184
Cocoa
Caramel-Chocolate Delights, 18
Choco-Caramel Delights, 126

Cocoa (*continued*)
Choco-Coco Pecan Crisps, 206
Chocolate Almond Buttons, 98
Chocolate & Vanilla Sandwich
Cookies, 146
Chocolate Biscotti, 209
Chocolate Cookie Pretzels, 130
Chocolate Frosting, 147
Chocolate Fruit Truffles, 197
Chocolate Kiss Cookies, 89
Chocolate Macaroon Cups, 147
Chocolate Madeleines, 142
Chocolate Rum Balls, 200
Chocolate Spice Cookies, 197
Chocolate Teddy Bears, 150
Cocoa Frosting, 142
Cocoa Gingerbread Cookies, 205
Cocoa Sandies, 139
Cocoa Shortbread, 71
Cocoa Snickerdoodles, 82
Cowboy Cookies, 23
Creamy Brownie Frosting, 160
Cut Out Chocolate Cookies, 152
Double Chocolate Banana Cookies,
156
Double Chocolate Cherry Cookies,
108
Double Chocolate Pecan Cookies,
108
Double Chocolate Raspberry Bars,
50
Double Mint Chocolate Cookies, 91
Easy Chocolate Frosting, 123
Giant Raisin-Chip Frisbees, 171
Greeting Card Cookies, 146
Hershey's® Vanilla Chip Chocolate
Cookies, 13
Holiday Chocolate Cookies, 199
Ivory Chip Strawberry Fudge Drops,
25
Kentucky Oatmeal-Jam Cookies, 102
Lemon Chocolate Bars, 75
Mocha Mint Crisps, 114
One-Bowl Buttercream Frosting, 45
Orange & Chocolate Ribbon Cookies,
138
Peanut Butter and Chocolate Cookie
Sandwich Cookies, 151
Quick Cocoa Glaze, 139
Reese's® Chewy Chocolate Cookies,
27
Satiny Chocolate Glaze, 131
Scrumptious Chocolate Fruit and Nut
Cookies, 29
Sour Cream Chocolate Cookies, 91
White Chocolate Biggies, 12
Coconut
Almond Macaroon Brownies, 40
Apricot Pinwheel Slices, 142
Buttery Caramel Crisps, 75
Cherry-Coconut Peanut Butter
Cookies, 184
Choco-Coconut Layer Bars, 57
Choco-Coco Pecan Crisps, 206

Coconut (*continued*)
Chocolate-Coconut Cookies, 107
Chocolate Macaroon Cups, 147
Chocolate Oat Chewies, 103
Coconut Macaroons, 95
Cowboy Macaroons, 174
Crisp 'n' Crunchy Almond Coconut
Bars, 79
Crispie Coconut Refrigerator Cookies,
101
Crumbly-Topped Lemon Mince Bars,
196
German Chocolate Oatmeal Cookies,
85
Granola Apple Cookies, 90
Holiday Pineapple Cheese Bars, 180
Island Treasure Cookies, 23
Layered Chocolate Cheese Bars, 58
Lemon Iced Ambrosia Bars, 57
Macaroon Almond Crumb Bars, 64
Macaroon Kiss Cookies, 102
Magic Rainbow Cookie Bars, 51
Marvelous Macaroons, 90
Oatmeal Chocolate Chip Cookies, 13
Petite Macaroon Cups, 147
Prized Peanut Butter Crunch Cookies,
111
Prune Bars, 63
tinting, 5
toasting, 5
Tropical Orange Coconut Drops, 99
Cookie Cutouts, 195
Cookies from Mixes
Any-Way-You-Like 'em Cookies, 100
Applesauce Fruitcake Bars, 179
Black Forest Brownies, 204
Cappucino Bon Bons, 33
Cheesecake Topped Brownies, 42
Chocolate Caramel Nut Bars, 76
Chocolate Chip 'n Oatmeal Cookies,
18
Chocolate Kiss Cookies, 89
Chocolate Oat Chewies, 103
Chocolate Peanut Butter Cookies, 156
Crunch Crowned Brownies, 161
Double Chocolate Black-Eyed Susans,
26
Double Chocolate Cookies, 22
Double Chocolate Fantasy Bars, 65
Double Nut Chocolate Chip Cookies,
20
Double Peanut-Choco Bars, 60
Easy Peanut Butter Cookies, 100
Easy Peanutty Snickerdoodles, 18
Fudgy Cookie Wedges, 53
Gingerbread Men, 211
Ice Cream Cookie Sandwich, 163
Lemon Cookies, 111
Macaroon Almond Crumb Bars, 64
Madison Avenue Mocha Brownies, 37
Peanut Blossoms, 100
Peanut Butter & Jelly Gems, 100
Pecan Date Bars, 200
Pinwheel Cookies, 143

Cookies from Mixes (*continued*)
Polka-Dot Cookies, 164
Quick and Easy Nutty Cheese Bars, 49
Quick Peanut Butter Chocolate Chip
Cookies, 28
Raspberry Meringue Bars, 64
Spicy Oatmeal Raisin Cookies, 106
Spicy Sour Cream Cookies, 90
Star Christmas Tree Cookies, 213
Swiss Chocolate Crispies, 86
Wheat Germ Cookies, 106
"Cordially Yours" Chocolate Chip Bars,
70
Cowboy Cookies, 23
Cowboy Macaroons, 174
Cranberries
Cranberry Orange Ricotta Cheese
Brownies, 187
Cranberry Walnut Bars, 211
Oatmeal Cranberry-Nut Cookies, 213
Cream Cheese
Almond Cream Cheese Cookies, 112
Almond Macaroon Brownies, 40
Apricot-Pecan Tassies, 127
Butterscotch Peanut Bars, 50
Cheesecake Topped Brownies, 42
Chocolate Candy Thumbprints, 193
Chocolate Cheese Ripple Bars, 49
Chocolate Fudge Filling, 198
Chocolate Macadamia Bars, 54
Chocolate Macaroon Cups, 147
Chocolate Mint Cutouts, 192
Choco-Orange Slices, 192
Cream Cheese Cookies, 110
Cream Cheese Cutout Cookies, 188
Cream Cheese Frosting, 195
Cream Cheese Pastry, 116
Double Peanut Butter Supremes, 106
European Kolacky, 120
Frosted Honey Bars, 80
Half-Hearted Valentine Cookies, 129
Holiday Pineapple Cheese Bars, 180
Kentucky Bourbon Pecan Tarts, 116
Layered Chocolate Cheese Bars, 58
Macaroon Kiss Cookies, 102
Madison Avenue Mocha Brownies, 37
Nut Cream Filling, 161
Oatmeal Lemon-Cheese Cookies, 105
Petite Macaroon Cups, 147
Philly Cream Cheese Cookie Dough,
192
Preserve Thumbprints, 192
Quick and Easy Nutty Cheese Bars, 49
Simply Delicious Minty Cookies, 15
Snowmen, 192
Tracy's Pizza-Pan Cookies, 15
Creamy Brownie Frosting, 160
Creamy Mint Frosting, 36
Creamy Vanilla Frosting, 123
Creative Pan Cookies, 62
Crisp 'n' Crunchy Almond Coconut Bars,
79
Crispie Coconut Refrigerator Cookies,
101

Crispie Treats, 173
Crisp Peanut Butter Cookies, 184
Crispy Chocolate Logs, 57
Crumbly-Topped Lemon Mince Bars, 196
Crunch Crowned Brownies, 161
Crunchy Chocolate Chipsters, 29
Crunchy Peanut Brickle Bars, 67
Crust, Bar Cookie, 211
Cut Out Chocolate Cookies, 152
Cut-Out Sugar Cookies, 123

D

Dates
Applesauce Fruitcake Bars, 179
California Apricot Power Bars, 76
Cherry Date Sparkle Bars, 77
Date Fudge Cookies, 101
Holiday Fruit Drops, 206
Old-Fashioned Harvest Cookies, 205
Pecan Date Bars, 200
Decorative Frosting, 146
Decorator Icing, 205
Decorator's Frosting, 199
Deep Dish Brownies, 36
Deep Fried Sour Cream Cookies, 121
Double Almond Butter Cookies, 92
Double Chocolate Banana Cookies, 156
Double Chocolate Black-Eyed Susans, 26
Double Chocolate Cherry Cookies, 108
Double Chocolate Cookies, 22
Double Chocolate Crispy Bars, 54
Double Chocolate Fantasy Bars, 65
Double Chocolate Pecan Cookies, 108
Double Chocolate Raspberry Bars, 50
Double Fudge Saucepan Brownies, 40
Double Mint Chocolate Cookies, 91
Double Nut Chocolate Chip Cookies, 20
Double Peanut Butter Supremes, 106
Double Peanut-Choco Bars, 60
Drop Cookies
Almond Chocolate Chip Cookies, 29
Apple Spice Cookies, 112
baking, 7
Banana Oatmeal Cookies with Banana Frosting, 166
Banana Orange Softies, 110
Beth's Chocolate Oatmeal Cookies, 115
Black Forest Oatmeal Fancies, 21
Brownie Cookie Bites, 25
Caramel-Chocolate Delights, 18
Cherry Oatmeal Cookies, 191
Chewy Cherry Chocolate Chip Cookies, 16
Chocolate Chip 'n Oatmeal Cookies, 18
Chocolate Chip Whole Wheat Cookies, 22

Drop Cookies (*continued*)
Chocolate Chunk Cookies, 161
Chocolate-Coconut Cookies, 107
Chocolate-Frosted Lebkuchen, 210
Chocolate-Frosted Marshmallow Cookies, 99
Chocolate-Orange Chip Cookies, 22
Chocolate Peanut Butter Cookies, 156
Chocolate-Peanut Cookies, 82
Chunky Fruit Chews, 26
Cinnamon-Apricot Tart Oatmeal Cookies, 112
Cocoa Snickerdoodles, 82
Coconut Macaroons, 95
Cowboy Cookies, 23
Cream Cheese Cookies, 110
Crunchy Chocolate Chipsters, 29
Date Fudge Cookies, 101
Double Chocolate Banana Cookies, 156
Double Chocolate Black-Eyed Susans, 26
Double Chocolate Cookies, 22
Double Mint Chocolate Cookies, 91
Double Nut Chocolate Chip Cookies, 20
Drop Sugar Cookies, 93
Famous Oatmeal Cookies, 108
Frost on the Pumpkin Cookies, 195
German Chocolate Oatmeal Cookies, 85
Giant Toll House® Cookies, 10
Ginger Snap Oats, 89
Granola & Chocolate Chip Cookies, 175
Granola Apple Cookies, 90
Health Nut Almond Oaties, 114
Hershey's® More Chips Chocolate Chip Cookies, 16
Hershey's® Vanilla Chip Chocolate Cookies, 13
Holiday Fruit Drops, 206
Honey 'n' Spice Cookies, 190
Island Treasure Cookies, 23
Ivory Chip Strawberry Fudge Drops, 25
Kentucky Oatmeal-Jam Cookies, 102
Maple Raisin Cookies, 87
Marvelous Macaroons, 90
Melting Moments, 134
Meringue Kisses, 210
Milk Chocolate Florentine Cookies, 126
Milky Way® Bar Cookies, 165
Mini Morsel Granola Cookies, 157
Mom's Best Oatmeal Cookies, 89
Nutty Clusters, 93
Oatmeal Apple Cookies, 107
Oatmeal Chocolate Chip Cookies, 13
Oatmeal-Chocolate Raisin Cookies, 174
Oatmeal Cranberry-Nut Cookies, 213
Oatmeal Lemon-Cheese Cookies, 105

Drop Cookies (*continued*)
Oatmeal Scotch Chippers, 16
Oatmeal Scotchies, 163
Old-Fashioned Harvest Cookies, 205
Original Toll House® Chocolate Chip Cookies, 10
Party Cookies, 17
Peanut Butter Chocolate Chip Cookies, 187
Peanut Butter Cremes, 153
Peanut Butter Jumbos, 12
Peanut Butter Sensations, 87
Peanut Butter Sunshine Cookies, 20
Peanut Buttery Cookies, 85
Pineapple Raisin Jumbles, 94
Pistachio Chip Cookies, 15
preparation, 5
Prized Peanut Butter Crunch Cookies, 111
Pudding Chip Cookies, 20
Quick Peanut Butter Chocolate Chip Cookies, 28
Reese's® Chewy Chocolate Cookies, 27
Ricotta Cookies with Chocolate and Pecans, 26
San Francisco Cookies, 17
Scrumptious Chocolate Fruit and Nut Cookies, 29
Simply Delicious Minty Cookies, 15
Sour Cream Chocolate Chip Cookies, 28
Sour Cream Chocolate Cookies, 91
Spiced Apple-Raisin Cookies, 164
Spicy Oatmeal Raisin Cookies, 106
Spicy Sour Cream Cookies, 90
storing, 7
Triple Chocolate Cookies, 10
Tropical Orange Coconut Drops, 99
Wheat Germ Cookies, 106
White Chocolate Biggies, 12
Whole Wheat Oatmeal Cookies, 86
Drop Sugar Cookies, 93

E

Easy Chocolate Frosting, 123
Easy Chocolate Icing, 93
Easy Lemon Icing, 165
Easy Peanut Butter Cookies, 100
Easy Peanutty Snickerdoodles, 18
Eggnog Snickerdoodles, 191
equivalents, 9
European Kolacky, 120

F

Fa-La-La-La-Las, 191
Famous Oatmeal Cookies, 108
Filled Almond Crisps, 141

Fillings
  Caramel Filling, 126
  Chocolate Filling, 180
  Chocolate Fudge Filling, 198
  Nut Cream Filling, 161
  Orange Butter Cream, 134
  Orange Liqueur Filling, 141
  Strawberry Filling, 141
Frosted Honey Bars, 80
Frostings & Icings (*see also* **Glazes**)
  Almond Frosting, 188
  Brown Butter Icing, 72
  Brown-Sugar Icing, 101
  Butterscotch Frosting, 50
  Chocolate Dream Frosting, 68
  Chocolate Frosting, 147
  Chocolate Icing, 199
  Cocoa Frosting, 142
  Cream Cheese Frosting, 195
  Creamy Brownie Frosting, 160
  Creamy Mint Frosting, 36
  Creamy Vanilla Frosting, 123
  Decorative Frosting, 146
  Decorator Icing, 205
  Decorator's Frosting, 199
  Easy Chocolate Frosting, 123
  Easy Chocolate Icing, 93
  Easy Lemon Icing, 165
  Holiday Icing, 203
  Lemon Creamy Frosting, 123
  Lemon Icing, 57
  Mint Frosting, 147
  One-Bowl Buttercream Frosting, 45
  Orange Creamy Frosting, 123
  Peanut Butter Chip Frosting, 130
  "Peanut Butter Special" Frosting, 68
  Vanilla Frosting, 147
Frost on the Pumpkin Cookies, 195
Fruit (*see also individual types*)
  Chunky Fruit Chews, 26
  Fruit and Chocolate Dream Bars, 48
  Fruit & Nut Snack Bars, 196
  Fruit Burst Cookies, 186
  Fruit Filled Thumbprints, 85
  Lebkuchen Jewels, 188
  Scrumptious Chocolate Fruit and Nut
    Cookies, 29
Fudge Topping, 32
Fudgey Microwave Brownies, 173
Fudgy Brownie Bars, 41
Fudgy Chocolate Glaze, 119
Fudgy Cookie Wedges, 53

G

Gaiety Pastel Cookies, 158
German Chocolate Oatmeal Cookies,
  85
Giant Raisin-Chip Frisbees, 171
Giant Toll House® Cookies, 10
Gingerbread Men, 211
Ginger Snap Oats, 89

Gingersnaps, 103
Glazed Rum Raisin Bars, 81
Glazes (*see also* **Frostings & Icings**)
  Bittersweet Glaze, 210
  Chocolate Chip Glaze, 118
  Chocolate Glaze, 36
  Fudgy Chocolate Glaze, 119
  Lemon Glaze, 188
  Microwave Chocolate Chip Glaze,
    68
  Peanut Butter Glaze, 68
  Quick Chocolate Drizzle, 75
  Quick Cocoa Glaze, 139
  Satiny Chocolate Glaze, 131
  Vanilla Glaze, 152
Graham Peanut Butter Crunchies,
  173
Granola
  Caramel Granola Bars, 56
  Granola & Chocolate Chip Cookies,
    175
  Granola Apple Bars, 151
  Granola Apple Cookies, 90
  Granola Bars, 170
  Mini Morsel Granola Cookies, 157
  San Francisco Cookies, 17
Greeting Card Cookies, 146

H

Half-Hearted Valentine Cookies, 129
Health Nut Almond Oaties, 114
Heath® Bars, 71
Hershey's® More Chips Chocolate Chip
  Cookies, 16
Hershey's® Vanilla Chip Chocolate
  Cookies, 13
Holiday Chocolate Chip Squares, 208
Holiday Chocolate Cookies, 199
Holiday Fruit Drops, 206
Holiday Hideaways, 202
Holiday Icing, 203
Holiday Pineapple Cheese Bars, 180
Honey
  Frosted Honey Bars, 80
  Honey 'n' Spice Cookies, 190
  Honey Brownies, 160
  Honey Orange Crescent Cookies,
    98
  Lebkuchen Jewels, 188

I

Ice Cream Cookie Sandwich, 163
Ice Cream Sandwiches, 100
Icings (*see* **Frosting & Icings**)
ingredients, measuring, 4
Island Treasure Cookies, 23
Ivory Chip Strawberry Fudge Drops,
  25

J

Jam-Filled Chocolate Sugar Cookies, 96
Jam-Filled Peanut Butter Kisses, 115
Jam-Up Oatmeal Cookies, 134

K

Kahlúa® Chocolate Nut Squares, 72
Kahlúa® Kisses, 190
Kentucky Bourbon Pecan Tarts, 116
Kentucky Oatmeal-Jam Cookies, 102

L

Layered Chocolate Cheese Bars, 58
Layered Lemon Crumb Bars, 61
Lebkuchen Jewels, 188
Lebkuchen Spice Spritz Cookies, 183
Lemons
  Almond Stars, 124
  Crumbly-Topped Lemon Mince Bars,
    196
  Easy Lemon Icing, 165
  Layered Lemon Crumb Bars, 61
  Lemon Chocolate Bars, 75
  Lemon Cookies, 111
  Lemon Creamy Frosting, 123
  Lemon Cut-Out Cookies, 165
  Lemon Cut-Out Sugar Cookies, 123
  Lemon Glaze, 188
  Lemon Iced Ambrosia Bars, 57
  Lemon Icing, 57
  Lemon Meltaways, 84
  Lemon Tea Cookies, 96
  Lemony Spritz Sticks, 119
  Oatmeal Lemon-Cheese Cookies,
    105
  Zesty Fresh Lemon Bars, 81
Linzer Bars, 200
Little Raisin Logs, 124
Lollipop Sugar Cookies, 171

M

Macadamia Nuts
  Chocolate Macadamia Bars, 54
  Holiday Pineapple Cheese Bars, 180
  Island Treasure Cookies, 23
  Scrumptious Chocolate Fruit and Nut
    Cookies, 29
Macaroon Almond Crumb Bars, 64
Macaroon Kiss Cookies, 102
Madeleines
  Almond Rice Madeleines, 125
  Chocolate Madeleines, 142
Madison Avenue Mocha Brownies, 37
Magic Rainbow Cookie Bars, 51

Maple Raisin Cookies, 87
Marbled Brownies, 160
Marshmallows
   Banana Split Bars, 60
   Buttery Caramel Crisps, 75
   Chocolate Dream Frosting, 68
   Chocolate-Frosted Marshmallow
      Cookies, 99
   Crispie Treats, 173
   Crispy Chocolate Logs, 57
   Double Chocolate Crispy Bars, 54
   Fudge Topping, 32
   Peanut Butter and Chocolate Cookie
      Sandwich Cookies, 151
   Peanut Butter Cremes, 153
   Rocky Road Bars, 170
   Rocky Road Brownies, 30
   Rocky Road Fudge Brownies, 44
Marvelous Macaroons, 90
measuring ingredients, 4
Melting Moments, 134
Meringue Kisses, 210
Microwave Chocolate Chip Glaze, 68
Milk Chocolate Brownies, 166
Milk Chocolate Florentine Cookies, 126
Milky Way® Bar Cookies, 165
Mincemeat
   Chocolate Fruit Truffles, 197
   Chocolate Spice Cookies, 197
   Crumbly-Topped Lemon Mince Bars,
      196
   Fruit & Nut Snack Bars, 196
Mini Morsel Granola Cookies, 157
Mint
   Chocolate Mint Bars, 61
   Chocolate-Mint Brownies, 36
   Chocolate Mint Cutouts, 192
   Chocolate Mint Pinwheels, 178
   Chocolate Mint Snow-Top Cookies,
      193
   Creamy Mint Frosting, 36
   Double Mint Chocolate Cookies, 91
   Half-Hearted Valentine Cookies, 129
   Mint Frosting, 147
   Mocha Mint Crisps, 114
   Simply Delicious Minty Cookies, 15
Mississippi Mud Bars, 66
Mocha
   Cappucino Bon Bons, 33
   Madison Avenue Mocha Brownies,
      37
   Mocha Almond Bars, 55
   Mocha Mint Crisps, 114
   Mocha Mint Sugar, 114
   Mocha Pecan Pinwheels, 137
Mom's Best Oatmeal Cookies, 89
Movietime Crunch Bars, 163

N

Naomi's Revel Bars, 55
Nestlé® Candy Shop Pizza, 154

New Wave Chocolate Spritz Cookies,
   178
Nutcracker Sweets, 208
Nut Cream Filling, 161
Nuts (*see also individual types*)
   Applesauce Fruitcake Bars, 179
   Caramel-Layered Brownies, 44
   Chocolate & Vanilla Sandwich
      Cookies, 146
   Chocolate Chip Rugalach, 203
   Chocolate Fruit Truffles, 197
   Chocolate Lace Cornucopias, 131
   Chocolate Pistachio Fingers, 136
   Chocolate-Topped Linzer Cookies, 132
   Crunch Crowned Brownies, 161
   Double Chocolate Fantasy Bars, 65
   Fruit Burst Cookies, 186
   Giant Toll House® Cookies, 10
   Holiday Chocolate Chip Squares, 208
   Holiday Fruit Drops, 206
   Kahlúa® Chocolate Nut Squares, 72
   Layered Chocolate Cheese Bars, 58
   Magic Rainbow Cookie Bars, 51
   Nutty Clusters, 93
   Oatmeal Caramel Bars, 73
   Original Toll House® Chocolate Chip
      Cookies, 10
   Pan Cookies, 10
   Peanut Butter Chocolate Chip
      Cookies, 187
   Prune Bars, 63
   Rocky Road Brownies, 30
   Rocky Road Fudge Brownies, 44
   Sour Cream Brownies, 33
   toasting, 5
Nutty Clusters, 93
Nutty Toppers, 105

O

Oats
   Apricot Oatmeal Bars, 80
   Banana Oatmeal Cookies with Banana
      Frosting, 166
   Banana Orange Softies, 110
   Beth's Chocolate Oatmeal Cookies,
      115
   Black Forest Oatmeal Fancies, 21
   Cherry Oatmeal Cookies, 191
   Chewy Fingers, 168
   Chocolate Chip 'n Oatmeal Cookies, 18
   Chocolate Chip Whole Wheat
      Cookies, 22
   Chocolate-Dipped Oat Cookies, 110
   Chocolate Mint Bars, 61
   Chocolate Oat Chewies, 103
   Chunky Fruit Chews, 26
   Cinnamon-Apricot Tart Oatmeal
      Cookies, 112
   Cocoa Snickerdoodles, 82
   Cowboy Cookies, 23
   Cowboy Macaroons, 174

Oats (*continued*)
   Crunchy Peanut Brickle Bars, 67
   Double Chocolate Banana Cookies, 156
   Famous Oatmeal Cookies, 108
   German Chocolate Oatmeal Cookies, 85
   Ginger Snap Oats, 89
   Granola Bars, 170
   Health Nut Almond Oaties, 114
   Jam-Up Oatmeal Cookies, 134
   Kentucky Oatmeal-Jam Cookies, 102
   Layered Lemon Crumb Bars, 61
   Milk Chocolate Florentine Cookies,
      126
   Mom's Best Oatmeal Cookies, 89
   Naomi's Revel Bars, 55
   Oatmeal Apple Cookies, 107
   Oatmeal Caramel Bars, 73
   Oatmeal Carmelita Bars, 168
   Oatmeal Chocolate Chip Cookies, 13
   Oatmeal-Chocolate Raisin Cookies,
      174
   Oatmeal Cranberry-Nut Cookies, 213
   Oatmeal Lemon-Cheese Cookies, 105
   Oatmeal Scotch Chippers, 16
   Oatmeal Scotchies, 163
   Oats 'n' Pumpkin Pinwheels, 127
   Old-Fashioned Harvest Cookies, 205
   Peanut Butter and Oatmeal
      Sandwiches, 119
   Peanut Butter Jumbos, 12
   Peanutty Crisscrosses, 86
   Prized Peanut Butter Crunch Cookies,
      111
   Santa Fe Sun Crisps, 109
   Snow Covered Almond Crescents, 196
   Spice 'n' Easy Apple Raisin Bars, 75
   Spiced Apple-Raisin Cookies, 164
   Spicy Oatmeal Raisin Cookies, 106
   Toffee Bars, 64
   Whole Grain Chippers, 27
   Whole Wheat Oatmeal Cookies, 86
Old-Fashioned Harvest Cookies, 205
Old-Fashioned Molasses Cookies, 143
One Bowl Brownies, 30
One-Bowl Buttercream Frosting, 45
Oranges
   Banana Orange Softies, 110
   Chocolate-Orange Chip Cookies, 22
   Choco-Orange Slices, 192
   Cranberry Orange Ricotta Cheese
      Brownies, 187
   Honey Orange Crescent Cookies, 98
   Orange & Chocolate Ribbon Cookies,
      138
   Orange Butter Cream, 134
   Orange Butter Cream Squares, 63
   Orange Creamy Frosting, 123
   Orange Cut-Out Sugar Cookies, 123
   Orange Liqueur Filling, 141
   Orange Pumpkin Bars, 209
   Tropical Orange Coconut Drops, 99
Original Toll House® Chocolate Chip
   Cookies, 10
Our Best Bran Brownies, 43

P

Pan Cookies, 10
Party Cookies, 17
P.B. Graham Snackers, 148
Peanut Blossoms, 100
Peanut Butter (*see also* **Peanut Butter Chips**)
Any-Way-You-Like 'em Cookies, 100
Breakfast Bars to Go, 70
Butterscotch Bars, 78
Butterscotch Frosting, 50
Cherry-Coconut Peanut Butter Cookies, 184
Chocolate Peanut Buddy Bars, 153
Chocolate Peanut Butter Bars, 58
Chocolate Peanut Butter Cookies, 156
Chocolatey Peanut Butter Goodies, 148
Cloverleaf Cookies, 184
Crispie Treats, 173
Crisp Peanut Butter Cookies, 184
Crunchy Peanut Brickle Bars, 67
Double Chocolate Crispy Bars, 54
Double Peanut Butter Supremes, 106
Double Peanut-Choco Bars, 60
Easy Peanut Butter Cookies, 100
Graham Peanut Butter Crunchies, 173
Jam-Filled Peanut Butter Kisses, 115
Nestlé® Candy Shop Pizza, 154
Nutcracker Sweets, 208
Nutty Toppers, 105
Oatmeal Scotch Chippers, 16
P.B. Graham Snackers, 148
Peanut Blossoms, 100
Peanut Butter & Jelly Gems, 100
Peanut Butter and Oatmeal Sandwiches, 119
Peanut Butter Bars, 68
Peanut Butter Bears, 158
Peanut Butter Chocolate Chip Cookies, 187
Peanut Butter Crackles, 184
Peanut Butter Cremes, 153
Peanut Butter Crunchy Surprises, 157
Peanut Butter Cutouts, 186
Peanut Butter Gingerbread Men, 185
Peanut Butter Glaze, 68
Peanut Butter Jumbos, 12
Peanut Butter Kisses, 115
Peanut Butter Secrets, 144
Peanut Butter Sensations, 87
"Peanut Butter Special" Frosting, 68
Peanut Butter Sunshine Cookies, 20
Peanut Butter Swirl Brownies, 30
Peanut-Layered Brownies, 38
Peanutty Crisscrosses, 86
Prized Peanut Butter Crunch Cookies, 111
Quick Peanut Butter Chocolate Chip Cookies, 28
Rocky Road Bars, 170
Santa Lollipop Cookies, 186
Teentime Dream Bars, 157
Wreath Cookies, 186

Peanut Butter Chips (*see also* **Peanut Butter**)
Chocolate Peanut Butter Cookies, 156
Easy Peanutty Snickerdoodles, 18
Peanut Butter and Chocolate Cookie Sandwich Cookies, 151
Peanut-Butter-Chip Brownies, 167
Peanut Butter Chip Frosting, 130
Peanut Butter Chips and Jelly Bars, 164
Peanut Butter Cut-Out Cookies, 118
Reese's® Chewy Chocolate Cookies, 27
Peanut Buttery Cookies, 85
Peanuts
Butterscotch Bars, 78
Butterscotch Peanut Bars, 50
Chocolate Meringue Peanut Squares, 73
Chocolate Peanut Butter Bars, 58
Chocolate-Peanut Cookies, 82
Crunchy Peanut Brickle Bars, 67
Double Peanut-Choco Bars, 60
Granola Bars, 170
Movietime Crunch Bars, 163
Peanut Buttery Cookies, 85
Peanut-Layered Brownies, 38
Prized Peanut Butter Crunch Cookies, 111
Peanutty Crisscrosses, 86
Pear Blondies, 51
Pecans
Apricot-Pecan Tassies, 127
Apricot Pinwheel Slices, 142
California Apricot Power Bars, 76
Caramel-Chocolate Delights, 18
Caramel Chocolate Pecan Bars, 56
Choco-Caramel Delights, 126
Choco-Coco Pecan Crisps, 206
Chocolate Pecan Pie Bars, 48
Cinnamon-Apricot Tart Oatmeal Cookies, 112
Cowboy Macaroons, 174
Crispie Coconut Refrigerator Cookies, 101
Double Chocolate Pecan Cookies, 108
Fruit & Nut Snack Bars, 196
Fruit Filled Thumbprints, 85
German Chocolate Oatmeal Cookies, 85
Honey Orange Crescent Cookies, 98
Jam-Up Oatmeal Cookies, 134
Kentucky Bourbon Pecan Tarts, 116
Lemon Iced Ambrosia Bars, 57
Mocha Pecan Pinwheels, 137
Mom's Best Oatmeal Cookies, 89
Nutty Toppers, 105
Oatmeal-Chocolate Raisin Cookies, 174
Pecan Date Bars, 200
Pecan Pie Bars, 71
Quick and Easy Nutty Cheese Bars, 49
Ricotta Cookies with Chocolate and Pecans, 26
Snowball Cookies, 206
Spicy Sour Cream Cookies, 90

Petite Macaroon Cups, 147
Philly Cream Cheese Cookie Dough, 192
Pineapple
Health Nut Almond Oaties, 114
Holiday Fruit Drops, 206
Holiday Pineapple Cheese Bars, 180
Marvelous Macaroons, 90
Oatmeal Chocolate Chip Cookies, 13
Pineapple Raisin Jumbles, 94
Pineapple Walnut Bars, 67
Pinwheel Cookies
Apricot Pinwheel Slices, 142
Chocolate Mint Pinwheels, 178
Mocha Pecan Pinwheels, 137
Oats 'n' Pumpkin Pinwheels, 127
Pinwheel Cookies, 143
Pistachio Chip Cookies, 15
Polka-Dot Cookies, 164
Preserve Thumbprints, 192
Prized Peanut Butter Crunch Cookies, 111
Prune Bars, 63
Pudding Chip Cookies, 20
Pumpkin
Frost on the Pumpkin Cookies, 195
Oats 'n' Pumpkin Pinwheels, 127
Old-Fashioned Harvest Cookies, 205
Orange Pumpkin Bars, 209
Slice 'n Bake Pumpkin Cookies, 181

Q

Quick and Easy Nutty Cheese Bars, 49
Quick Chocolate Drizzle, 75
Quick Cocoa Glaze, 139

R

Raisins
Applesauce Fruitcake Bars, 179
Giant Raisin-Chip Frisbees, 171
Ginger Snap Oats, 89
Glazed Rum Raisin Bars, 81
Granola Bars, 170
Health Nut Almond Oaties, 114
Lebkuchen Jewels, 188
Little Raisin Logs, 124
Maple Raisin Cookies, 87
Mini Morsel Granola Cookies, 157
Movietime Crunch Bars, 163
Oatmeal-Chocolate Raisin Cookies, 174
Pineapple Raisin Jumbles, 94
Spice 'n' Easy Apple Raisin Bars, 75
Raspberries
Almond Raspberry Thumbprint Cookies, 92
Chocolate Raspberry Linzer Cookies, 176

Raspberries (*continued*)
Chocolate-Topped Linzer Cookies, 132
Double Chocolate Raspberry Bars, 50
Linzer Bars, 200
Raspberry-Filled Chocolate Ravioli, 120
Raspberry Fudge Brownies, 37
Raspberry Meringue Bars, 64
Raspberry Pyramids, 133
Reese's® Chewy Chocolate Cookies, 27
Refrigerator Cookies
Almond Cream Cheese Cookies, 112
Apricot Pinwheel Slices, 142
baking, 7
Black Walnut Refrigerator Cookies, 109
Choco-Coco Pecan Crisps, 206
Chocolate Mint Pinwheels, 178
Choco-Orange Slices, 192
Crispie Coconut Refrigerator Cookies, 101
Ice Cream Sandwiches, 100
Lemon Meltaways, 84
Mocha Pecan Pinwheels, 137
Oats 'n' Pumpkin Pinwheels, 127
Orange & Chocolate Ribbon Cookies, 138
Pinwheel Cookies, 143
preparation, 6
Slice 'n Bake Pumpkin Cookies, 181
storing, 7
Ricotta Cookies with Chocolate and Pecans, 26
Ricotta Crescents, 133
Rocky Road Bars, 170
Rocky Road Brownies, 30
Rocky Road Fudge Brownies, 44
Rolled Cookies
Almond Stars, 124
Austrian Tea Cookies, 144
baking, 7
Buttery Butterscotch Cutouts, 167
Buttery Jam Tarts, 175
Chocolate & Vanilla Sandwich Cookies, 146
Chocolate Chip Rugalach, 203
Chocolate Kahlúa® Bears, 199
Chocolate Mint Cutouts, 192
Chocolate Raspberry Linzer Cookies, 176
Chocolate-Topped Linzer Cookies, 132
Cocoa Gingerbread Cookies, 205
Cocoa Sandies, 139
Cookie Cutouts, 195
Cream Cheese Cutout Cookies, 188
Cut Out Chocolate Cookies, 152
Cut-Out Sugar Cookies, 123
Deep Fried Sour Cream Cookies, 121
European Kolacky, 120
Gingerbread Men, 211
Greeting Card Cookies, 146
Half-Hearted Valentine Cookies, 129
Holiday Chocolate Cookies, 199
Jam-Up Oatmeal Cookies, 134
Lemon Cut-Out Cookies, 165

Rolled Cookies (*continued*)
Lemon Cut-Out Sugar Cookies, 123
Old-Fashioned Molasses Cookies, 143
Orange Cut-Out Sugar Cookies, 123
Peanut Butter Bears, 158
Peanut Butter Cut-Out Cookies, 118
Peanut Butter Cutouts, 186
Peanut Butter Gingerbread Men, 185
Philly Cream Cheese Cookie Dough, 192
preparation, 6
Raspberry-Filled Chocolate Ravioli, 120
Raspberry Pyramids, 133
Ricotta Crescents, 133
Santa Lollipop Cookies, 186
Snowmen, 192
Sparkly Cookie Stars, 204
Star Christmas Tree Cookies, 213
storing, 7
Tea-Time Sandwich Cookies, 138
Wreath Cookies, 86
Rosettes, 139

S

Sandwich Cookies
Almond Stars, 124
Banana Cream Sandwich Cookies, 141
Buttery Jam Tarts, 175
Chocolate & Vanilla Sandwich Cookies, 146
Chocolate Raspberry Linzer Cookies, 176
Chocolate-Topped Linzer Cookies, 132
Jam-Up Oatmeal Cookies, 134
Melting Moments, 134
Milk Chocolate Florentine Cookies, 126
Peanut Butter and Chocolate Cookie Sandwich Cookies, 151
Peanut Butter and Oatmeal Sandwiches, 119
Raspberry-Filled Chocolate Ravioli, 120
Tea-Time Sandwich Cookies, 138
Walnut Christmas Balls, 180
San Francisco Cookies, 17
Santa Fe Sun Crisps, 109
Santa Lollipop Cookies, 186
Satiny Chocolate Glaze, 131
Scrumptious Chocolate Fruit and Nut Cookies, 29
Semi-Sweet Chocolate Brownies, 43
sending, 7
Shaped Cookies
Almond Raspberry Thumbprint Cookies, 92
Almond Rice Madeleines, 125
Any-Way-You-Like 'em Cookies, 100
Apricot-Pecan Tassies, 127
baking, 7

Shaped Cookies (*continued*)
Banana Cream Sandwich Cookies, 141
Bavarian Cookie Wreaths, 202
Brandied Buttery Wreaths, 183
Brandy Lace Cookies, 118
Cherry-Coconut Peanut Butter Cookies, 184
Chewy Fingers, 168
Choco-Caramel Delights, 126
Chocolate Almond Buttons, 98
Chocolate Biscotti, 209
Chocolate Candy Thumbprints, 193
Chocolate-Caramel Sugar Cookies, 96
Chocolate Cherry Cookies, 136
Chocolate Cookie Pretzels, 130
Chocolate-Dipped Almond Horns, 130
Chocolate-Dipped Oat Cookies, 110
Chocolate Fruit Truffles, 197
Chocolate-Gilded Danish Sugar Cones, 121
Chocolate Kiss Cookies, 89
Chocolate Lace Cornucopias, 131
Chocolate Macaroon Cups, 147
Chocolate Madeleines, 142
Chocolate Mint Snow-Top Cookies, 193
Chocolate Oat Chewies, 103
Chocolate Pistachio Fingers, 136
Chocolate Pixies, 109
Chocolate Rum Balls, 200
Chocolate Spice Cookies, 197
Chocolate Spritz, 136
Chocolate Sugar Cookies, 96
Chocolate Teddy Bears, 150
Cloverleaf Cookies, 184
Cowboy Macaroons, 174
Crispie Treats, 173
Crisp Peanut Butter Cookies, 184
Double Almond Butter Cookies, 92
Double Chocolate Cherry Cookies, 108
Double Chocolate Pecan Cookies, 108
Double Peanut Butter Supremes, 106
Easy Peanut Butter Cookies, 100
Easy Peanutty Snickerdoodles, 18
Eggnog Snickerdoodles, 191
Fa-La-La-La-Las, 191
Filled Almond Crisps, 141
Fruit Burst Cookies, 186
Fruit Filled Thumbprints, 85
Gaiety Pastel Cookies, 158
Giant Raisin-Chip Frisbees, 171
Gingersnaps, 103
Graham Peanut Butter Crunchies, 173
Holiday Hideaways, 202
Honey Orange Crescent Cookies, 98
Ice Cream Cookie Sandwich, 163
Jam-Filled Chocolate Sugar Cookies, 96
Jam-Filled Peanut Butter Kisses, 115
Kahlúa® Kisses, 190
Kentucky Bourbon Pecan Tarts, 116
Lebkuchen Spice Spritz Cookies, 183
Lemon Cookies, 111

Shaped Cookies (*continued*)
Lemon Tea Cookies, 96
Lemony Spritz Sticks, 119
Little Raisin Logs, 124
Lollipop Sugar Cookies, 171
Macaroon Kiss Cookies, 102
Mocha Mint Crisps, 114
Nestlé® Candy Shop Pizza, 154
New Wave Chocolate Spritz Cookies, 178
Nutty Toppers, 105
P.B. Graham Snackers, 148
Peanut Blossoms, 100
Peanut Butter and Chocolate Cookie Sandwich Cookies, 151
Peanut Butter & Jelly Gems, 100
Peanut Butter and Oatmeal Sandwiches, 119
Peanut Butter Crackles, 184
Peanut Butter Crunchy Surprises, 157
Peanut Butter Kisses, 115
Peanut Butter Secrets, 144
Peanutty Crisscrosses, 86
Petite Macaroon Cups, 147
Polka-Dot Cookies, 164
preparation, 6
Preserve Thumbprints, 192
Rosettes, 139
Santa Fe Sun Crisps, 109
Snickerdoodles, 94
Snowball Cookies, 206
Snow Covered Almond Crescents, 196
Spumoni Bars, 129
storing, 7
Swiss Chocolate Crispies, 86
Tracy's Pizza-Pan Cookies, 15
Walnut Christmas Balls, 180
Whole Grain Chippers, 27
Simply Delicious Minty Cookies, 15
Slice 'n Bake Pumpkin Cookies, 181
Snickerdoodles, 94
Snowball Cookies, 206
Snow Covered Almond Crescents, 196
Snowmen, 192
Sour Cream
Apricot Pinwheel Slices, 142
Chewy Cherry Chocolate Chip Cookies, 16
Deep Fried Sour Cream Cookies, 121
Double Peanut Butter Supremes, 106
Pineapple Walnut Bars, 67

Sour Cream (*continued*)
Sour Cream Brownies, 33
Sour Cream Cherry Bars, 77
Sour Cream Chocolate Chip Cookies, 28
Sour Cream Chocolate Cookies, 91
Sparkly Cookie Stars, 204
Spice 'n' Easy Apple Raisin Bars, 75
Spiced Apple-Raisin Cookies, 164
Spicy Oatmeal Raisin Cookies, 106
Spicy Sour Cream Cookies, 90
Spritz Cookies
Chocolate Spritz, 136
Fa-La-La-La-Las, 191
Lebkuchen Spice Spritz Cookies, 183
Lemony Spritz Sticks, 119
New Wave Chocolate Spritz Cookies, 178
Spumoni Bars, 129
Star Christmas Tree Cookies, 213
Strawberries
Ivory Chip Strawberry Fudge Drops, 25
Strawberry Filling, 141
Strawberry Wonders, 78
substitutions, 8
Swiss Chocolate Crispies, 86

T

Tartlets
Apricot-Pecan Tassies, 127
Chocolate Macaroon Cups, 147
Kentucky Bourbon Pecan Tarts, 116
Petite Macaroon Cups, 147
Tea-Time Sandwich Cookies, 138
Teentime Dream Bars, 157
Toffee
Blonde Brickle Brownies, 41
Crunchy Peanut Brickle Bars, 67
Heath® Bars, 71
Toffee Bars, 64
Toffee-Bran Bars, 46
Toffee Brownie Bars, 35
Topping, Fudge, 32
Tracy's Pizza-Pan Cookies, 15
Triple Chocolate Cookies, 10
Tropical Orange Coconut Drops, 99

U

Ultimate Chocolate Brownies, 45

V

Vanilla Frosting, 147
Vanilla Glaze, 152

W

Walnuts
Beth's Chocolate Oatmeal Cookies, 115
Black Walnut Refrigerator Cookies, 109
Brownie Fudge, 32
Chewy Bar Cookies, 46
Chewy Chocolate Brownies, 35
Chocolate Caramel Nut Bars, 76
Chocolate Chunk Cookies, 161
Chocolate Rum Balls, 200
Cranberry Walnut Bars, 211
Fudge Topping, 32
Lebkuchen Jewels, 188
Linzer Bars, 200
Little Raisin Logs, 124
Oatmeal Scotch Chippers, 16
Pineapple Walnut Bars, 67
Raspberry Meringue Bars, 64
Sour Cream Chocolate Chip Cookies, 28
Sour Cream Chocolate Cookies, 91
Tracy's Pizza-Pan Cookies, 15
Walnut Christmas Balls, 180
Walnut Crunch Brownies, 38
Zesty Fresh Lemon Bars, 81
weights and measures, 8
Wheat Germ Cookies, 106
White Chocolate & Almond Brownies, 32
White Chocolate Biggies, 12
Whole Grain Chippers, 27
Whole Wheat Oatmeal Cookies, 86
Wreath Cookies, 186

Z

Zesty Fresh Lemon Bars, 81

Chocolate Chip Cookies
∗ The Best ∗

- 1 cup solid shortening
- ½ cup (¼ lb.) butter or margarine, softened
- 1⅓ cups granulated sugar
- 1 cup firmly packed brown sugar
- 4 eggs
- 1 tablespoon vanilla
- 1 teaspoon lemon juice
- 2 teaspoons baking soda
- 1½ teaspoons salt
- 1 teaspoon ground cinnamon
- ½ cup regular or quick-cooking rolled oats
- 3 cups all-purpose flour
- 2 large packages (12 oz. *each*) semisweet chocolate chips
- 2 cups chopped walnuts

In large bowl of an electric mixer, beat shortening, butter, granulated sugar, and brown sugar at high speed until light and fluffy (about 5 minutes). Add eggs, one at a time, beating well after each addition. Beat in vanilla and lemon juice.

In another bowl, stir together baking soda, salt, cinnamon, oats, and flour. Beat into creamed mixture until well combined; stir in chocolate chips and nuts.

For each cooky, drop a scant ¼ cup dough on a lightly greased baking sheet, spacing cookies about 3 inches apart. Bake in a 350° oven for 16 to 18 minutes or until golden brown. Transfer to racks and let cool. Makes about 3 dozen large cookies.

From *Sunset's* FAVORITE RECIPES II copyright © 1982, Lane Publishing Co.

The Chewy Oatmeal Cookie

- ¾ cup Butter Flavor† Crisco
- 1¼ cups firmly packed light brown sugar
- 1 egg
- ⅓ cup milk
- 1½ tsps. vanilla

- 3 cups quick oats
- 1 cup all-purpose flour
- ½ tsp. baking soda
- ½ tsp. salt
- ¼ tsp. cinnamon

- 1 cup raisins
- 1 cup chopped walnuts

Yield: About 2 1/2 Dozen Cookies.

1. Heat oven to 375° F. Grease baking sheet with Butter Flavor Crisco.
2. Combine Butter Flavor Crisco, light brown sugar, egg, milk and vanilla in large bowl.
3. Beat at medium speed of electric mixer until well blended.
4. Combine oats, flour, baking soda, salt and cinnamon.
5. Mix into creamed mixture at low speed just until blended.
6. Stir in raisins and nuts.
7. Drop rounded tablespoonfuls of dough 2 inches apart onto baking sheet.
8. Bake at 375° F for 10 to 12 minutes, or until lightly browned.
9. Cool 2 minutes on baking sheet. Remove to foil on countertop.

ALL-VEGETABLE
Crisco
BUTTER FLAVOR

...LAMOOK
...ER COOKIES

...amook Butter and
... Add 1 beaten egg, 1/2
...nd 1/2 tsp. almond ex-
...ell. Sift 2-1/2C. flour, 1/2
...d 1/2 tsp. cream of tartar
...d and mix thoroughly.
...into 1/2 inch balls, roll
...y chopped almonds or
...a ball with an almond or
...e at 350° for 10 minutes.
...r cook and do not brown.

...he Ultimate Chocolate Chip Cookie

...avor Crisco®	1 Tbsp. vanilla	1 tsp. salt
...y packed	1 egg	3/4 tsp. baking soda
...gar	1–3/4 cups all-purpose flour	1 cup semi-sweet chocolate chips
2 Tbsps. milk		1 cup pecan pieces (optional)**

Heat oven to 375°F. **Combine** Butter Flavor Crisco, brown sugar, milk and vanilla in large bowl. Beat at medium speed of electric mixer until creamy. **Beat** egg into creamed mixture. **Combine** flour, salt and baking soda and mix into creamed mixture until just blended. **Stir** in chocolate chips and pecan pieces. **Drop** rounded tablespoonfuls (about 2 measuring tablespoons of dough) 3 inches apart on ungreased baking sheet. **Bake** at 375°F for 8 to 10 minutes for chewy cookies (cookies will appear moist— DO NOT OVERBAKE), or 11 to 13 minutes for crisp cookies. **Cool** on baking sheet 2 minutes. **Remove** to cooling rack.

3 Dozen 3-Inch Cookies

**Note: If nuts are omitted, use 1-1/2 cups semi-sweet chocolate chips.